More praise for
ONE TOUGH MARINE

"I have been associated with countless service personnel during my lifetime and Sergeant Hamblen tops the list of selfless, dedicated, all-American tough Marines. Words are inadequate to portray his life as fully as he has lived it, but his biography will serve as an inspiration and be a worthy model to be emulated by all who would aspire to be among the few good men—the Marines. As one of the 'Godfathers' of the Marine Corps deep reconnaissance, it has been a privilege to have known and served with Woody Hamblen. *Semper Fidelis*."

—HERMAN NICKERSON, JR.
Lt. Gen. USMC (Ret.)

Also by Major Bruce H. Norton, USMC (Ret.)
Published by Ivy Books:

FORCE RECON DIARY, 1969
FORCE RECON DIARY, 1970

ONE TOUGH MARINE

The Autobiography of First Sergeant Donald N. Hamblen, USMC

First Sergeant Donald N. Hamblen, USMC (Ret.)

Major Bruce H. "Doc" Norton, USMC (Ret.)

IVY BOOKS • NEW YORK

Ivy Books
Published by Ballantine Books
Copyright © 1993 by Donald N. Hamblen and Bruce H. Norton

Library of Congress Catalog Card Number: 93-70006

ISBN 0-8041-1031-X

Manufactured in the United States of America

First Hardcover Edition: November 1993
First Mass Market Edition: October 1994

10 9 8 7 6 5 4 3 2 1

This book is dedicated to the memory of my mother and father and to my wife, Reiko.

—Don "Woody" Hamblen

and

To Darice, who has always stood by me.

—Bruce H. Norton

Contents

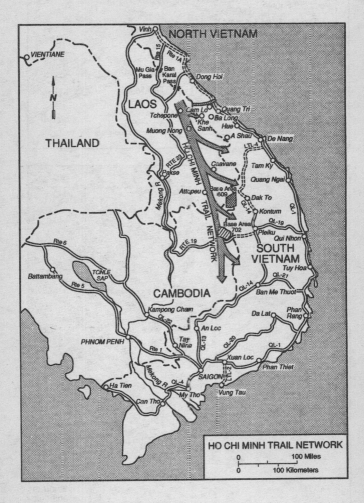

VIENTIANE

NORTH VIETNAM

Vinh

Rte 15

Mu Gia Pass

Ban Karai Pass

Rte 1A

Dong Hoi

LAOS

THAILAND

N

Tchepone

Cam Lo

Quang Tri

Ba Long

Khe Sanh

Hue

Muong Nong

A Shau

De Nang

LTL-4

HO CHI MINH TRAIL NETWORK

RTE 23

Chavane

Tam Ky

Quang Ngai

Pakse

Attopeu

Base Area 609

Dak To

QL-14

QL-1

Mekong R.

Kontum

Base Area 702

Pleiku

Qui Nhon

RTE 19

SOUTH VIETNAM

Rte 6

Tuy Hoa

Battambang

Rte 5

TONLE SAP

CAMBODIA

QL-14

QL-21

Ban Me Thuot

Kampong Cham

Da Lat

Phan Rang

QL-22

An Loc

QL-13

PHNOM PENH

Rte 1

Tay Ninh

QL-20

QL-1

Xuan Loc

Phan Thiet

Mekong R.

SAIGON

QL-4

Ha Tien

My Tho

Vung Tau

Can Tho

HO CHI MINH TRAIL NETWORK

0   100 Miles

0   100 Kilometers

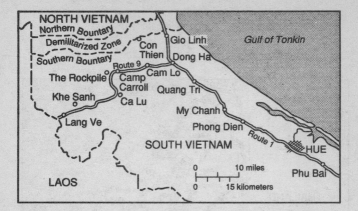

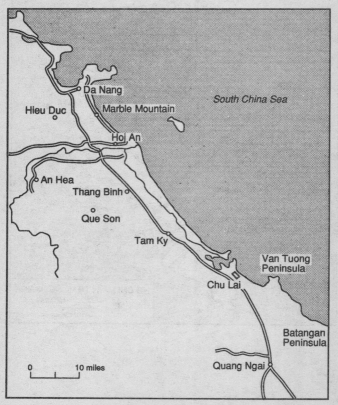

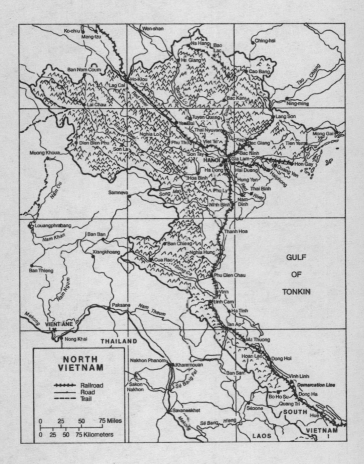

NORTH
VIETNAM

+++++ Railroad
——— Road
----- Trail

0   25   50   75 Miles
0   25   50   75 Kilometers

Foreword

My first contact with then–Staff Sergeant Donald N. Hamblen was shortly after the tragic circumstances in 1962 when high winds drove his parachute into high-tension wires at Camp Pendleton, California, where I was commanding general of the 1st Marine Division. He requested an interview with me to express his strong desire to somehow remain in active service to his country. His record showed that he had been severely wounded twice by mortar fire at "Bunker Hill" in Korea, and now, as a result of his accident, he was an amputee facing a medical discharge. His dedication and determination were evident throughout the interview. He wanted a chance to prove that after rehabilitation he could remain on full duty with the Corps. This was one amazing Marine!

I wondered why he didn't quit this rugged life and take his many talents of leadership and experience into the civilian world, but he had only one goal—to live his life as a Marine, and he left no stone unturned to convince others that he could accomplish the near impossible. The Marine Corps gave him that chance, and by sheer willpower he qualified for full duty.

In 1966, while in Vietnam, I was again commanding officer of the 1st Marine Division and became aware that Staff Sergeant Hamblen was there, too, having done many months of outstanding long-range patrol duty. I asked even

more of him: to accompany me on visits to the Naval Hospital in Danang and to the hospital ship offshore. His presence among the severely wounded, many of whom were amputees, did greater good than any medication. He could—and did—"show-and-tell," using his own artificial leg to demonstrate what could be accomplished. He moved from one hospital bed to another, encouraging the men by proving that severe handicaps could be overcome.

I have been associated with countless service personnel during my lifetime and Sergeant Hamblen tops the list of selfless, dedicated, all-American tough Marines. Words are inadequate to portray his life as fully as he has lived it, but his biography will serve as an inspiration and be a worthy model for emulation by all who would aspire to be among the few good men—the Marines. As one of the "godfathers" of Marine Corps deep reconnaissance, I have been privileged to have known and to have served with "Woody" Hamblen.

Semper Fidelis

Herman Nickerson, Jr.
Lt. Gen. USMC (Ret.)

Introduction:
Mentors

During the 216-year history of the United States Marine Corps many men have stood proudly at attention before their fellow Marines as they were recognized for making some lasting contribution that bettered our Corps or for having distinguished themselves in acts of great personal courage on the battlefield. Their individual achievements and moments of bravery have become a lasting part of our military history; these accomplishments serve as examples for all to follow. However, the pedestal of recognition on which these Marines have stood often seems to be made of a very delicate, shifting sand as their moments of recognition, being much too brief, are quickly eroded by time.

Occasionally, a very few Marines find themselves having to stand tall more than once, as again they are recognized for their sustained exemplary service or for their repeated demonstrations of personal courage during combat. These Marines are an extremely rare breed and they become our mentors and our heroes. This is the story of one such individual.

In 1950, an eighteen-year-old boy from the small New England farming community of Winthrop, Maine, questioned whether or not he was man enough to "wear the Greens" and enlist in the ranks of the United States Marine Corps. He heard that Marines were tough and wanted to join "with the best." He went to boot camp at Parris

Island and he got his first taste of combat serving in Korea from 1951 to 1952 as a rifleman assigned to D Company, 2nd Battalion, 5th Marine Regiment. He was wounded two times in one day during fighting against the North Korean Army.

Following the Korean War he chose service with the Marine Corps as his life's profession and learned his trade serving with the infantry at Camp Lejeune, at the Marine Barracks, New London, Connecticut, and with the 1st Marine Brigade in Hawaii. Subsequently, he returned to Camp Pendleton, California, and volunteered for duty with a Marine force reconnaissance company and honed his combat skills at the Army's Airborne School, at Fort Benning, Georgia, the Marine Corps' Mountain Leadership School in California's High Sierras, and the Navy's Underwater Swimmer's School in Key West, Florida.

In September 1962, while assigned as the pathfinder platoon sergeant in 1st Force Reconnaissance Company, he was making his two hundred and fifteenth parachute jump over Camp Pendleton, California, when strong, gusting winds caused him to drift down and away from his designated drop zone. His nonsteerable parachute canopy became entangled in a series of three sixty-nine-thousand-volt electrical lines, and while suspended helplessly beneath those high-tension cables he swayed back and forth until his left jump boot made contact with a lower twelve-thousand-volt line, causing him to be electrocuted.

His green parachute canopy sparked into a ball of orange and blue flames and melted as fire swept over him. His jump boot burned around his foot and he fell more than thirty feet to the ground in a smoking heap. Badly burned, but still alive and fully conscious, he was taken by rescue helicopter to the base hospital where five days later, his blackened left leg was amputated six inches below his knee.

But the story does not end here with this injured Marine staff sergeant being discharged from the Corps with a medical disability, receiving an artificial leg, and left with the feeling of being someone less than whole. This Marine noncommissioned officer embarked on a personal crusade to recover from what he believed was only a "temporary" handicap and requested that he be given the chance to prove that he was physically fit and be allowed to stay on active duty in the Corps. While he waited for an official reply, he learned how to stand, how to walk, and how to run. He soon demonstrated that he was able to scuba-dive and return to parachuting. The story of his remarkable recovery soon became newsworthy and he had the opportunity to represent our country's disabled veterans when he was invited to Washington, D.C, to attend the annual meeting of the President's Committee on Employment of the Handicapped. There, he met with Commandant of the Marine Corps General Wallace M. Greene, and with various state senators and members of Congress. He was honored by the President of the United States, Lyndon B. Johnson. To these leaders and to thousands of others, his remarkable recovery was an incredible example of personal courage.

Returning to full-duty status with 1st Force Reconnaissance Company in 1963, he became the first United States Marine wearing a prosthesis assigned to combat duty. He spent thirty consecutive months in Vietnam operating as a reconnaissance specialist and Studies and Operations Group (SOG) Team adviser operating in both the southern and northern part of the country, and he was wounded again, twice.

This is the story of one dedicated individual who simply would not quit in the face of tremendous adversity and who repeatedly demonstrated that he had the courage, spirit, and the self-determination to overcome his misfortune. His extraordinary example of tenacity is personified in the phrase one tough Marine. This is the biography of 1st Sergeant Donald N. Hamblen, United States Marine Corps.

1

My Early Years

Memories of my youth are centered around those wonderful years spent growing up on my family's 190-acre farm, located three miles outside the township of Winthrop, Maine. The closest city, our state capital Augusta, was just ten miles northeast of the farm.

I was born on July 7, 1932, the youngest of four children. I have two older brothers, Edward and Dick, and a sister named Gloria. The farm had belonged to our family for more than six generations and headstones are still standing in our cemetery that record the deaths of Hamblens back to the late seventeenth century. My mother brought me into the world in the same house where my father was born in 1887.

Our farm was self-sustaining: We had eleven good milking cows, mostly Guernseys and Jerseys, with an assortment of pigs, Rhode Island Red chickens, white Peking ducks and guinea hens, and a large garden that provided us with an abundance of fresh vegetables. An apple orchard supplied us with fruit and hardwood, and those sections of land cleared of trees and stone were used to grow hay that was later harvested to become feed for the dairy cows. Every summer we would trade produce for a couple of small pigs. The pigs were butchered, usually in late November, and whoever butchered them would receive half of one in payment, while the other half was used in trade to get the remaining pig smoked. There wasn't too much money that switched hands when you lived on a farm. The rule was to trade first for what could not be produced on the farm.

I remember my father, George Hamblen, as an honest, fair, and kind man. He was very big and exceptionally strong. He once told us that when he worked off the farm he was paid double wages because he did the work of two men. He said that hard, out-of-doors work always kept him healthy. I have a cherished black-and-white photograph of my father standing in the snow, holding his saw while cutting ice out on Lake Cobbosseecontee. Using a horse-drawn sled, he hauled those long blocks of cut ice into one of the barns, where he'd cover them with layers of dry sawdust, stacking them several inches apart. Come summertime, we would take a snow shovel and scrape off the sawdust, hose off any remaining dirt, and cut the blocks of ice into smaller pieces that were taken into the house and placed in the top compartment of our icebox. As the ice slowly melted inside, the water ran out through a hole cut into the floor to a drain in the cellar. Many of the old farm houses had this unique feature. We also had electricity in our farmhouse while many of the other farms didn't, and we felt quite fortunate in not having to rely on a system of kerosene lamps for our lighting.

One of the more interesting curiosities I recall was the old lightning arrester positioned on top of our house. Lengths of iron rod had been placed at opposite ends of our roof, with a flat cable running down from the rooftop to a grounding rod hammered into the earth some distance from the house. The system was old and worn, but on several occasions, when summer thunderstorms rolled across the open farmland, lightning struck one of the electrical lines and a flash of electric current would race down that cable on the side of the house, shoot into our kitchen from an electrical outlet, producing a ball of flame that shot straight across the room and struck the drain on our cast-iron kitchen sink. The entire phenomenon would take only a few seconds, but it scared the hell out of everyone who witnessed it.

We had a telephone that we'd crank up to reach the town

operator, whose switchboard was located inside her home in Winthrop. Seven other families were on our party line for most of the year, but during the summer months, when the city folks came up from New York to vacation near Winthrop, their phones were added to our line. Our telephone number was 21 and the operator would ring us using two long rings, followed by one short ring. When the telephone rang you'd pick up the receiver and hear the additional *click, click, click,* as the other residents quietly lifted their receivers to secretly listen in on what was being said. There were damned few secrets ever kept in the township of Winthrop, Maine.

I got my very first white-tailed deer when I was nine years old, thanks in part to our party-line telephone. On that particular Thanksgiving morning most of the men were home from work and had organized a big deer drive to insure a successful hunt for part of the winter meat supply. Before the sun had risen, half of the men had positioned themselves at one end of a huge open field, waiting for a possible shot, while the other half of the group had entered the woods adjacent to the field and begun their long walk, driving any deer toward the waiting shooters. When the first deer were spotted, one of the drivers ran to the nearest farmhouse having a telephone and called the farm closest to the shooters, alerting them that the deer were on the move. I listened in on that conversation and learned of the location of the moving deer, then picked up my lever-action Winchester .25-35 rifle and ran from our farmhouse, positioning myself between the drivers, the shooters, and the moving white-tails. This ambush technique guaranteed that fresh venison was on our dining room table.

We had a deep, gravity-fed well that provided us with clean, fresh water, pumped right into the kitchen, but we didn't have a flush toilet in our home. We used an outhouse located near the back of the farmhouse; inside were three "sitters" and one "pointer" for the men. Remembering just how cold winter nights could get, I'm still grateful that I didn't have to travel any great distance from the house to get there. When any of us used the outhouse during the wintertime we'd make a run for it and, once finished, race back into the kitchen to bend over the wood stove and warm our cold backsides.

Our farmhouse was big, standing two stories tall, with five bedrooms upstairs, three more downstairs, a good-sized living room, a big country kitchen, and a pantry. It was heated entirely by a wood stove, as we had no furnace and no boiler. My father would get up every morning at four A.M. and, if he knew that the temperature was going to dip way below freezing, he would use only those logs that had big knots in them because they produced extra heat. When he had the fire going he would holler upstairs for my brothers and sister, giving them just ten minutes to get dressed and be downstairs to help with breakfast.

That big stove had a chimney that helped to heat the upstairs bedrooms, but there were many nights when the winter temperature dipped to thirty degrees below zero and no amount of wood shoved into that cast-iron stove could keep the farmhouse warm. It was not uncommon, on those freezing cold nights, to use a chamber pot kept under the bed, and in the morning find the contents completely frozen.

Nearly every room in our house was wallpapered, the walls of each room constructed of white plaster and horsehair. The horsehair served to bind with the plaster and acted as an early form of insulation. The downstairs floors were covered with linoleum and the settling of the old house had caused gaps along the tongue-and-groove joints between the wooden floor boards and the linoleum tiles. Those gaps were most apparent in doorways and allowed the cold winter air to blow inside, but my mother had solved this problem by taking excess dress material and sewing it into three-foot-long tubes that were filled with sand and then sewn shut. We called these tubes "sand eels" and they were strategically placed in the gaps under the doors and worked very well to block the passage of cold air. If we didn't have sand eels we'd use the dirtiest towel in the house or an old farm jacket and jam it over the worn threshold. We had thick glass storm windows that were used to insulate the farmhouse during the winter months. Kept in the barn for six months out of the year, each of the storm windows was matched to a corresponding farmhouse window and marked accordingly to simplify the job of hanging them up each fall.

Life for a boy on a New England farm was a combination of hard work, increasing responsibilities, and sheer fun. The chores that I was given were dependent upon the season. In the wintertime the walkways had to be shoveled clear of ice and snow. First, a long path was cut through the snowdrifts in order to let the mailman reach our mailbox. No path, no mail. Then, a wide path was necessary for my mother to walk out to her clothesline. I can still picture my mother coming back into the farmhouse carrying several pairs of long johns and several sets of sheets, all frozen stiff, then propping them up in a corner of the kitchen until they thawed.

The chickens, pigs, and ducks had to be fed every morning, and after my father and older brothers had milked the cows by hand, the stalls had to be cleaned out and covered with fresh hay. That was also one of my jobs. The school bus arrived in front of our farmhouse at exactly seven-fifteen and the assigned chores had to be completed before we went off to school. Those were the house rules.

As I grew older, I was able to complete my household chores more quickly and I took on the responsibility of after-school jobs to help put a little money in my pocket. In the springtime, I'd walk behind a spring-toothed harrow clearing stones from the freshly turned soil and breaking up the big clods of earth. This job netted me twenty-five cents per day. To supplement my springtime job I caught frogs and hellgrammites, and dug nightcrawlers to be used as bait during the trout and bass season. When summer finally came to Maine I picked snow peas and green beans that sold for three cents a pound. I dug potatoes for fifteen cents a barrel, cut hay and stacked it in windrows for thirty cents a day, and in the fall, for the mighty sum of five cents a bushel, I worked picking up apples that had fallen from the trees.

Growing up on that wonderful farm taught me responsibility and never allowed me to become a stranger to hard work.

By the time I had reached my early teens I had learned enough about the complexities of fishing, hunting, and trapping from my father to be hired on as a camp guide taking hopeful nonresidents out onto the surrounding lakes to catch their limits of perch, trout, pickerel and small-mouth bass. I knew how to handle both an "Old Town" canoe and a rowboat. I could swim extremely well and learned how to do so at an early age thanks to my father's simple swim test: When we felt that we were ready to be tested, he'd row us out to the center of the lake, we'd jump out of his boat, and then swim for shore. He believed that motivation was more the mother of invention than necessity. It was sink or swim.

I could tell what the New England weather was about to do by reading the signs of nature and I learned how to be handy as the camp's carpenter and plumber. The best part of all was that I was now getting paid for doing what I enjoyed the most: working in the outdoors with my constant companion, an English setter named Tippy. As a present from Mr. Nash, a wealthy printer whom my father always guided, I was given the pick of his litter of hunting dogs and this particular dog proved to be the very best setter I ever owned. What endeared me to this dog was his loyalty and devotion to me. As an example, I can remember riding my bicycle into Winthrop one winter afternoon to go to the movies, having left Tippy tied up at home. I parked my bike next to the theater and during my time inside a heavy snow began to fall. When I came out of the movie house, there was Tippy curled up next to my bike, covered with snow. He had chewed through his leash and made the trip to town on his own.

Winthrop was a small rural town of perhaps two thousand people. There was only one car dealership, one good hardware store, and just one barbershop. I remember my parents taking my brothers and me to the barbershop in Winthrop, always on a Saturday night. My father would park the car in front of the barbershop and wait patiently for us while we'd go into the shop, take out our egg money—the change that we'd taken in selling fresh eggs— and pay the barber fifteen cents for a crew cut. I can recall my mother saying to my father, "Now George, school's started and the cold weather is coming, so don't peel their heads anymore." However, we never had the luxury of long hair. In fact, any boy who sported long hair was considered to be a sissy or a violin player. Maybe both.

I was brought up as a Quaker, but I must admit that I wasn't a very strong one. My father's parents were strong Quakers, but he wasn't, because he believed in fighting for what he considered right. Obviously, that differed from the accepted views of the church. The Quaker church was called the Friends Church and I had several experiences with it that left a lifelong impression on me.

Our farmhouse was located about a mile away from the Friends Church and as a part of my winter chores it was my responsibility, after each new snow, to shovel off the walkways around the church and clear the parking lot. I had maintained a perfect attendance record at Sunday school and this small chore simply insured that I would keep my attendance record clean. Our Quaker church promised a small leather-bound Bible to any boy or girl who had a perfect attendance record and my first goal was to get that Bible. On my hundred and seventh consecutive Sunday a great blizzard covered eastern Maine and because of the high snow drifts we couldn't get a car or a truck down the road, so I strapped on my skis and went over to the church. There I met the Reverend Jones as he was coming out of his nearby house. He said, "Don, you know that there's no church services or Sunday school today, but if you still want to go over to the church with me, you can help add some coal to the furnace and bank the fire." So, I counted that Sunday as still having gone to church and I also attended church services on the following two Sundays. On that last Sunday, I felt very proud of myself for having completed 109 consecutive services as I went forward to put my five-cent offering in the collection basket, hoping to receive my leather-bound Bible. But, to my absolute amazement, one of the elders took me aside and told me that I wouldn't be receiving my prized Bible, because, according to church records, I had missed attendance on the day of the blizzard. Back then, children didn't question the authority of the church elders, so I waited until after the service had ended and went directly to the Reverend Jones, asking him to please help me and correct this problem, verifying the fact that I had not missed church on that Sunday two weeks earlier. But no matter how much protesting and explaining I did, it made no difference. The Reverend Jones said that he just "didn't recall my being there" and he couldn't help me. That was the last day I ever stepped inside the Friends Church.

Years later, when I was a Marine infantryman fighting in Korea, a friend of mine showed me a newspaper and said, "Hey, look, Ham. You're a Quaker aren't ya? Look what those bastards are doing. It says right here that the Quakers are sending medical supplies out of San Francisco to the damned North Koreans." I just couldn't believe what he was saying until I read that newspaper, but it was true. I walked straight back to the company area and told one of the administrative clerks that I'd lost my dog tags and needed a brand new pair. From that day on my dog tags were stamped with an NP indicating "no preference" in place of a religious affiliation. Unfortunately, that wasn't the last that I heard about the Quakers. When I went to Vietnam I had the distasteful job of having to strip-search some North Vietnamese and Vietcong prisoners we'd taken in a firefight. We found tubes of Pepsodent toothpaste and bags of fresh medical supplies labeled FROM THE FRIENDS CHURCH. In two separate wars I was shot at by a very determined enemy, who were supported by my own church.

My formal education in Maine was much different from the education that I enjoyed working and playing in the fields and woods around our farm. I started sub-primary school (kindergarten) and during my first few years I did well. However, a sudden case of appendicitis and surgery with six weeks of required recovery time caused me to have to repeat third grade.

In our rural schoolhouse, grades one through six usually accommodated forty to fifty students, while grades seven and eight would have less than thirty. The number of students in grades nine through eleven were less than thirty, and the graduating high school class usually consisted of less than two dozen students. The reason for the significant decrease in numbers was due to the fact that older students left school early and went to the city to work.

Mathematics, science, geography, and mechanical drawing were some of my favorite subjects, while English, spelling, and reading were difficult for me. There was a very good reason for this—I was dyslexic, but didn't know it. My poor progress was considered to be nothing less than laziness on my part. In my early grades I could memorize what needed to be learned, but as subjects became more complicated, my inability to read well and to comprehend what I was reading caused my grades to suffer badly.

One of my teachers, a Mrs. Davis, made matters worse for me because she routinely catered to the brighter students in the class, particularly to students from the more affluent families of Winthrop. I didn't fall into her category of preferred students and, being a farm kid, I was made to feel that no matter how hard I tried to improve my grades, my efforts would always fall short of the mark. In defense of the public school system, however, there was one teacher, Mrs. Lawrence Hersom, who I remember as being the finest I have ever known. Fortunately, she recognized that I had a learning problem and took me under her wing as though I was one of her own children. She worked with those of us who had difficulties and made us feel that we were just as competent—and equals of any other student. Working with her was the only time that I truly enjoyed school. Despite my efforts to learn, though, I eventually came to the self-proclaimed realization that I was as knowledgeable as any of my teachers and decided to quit high school in the tenth year, 1949. I started to work full time, hauling trash and cutting wood.

I had a pet bull that I'd raised from a calf. Because I had spent so much time with him he was easy for me to handle. When he was small I could take him by the horns and wrestle him to the ground, but if anyone else got near him he'd lower his head, turn up the ground with his front hooves, and come after them. I used that bull to haul cut wood that I dragged on a sled from the hardwood stands on nearby farms, but because of his unpleasant disposition no one else wanted to ride on the drag sled with me. Finally, I had to have a ring placed through his nose—a common practice to control difficult animals. If a particular bull was really difficult to handle, a length of chain was placed behind the bull's horns and then threaded through the ring in his nose. A clip-on shovel handle was attached to the free end of the chain and the bull was led around in this manner. The only drawback to this arrangement was that once the bull was set free to graze it was no easy task to approach him.

When springtime came, I augmented my wood-cutting job by trapping and I felt lucky when I took some mink or a few foxes, though the foxes were usually too smart for me. I had to compete against the local professional trappers to make any money and that meant having to walk out onto the ice pulling a small boat behind me as I headed for the open water areas where the muskrats lived. I didn't consider this too dangerous, but one day a woman who lived out on one of the islands happened to be watching me through her binoculars and the thought of me falling through the soft ice and drowning scared her so badly that she called my mother and begged her not to allow me to continue trapping.

The coming of spring also meant that it was time to start preparing the ground for planting, and with Maine having such a very short growing season we took every opportunity to get a head start in preparing our family garden. We would start our tomatoes in the early spring by placing sev-

eral rows of fertilized seed beds beneath a line of storm
windows that were angled up toward the sun. This Yankee
"hothouse" enabled us to produce an ample number of
healthy starter plants. After the spring thaw had passed
we'd still wait a few more weeks before putting seedlings
into the ground as it was not uncommon for a freak snow-
storm to blanket the countryside even as late as the end of
April. By mid-May, the spring planting was usually completed and then it was the matter of constantly tending to
the daily needs of the gardens—weeding, hoeing, and
watering—that occupied much of my time.

In the summer of 1949, two unrelated events occurred
that changed my life forever. The first of these events was
watching the Augusta Air Show. For some unexplainable
reason I was fascinated with the concept of flight and when
I learned that an air show was being held in Augusta,
Maine, I made it a point to be there. The old air shows
were a much different event than the choreographed specta-
cles of today. The price of admission was only twenty-five
cents and everyone got their money's worth of entertain-
ment. One of the highlights of the air show I saw involved
an apparently drunken local resident, dressed in bib over-
alls, who staggered through the crowd to accept his prize of
a free airplane ride. The crowd watched in amazement as
the local farmer walked around the little J-3 Piper Cub
looking as though he'd never seen a plane close-up. The
pilot instructed his passenger to climb into the cockpit, explained the simple instrumentation to him, and then cautioned him not to touch anything, unless he was told to do
so. After a quick preflight inspection for the benefit of the
admiring crowd, the pilot spun the plane's propeller to
crank the engine. Just then the frightened passenger pushed
forward on the throttle and accidentally ran over the pilot.
The little J-3 raced away from the stunned crowd and took
off, barely making it over a stand of elm trees at the end of
the runway. The air-show announcer cautioned the crowd
not to panic, but asked if anyone had a twelve-gauge shotgun handy to shoot down the helpless passenger. Miracu-

lously, a shotgun appeared, and as several men ran to the far end of the runway the crowd watched as the passenger rolled, looped, and spun the Cub across the sky. Each time the plane buzzed the field the spectators would duck down and scream until the plane was shot at. Finally, the engine sputtered dead. The Cub made its final approach, first touching down on one wheel, then the other, until it came to rest directly in front of the crowd. The "passenger" jumped from the cockpit and was then properly introduced as "Mr. John C. Weir, New England's most daring stunt pilot." The people loved it.

The final event of the show was similar in its execution to the first one: A parachutist dressed in new white coveralls was introduced to the crowd before he went up to make his jump, and while his plane took off and gained altitude the announcer added to the excitement by explaining just how difficult it was for the jumper to exit the aircraft properly and how the slightest mistake would spell certain disaster. As the aircraft turned to make its pass over the airfield, the parachutist pulled out a mannequin dressed in white coveralls from a storage compartment behind his seat and, at just the right moment, the pilot banked away from the crowd while the parachutist threw his dummy from the plane. Of course, the folks on the ground assumed that the falling body was that of the man they had just been introduced to earlier, and they stood there, frozen in fear, waiting for his parachute to open. The "body" slammed into a nearby cornfield, but before anyone in the crowd could reach the place of impact another member of the air show, who had hidden himself in the cornfield dressed just like the jumper, stood up and wobbled out of the field toward the runway. The crowd went wild in disbelief and the announcer commented that only a man in great physical shape and helped by God could have survived such a fall.

It's a shame that they don't put on air shows like that anymore because the experience certainly left its mark on me. I left that air show determined that someday I would learn how to fly and how to jump from a plane.

The second event that served to change my life began while I was listening to one of my best friends, a boy named Ronnie Bailey, talk about the possibilities of the two of us joining the United States Marine Corps.

My oldest brother, Edward, had been studying forestry at the University of Maine when the United States entered World War II, and our family was surprised to find that his date of graduation was accelerated to allow him and other college seniors to quickly graduate and join the ranks of the United States Army. Based on Edward's qualifications he was assigned as a surveyor to a field artillery unit headed for duty in Europe. During the Army's amphibious assault across the beaches at Anzio, the truck that Edward was riding ran over a land mine and exploded, fracturing Edward's pelvis. Hospitalized for several months in England, he was fortunate to have lived to return home.

While our nation was united in its goal to achieve victory in Europe and in the Pacific, this effort filtered all the way down to touch those of us in elementary school. Before the war, we began each school day by pledging our allegiance to the flag. We would place our right hand over our heart and begin, "I pledge allegiance to the flag," at which point we would remove our hands from over our hearts and, with our fingers held close together and with palms down, finish the pledge with our arms elevated toward the flag. When it was learned that our style of pledging allegiance to the flag was so similar to the salute used by the citizens of Nazi Germany the practice was changed forever.

I can recall collecting countless onion sacks that we then filled with milkweed pods, which we later hung out to dry. The milkweed fiber, known as kapok, was used in the manufacturing of life-preserver vests for sailors and pilots. With the money that we received for collecting the milkweed pods, two cents a pound, we would run down to the local post office and buy ten-cent stamps. Each stamp equated to the value of one bullet, and we were told by the postman that each new bullet would be used to "kill a Jap or a German."

As the war progressed we continued to support the national effort in every way possible. When the annual carnival came to Augusta, the price of general admission was one aluminum pot or pan ultimately destined to become some part of a new aircraft. It became our duty as citizens to sacrifice whatever we had in excess to help win the war, and when the conflict finally ended we were happy in knowing that we had all contributed in some small way to Allied victory.

So, in the summer of 1949, my friend Ronnie Bailey and I happened to go to the main post office in Augusta, and saw two United States Marines who had come down from Portland to talk with prospective volunteers. Ronnie walked up to them and asked some questions about a place called Parris Island. I had no idea what he was talking about or where this unknown island was located, but after his opening comments one of the Marines looked down his nose at Ronnie and said, "I want you to know, lad, Parris Island is no goddamned paradise. In fact, the M-1 Garand rifle that we use is just about twice your size. So why don't you and your buddy either get lost or—if you think that you're man enough to wear the Greens—come in and talk to us at the recruiting station in Portland." Feeling somewhat humiliated by the Marine's comments, Ronnie thought that the United States Navy would be more to his liking, but I accepted the Marine's challenge and decided to enlist.

I remember listening to the famous radio announcer, Walter Winchell, as he would sign off from his show, saying, "Folks, if you have a son serving in Europe, send him a letter and let him know that you're thinking about him, but if you have a son in the Marine Corps boot camp at Parris Island, South Carolina, send him a prayer." I was about to learn what he meant by that remark.

The requirements to join the Marine Corps began with my parents agreeing to sign a letter of consent allowing me to enlist because I was not yet eighteen years old. Additionally, I was required to collect three letters of personal recommendation that would vouch for my good character. The first letter was written by the principal of my school, the second letter came from Mr. Paul Bailey, our town's elected representative, and the third letter, ironically, was written on my behalf by the Reverend Jones from the Friends Church. I was then notified by mail to report to the recruiting office in Augusta, where a Marine Corps truck would take me to Waterville and then by train to Portland, where I would begin my preliminary physical examination, which was conducted inside the recruiting station.

The requirements for completing induction were rather simple: no prospective recruit could be missing more than two teeth, and the remaining ones had to be in A-1 condition. I passed that test and then went on to pass the color-blindness test and a simple vision exam. I was required to take several multiple-choice intelligence tests that I somehow managed to pass, and then returned home, having been told by the recruiter to wait there until I heard from him, at which time I would be given a date to return to the recruiting office to be sworn into the Marine Corps. I spent the winter months of 1949 working in a canning factory that processed corn. In February 1950, I received that long-awaited telephone call from the recruiting station telling me to report to their office.

After the formal swearing-in ceremony, I spent the night in a nearby hotel along with a dozen other volunteers, and early the next morning we boarded a train for the long ride to Parris Island. A Marine reservist, wearing the stripes of a private first class, was placed in charge of our group; it was his responsibility to insure that all of us arrived at Parris Island together and on time. That long train ride took us from Portland to Boston's South Station, where we were transferred to another train, and then continued south to Baltimore where we again transferred to the train that would complete our trip to the town of Beaufort, South Carolina.

It was this train ride that provided me with a learning experience that would last for a very long time, for in not being a very well-traveled young man, I was amazed to discover that separate passenger cars were designated "For Whites Only" and "For Negroes Only."

Up until this time, Mr. Johnny McCauley was the only Negro I had ever known. He and his family owned and operated a restaurant near Augusta, and the two of us had hunted deer together each fall since I was fourteen years old. For two reasons, I was always amused on these hunting trips with Johnny—he was particularly easy to see in the woods, sporting a full head of snow-white hair, and he was terrified of being out on the open water. When I'd take him in my canoe to one of our favorite hunting spots, a place called Horseshoe Island, Johnny would sit motionless in the front of the canoe, concerned not only with the prospect of drowning, but also worried by the fact that he felt he was never wearing enough red clothing to prevent him from being mistaken for a white-tailed deer.

Mr. Johnny McCauley and I got along very well together because we respected one another, but I was young and very ignorant of the differences that were considered to exist by some between whites and Negroes outside of Maine. The farther south from the Mason-Dixon Line we traveled, the more frequent were the stops that allowed us to move freely about the train, taking in new sights. Soon we began to hear whispered remarks about those "goddamned dumb Yankees" walking through the "niggers-only" railroad cars. I may have appeared dumb, but I wasn't stupid: I learned that segregation and racism were very much alive and in practice in the South in 1950.

After we arrived in Beaufort, we boarded a public bus that was to take us to our final destination, Parris Island. Just before we crossed the two-lane bridge that led onto the base, our bus stopped and a Marine Corps drill instructor, a sergeant, climbed aboard. He looked around at the faces on the bus and finally spoke. "All right, all of you civilians can get off of this bus, *now*, and the rest of you almost-Marines will remain seated."

Then the sergeant walked up and down the aisle and asked each and every person who remained, "Are *you* down here for recruit training, son? Are *you* here to become a Marine?" When he was finally satisfied that only those of us who remained aboard the bus were, in fact, recruits, he moved to the front of the bus and motioned to the driver to proceed. Then he turned and faced us and in a voice loud enough to be heard a half-mile away he screamed, "When I say get off the bus, I want everyone to get off this damned bus! I want you to line up outside in three columns. If you don't know what a column is, it's like a row of corn. I want three rows of corn out there. I don't want to see nothin' but assholes and elbows flying off this damned bus as fast as is humanly possible."

By this time our bus had been waved through the front gate of the Marine Corps Recruit Depot, Parris Island, South Carolina, and had rolled to a slow stop. The sergeant turned and faced us. "You bastards get off this bus, now! Move, move, move! I said get off this goddamned bus, *now!*" Two drill instructors were waiting for us as we tried to scramble off of that bus, but no one moved fast enough to satisfy them. We were pushed, kicked, and pulled from the bus. "You, come here. You, stand here. Shut your goddamned mouths. I said fall in, you dumb sons o' bitches. Don't you understand *me?*"

When we had finally managed to arrange ourselves into the desired column of threes, one of the drill instructors stepped directly in front of the largest recruit in our formation and, placing his nose less than an inch away from the boy's face, he screamed, "What the hell are you lookin' at, *boy?* Do *you* think that I'm pretty, *boy?* You're not queer, are ya, *boy?*"

The boy began to shake with fright, not knowing exactly how to answer the rapid-fire questions, which was when the senior drill instructor centered himself in front of our formation. "All right, listen to *me.* Welcome to Parris Island."

Cocking his head toward one of his assistant drill instructors, he said, "Now take these assholes away from me, on the double."

My life as a Marine recruit had just begun.

2

Boot Camp

Our platoon, consisting of seventy-four recruits, was run directly into the receiving barracks where we were quickly introduced to that age-old Marine Corps ritual known as "processing." This began with stripping ourselves of every semblance of having once been associated with what was regarded by Marine drill instructors as the lowest form of human life—a civilian.

Standing at attention in three-foot-square blocks painted on the wooden floor, we were ordered to look down and memorize our individual block's number, which we were to use throughout our processing. No orders or verbal commands were just spoken by the drill instructors—they were screamed, shouted, or hissed at us, so that no man would dare to forget what was being said. We were in constant fear and total shock. We were instructed to remove everything from our pockets and to place whatever we had on the floor directly in front of our shoes. This search was to insure that no contraband was smuggled aboard at the depot and since everything was considered to be contraband, harsh examples were made of those individuals thoughtless enough to have kept possession of anything, particularly pornographic material.

"What the hell are you doin' with this here magazine full o' pictures of these dirty women, *boy*? This stuff is filth! Is that a picture of your girlfriend or a picture of your mother?

21

Answer me, *boy*! Are you some kind o' sick pervert? Were you sent here to make my life miserable? Are you some kind of criminal? Answer me, *boy*! Answer me!"

Anyone who committed such an unthinkable offense was so terribly humiliated by the drill instructors that the experience was never forgotten. No one dared so much as to steal a look at any of the drill instructors, let alone give them any smart back talk. However, there was one big guy who, we later learned, had been in the Air Force prior to coming to Parris Island and who made the error of daring to talk back to one of the drill instructors, challenging his authority. Within seconds this idiot was surrounded by screaming, punching Marines, who physically beat him out of the receiving barracks. We never saw him again, but instantly learned from his costly mistake.

Following the search for contraband, we were told to undress and to box up our civilian belongings and address them for the return trip back to wherever we had come from. Then we were herded directly into the showers. Upon emerging clean on the other side of the barracks, each man was subjected to yet another inspection that identified those who had infections, skin disorders, and even hemorrhoids. The pace was exhausting as we were moved on the double from one place to the next. When all of these preliminary events were completed, we lined up to receive our first Marine Corps haircuts. We were told that when we sat in the barber's chair there would be absolutely no talking or movement—we would only be allowed to place our fingers on any existing moles or pimples growing beneath our hair. This would alert the barber to their location and, hopefully, prevent him from jamming up his clippers with human flesh.

"If you have more than ten o' them things, *boy*, then you *will* tell the recruit standing directly behind you to place *his* fingers on them."

The barbers at Parris Island knew of only one way to cut hair—off, and no one was spared from this swift, twelve-second ordeal. The result was a mob of scared young men sporting shaved heads and waiting to be moved to the "inoculation" room, where two lines of Navy hospital corpsmen stood waiting anxiously to inoculate us against every disease known to man. These corpsmen had invented something of a game at our expense. Each recruit's upper arm was painted with an antiseptic "bull's-eye" to assist the corpsmens' aim, and as we passed through the gauntlet of waiting needles, many of the recruits simply fainted out of fear.

Moving at a dogtrot away from the inoculation room, we were run inside of another large warehouse to receive and be fitted with our initial issue of uniforms. In 1950, the size of a particular uniform was given with only a number: size small was usually a 2 or 3, medium sizes were a 4 or 5, and size large was a 6 or 7. As each of us approached the large wooden counter that ran down the entire length of the warehouse we shouted out our last name and our size number. The Marines who worked in the sweltering structure threw shirts, trousers, shoes, heavy woolen overcoats, and socks in our direction, and we grabbed at our new clothing as it came flying at us. Included in this flurry of uniforms were two pairs of black-leather dress shoes and two pairs of three-quarter-height leather work boots called boondockers. As quickly as we could account for our mountainous issue we were required to try on each new article of clothing in the presence of a tailor who made his alteration marks with a sliver of white soap.

I don't believe that anyone ever got his correct issue that first day at Parris Island. The heat and humidity of the South, the never-ending screams of dissatisfied drill instructors, and the constant state of total confusion were masterfully designed to keep us in shock. As the final part of the growing list of our equipment we received our "bucket issue," one large, silver, galvanized-metal bucket, one new toothbrush, one solid-brass padlock with two keys, and one new wooden-handled scrub brush. Carrying in our outstretched arms everything we had been issued, we were run over to the old, two-story wooden barracks that would be our home for the next twelve weeks.

Once inside the squad bay we were told to line up in front of the metal bunk beds that ran down both sides of the barracks. On command, we were told to quickly stuff everything we had just been issued inside our wooden footlockers, located at the end of our bunks. Once that job was completed we were told to remove the brass padlocks from our buckets, lock them to our footlockers and then stand at attention in front of our bunks, holding out one of our two keys. The other key was taken from each man, placed on a coat hanger, and presented to one of the drill instructors.

A bobbin of string was produced and each recruit was required to cut a length of string that was then used to keep his padlock key secured tightly around his neck. When the last recruit in our platoon had finished threading his key on his piece of string, a sharp whistle blast gained everyone's attention. Two drill instructors stood glaring at us from the far end of our barracks.

"All right, you people, listen up. My name is Staff Sergeant Trope. T-R-O-P-E. I am your drill instructor. My assistant here is Sergeant Kerton and you people will listen to everything that he and I say, and you will do everything that we tell you to do. You are recruits, not Marines, and while you are here you will not refer to yourselves as Marines. The training here is tough. It is meant to be that way so that we can separate the men from the boys. To us, you people are nothing more than whaleshit, and whaleshit is the lowest thing on the bottom of the ocean. When I speak, you will function. If any one of you fails, than you will all pay the price for that failure. You will learn to function together, as a team. Is that clear?"

"YES SIR!"

"Now, when I say *move*, you will get down in a push-up position in front of your footlockers, open them up, and remove from your footlocker *The Guide Book for Marines*. Is that clear?"

Seventy-four frightened voices screamed in unison, "Yes, sir."

"Move!"

From a push-up position it was a lesson in absolute futility to try and fit that key, hanging from around my neck, into the padlock. Fortunately, I was not alone. My jabbing at the lock was interrupted.

"I didn't say take all day long. I said do it now. Stop. Get on your goddamned feet! You people are just *too* slow. Let's try it again. Move!"

Again we hit the deck and wormed our way forward into position. With seventy-four faces pressed against our footlockers, padlocks began to spring open until every recruit stood in front of his bunk holding *The Guide Book for Marines* in his right hand.

"This book is now your Bible. You will study this book at every opportunity. You will learn from it. You will carry it with you, and not separate yourself from this book. Everywhere you go, from now on, you will have your Bible with you. When you are not reading from it, it will be placed in the right cargo pocket of your utility uniform. Do you understand this? I will never see any one of you with nothing to do. There is always your guidebook to read."

My life during boot camp was always a fresh and difficult challenge, but I looked forward to each day because for the first time I was impressed by the fact that I was always learning something. From my first day in the Corps until the day that I retired, I was either learning something new or teaching something I had learned. Of course, in boot camp there were ingenious systems designed to help reinforce our learning potential. Those of us who made mistakes during close-order drill were not allowed to march with the platoon, but were required to walk ten paces behind. They were deemed "unworthy" of being a part of the platoon. Those individuals who had difficulty in remembering the left foot from the right had the offending foot promptly stomped on by their watchful drill instructor. So, when "Left face!" was ordered, a constantly throbbing left foot was a reminder to "do it right." If the platoon as a unit was unable to master a particular movement during close-order drill, we were hurriedly ordered into the barracks and, once all of the squad-bay windows were tightly shut, we corrected our mistakes wearing our heavy wool "horse-blanket" overcoats. The unbearable heat and humidity of South Carolina, coupled with the weight and warmth of the overcoat quickly focused our minds on how to do things as a platoon to the satisfaction of our drill instructor.

Another ritual of Marine Corps boot camp was the weekly cleaning of our barracks, known forever as "field day." It was during our first field day that we were introduced to the nautical terminology that was to become a part of our daily vocabulary. The floor became the deck, a pail became a bucket, a mop was now a swab, the walls were known as bulkheads, and the stairs were referred to as ladderwells. We learned to clean every inch of our barracks as a team. We began our field day by first removing everything from inside of the barracks so that we could clean the deck. Our spotless deck was made from oak slats and it was not by accident that it had become a bleached-out white.

Our platoon was divided into three groups of men wearing blue wool bathing suits, who were positioned shoulder to shoulder across the width of the barracks. The first line was manned by recruits wielding swabs of hot soapy water; and it was their job to wet the floor for the kneeling, second echelon. Each of these individuals was armed with a toothbrush used to scrub every square inch of the deck to the satisfaction of Sergeant Kerton. When one foot-wide swath of the deck was "clean" the third echelon of recruits, armed with squeegees, wiped the soap and water from the floor. This process was repeated from one end of the squad bay to the other at least once a week for the entire time that we occupied the building. When the deck was clean, our bunk beds and footlockers were repositioned and the detailed interior cleaning began. It was only through this type of teamwork that the desired results were ever accomplished—just one of the many lessons learned that we would carry with us for the remainder of our time in the Corps. For our first four weeks we learned how to respond immediately to orders, how to accept the strict discipline that was used to correct our many deficiencies, and how to come together and act as a team. Recruits who could not deal with the stress were removed from the platoon.

Our remaining weeks were filled with classes on individual first aid, sanitation and hygiene, and on the laws of warfare. We also learned the history of the Marine Corps and how our unique customs and traditions came to be. Physical fitness exercises and close-order drill were a daily ritual designed to build our bodily strength and to reinforce teamwork.

Our introduction to life in the infantry began with studying weapons nomenclature, basic communications, and how to use a map and a compass to navigate. All of these classes were the basic foundation of our learning how to be prepared for combat at any time.

The issue of the M-1 Garand service rifle was a moment that I had looked forward to since arriving at Parris Island, but much to my surprise and disappointment no recruit received a completely functional weapon. The firing pins had been purposely removed from every rifle to prevent any recruit from accidentally shooting either himself or the drill instructors. While the M-1 rifle was regarded as the principal tool of our trade, it also served a multitude of purposes that were not directly related to marksmanship. The M-1 was used to strengthen our arms during physical fitness classes and during all phases of close-order drill. We learned how to crawl with the rifle, how to walk with the rifle, and how to drill with the rifle. We learned how to strip it down, piece by piece, clean and oil it properly, and how to reassemble it. We began this inseparable love affair with the M-1 by first memorizing the official description of the rifle. It wasn't very long before I could repeat the textbook description of my weapon to the unswerving satisfaction of Staff Sergeant Trope.

"Sir, the U.S. rifle, .30 caliber, M-1 Garand, is a lightweight, air-cooled, gas-operated, clip-fed, semiautomatic shoulder weapon. This means that the air cools the barrel; that the power to cock the rifle and chamber the succeeding round comes from the expanding gas of the round fired previously; it is loaded by inserting a metal clip containing eight rounds into the receiver; the rifle fires one round each time the trigger is pulled, sir."

By the end of the eighth week of recruit training, our platoon size had dwindled to only fifty-nine recruits, but, for the first time, we were responding to the orders and demands of Staff Sergeant Trope and Sergeant Kerton as a platoon. It was during this time that we received the word that we would be moving to the rifle range for the two weeks of marksmanship training that would prepare us to qualify for the record with the M-1 rifle. This opportunity to excel as a shooter was more than a matter of personal pride—it was also a matter of additional pay. Marines who qualified as expert riflemen received an additional five dollars a month and would be distinguished by the crossed-rifles badge of an expert; sharpshooters received an extra three dollars a month and wore a Maltese cross–like device; marksmen received no extra monthly pay, and had the dubious honor of wearing the circular shooter's badge known throughout the Marine Corps as the "toilet seat." Our normal pay as recruits was a maximum of sixty-five dollars a month and the opportunity to receive an additional five dollars monthly for shooting expert was considered to be a very serious affair.*

The responsibility for our platoon was turned over to the marksmanship instructors during the time that we spent on the rifle range, the reasoning being that our minds should be concentrated on this—and only this—important training

---

*Those recruits who admitted to smoking had two dollars automatically deducted from their monthly pay. Even though they were allowed to purchase two cartons of cigarettes during their twelve weeks at Parris Island, I seriously doubt that any recruit ever smoked more than two packs of cigarettes during the entire time he was there.

evolution. We spent our first week snapping-in—learning the correct methods of positioning ourselves for shooting in the prone, kneeling, sitting, and offhand positions, how to hold the rifle, and to properly squeeze the trigger. Additional classes were conducted that explained the correct use of the rifle sling, how to call shots on the target, and how to use the flags positioned on the two hundred–, three hundred–, and five hundred–yard lines of rifle range to judge changes in the wind.

By the time our coaches had finished with us our bodies ached from the constant struggle to assume the correct firing positions, but we each felt confident that we had received the best marksmanship instruction possible. We looked forward to the chance to put to practice what we had learned. With our platoon divided into "relays," we alternated between firing on the one hundred–, three hundred–, and five hundred–yard lines and working in the target area, known as the "butts." As the targets were hit by shooters on the firing line we would pull the target carriage down, signal to the shooter where his shot had struck the target, patch up the hole, and then raise up the target for succeeding shots. This was the first time that most of us had ever been on the receiving end of rifle fire and the loud bullwhip snap and crack of .30-caliber bullets cutting through the paper targets just inches above our heads and impacting into the embankment behind us created a lasting audible and visual impression. Overall, our platoon did a fine job qualifying with the M-1 rifle; no one failed and a feeling of personal accomplishment spread throughout the platoon. We marched back to the squad bay with our chests stuck out and heads held high. I shot a score of 224 out of a possible 250 points and would reap the benefits of five more dollars a month.

All that remained for us to do was pass our final personnel inspection, turn in our rifles to the armory, and receive our individual orders to our next command. Our formal graduation from boot camp into the ranks of the real Marine Corps was nothing like the recruit-graduation parades that are currently performed each Friday morning aboard the recruit depots at Parris Island or San Diego. Following our final inspection and some encouraging words from our training battalion commanding officer, we received three metal Marine Corps emblems—the coveted eagle, globe, and fouled anchor. One went on our cover and the other two were worn as collar devices on the lapels of our woolen Dress Green uniforms. For the very first time we were addressed as "Marines" when Staff Sergeant Trope read off our new duty assignments.

"Private First Class Hamblen, you're going up north to Camp Lejeune and become a member of the 6th Marines. Well done and good luck, Marine."

In looking back on what had happened to me during those twelve hellish weeks at Parris Island, I am pleased to say that for the first time I had learned how to function as a part of a whole. Our individuality had been stripped away, and from a mob of shocked, scared, and bald young men our drill instructors had begun the process of molding us into a living, breathing, and hardworking unit. We accepted the discipline, learned how to immediately respond to the orders of those in command, and learned that we could depend upon our fellow Marines. Truthfully, I enjoyed boot camp. I had experienced some very hard times growing up in Maine, but I hadn't realized how well those difficult experiences would prepare me for what lay ahead. I took what the drill instructors dished out and I became a better Marine and a better man because of it. I firmly believe that the drill instructors at Parris Island—those who had been veterans of combat in World War II and Korea—knew the demands of war and did the very best job of weeding out the weak from those of us who were determined to see through what we had begun. What remained was a platoon of fifty-nine proud, young, and physically fit Marines eager to get away from Parris Island and to their next duty assignment.

With my seabag fully packed, and wearing the stripes of a Marine private first class, I boarded the bus destined for Camp Lejeune and the 6th Marine Regiment.

3

Training for Korea

Background . . .

On March 28, 1949, Louis A. Johnson was sworn in as President Harry S. Truman's secretary of defense and, with the President's blessing, started to reduce the size of the United States Navy and the Marine Corps. As had happened so many times in the past, the Marine Corps was under siege. Secretary Johnson's attitude was expressed to Admiral Richard L. Connally shortly after his appointment. He said:

Admiral, there is no reason for having a Navy and a Marine Corps. General Bradley tells me amphibious operations are a thing of the past. We'll never have any more amphibious operations. That does away with the Marine Corps. And the Air Force can do anything the Navy can do, so that does away with the Navy.*

Although the United States Congress had voted shortly after the end of World War II to restrict all appropriations for military purposes, those of its members who had served in the military interceded on behalf of the Department of the Navy and to some extent prevented this from happen-

*U.S. Marine Operations in Korea 1950–1953, vol. V, Historical Branch G-3, Headquarters, U.S. Marine Corps, p. 257

ing. However, the wheels were set in motion to reduce the
Marine Corps from 75,000 to 65,000 Marines. Infantry battalions would be reduced from eleven battalions to eight,
and aviation squadrons would be reduced from twenty-three
to twelve. The war in Korea helped to turn things around.

When the Korean War began on June 25, 1950, the 1st
and 5th Marine Regiments were stationed at Camp Pendle-
ton, California. The Commandant of the Marine Corps,
General Clifton B. Cates, offered to the Joint Chiefs of
Staff one regimental combat team and one Marine aircraft
group for immediate service. The United States Navy,
Army, and Air Force made no such offers. Finally, General
Cates persuaded the Chief of Naval Operations to give the
Commander in Chief, U.S. Naval Forces Far East, authori-
zation to offer General Douglas MacArthur, Commander in
Chief Far East, a Marine air-ground brigade. General
MacArthur sent an immediate request to the Joint Chiefs of
Staff asking for the Marines, but it was not until July 3 that
the approval was granted.

With the Marine Corps under great pressure from General MacArthur to quickly build up the 1st Marine Division
for deployment to the Far East, unusual methods were used
to accomplish the task. The 1st Marine Division, based at
Camp Pendleton, was commanded by Major General
Graves B. Erskine; his assistant division commander was
Brigadier General Edward A. Craig. Comprised of Marines
from the 1st, 5th, and 7th Marine Regiments, the 1st Provisional Marine Brigade was organized on July 7, 1950, as a
heavily armed advance component of the 1st Marine Division. The brigade also included one company each from the
division's signal, motor transport, medical, shore party, engineer, ordnance, and tank battalions, as well as a detachment from the service battalion, combat service group,
reconnaissance, and military police companies, and the
1st Amphibian Tractor Company and amphibian truck platoon. The 1st Battalion, 11th Marines, an artillery battalion
with three firing batteries, was also attached. In all, the Marine brigade ground forces numbered 266 officers and 4,503

men. The brigade's air component from the 1st Marine Air Wing of three fighter squadrons and an observation squadron amounted to 192 officers and 1,358 men.

The newly formed 1st Provisional Marine Brigade was placed under the command of Brigadier General Craig, with the core of the ground-combat element to be the 5th Marine Regiment under the command of Lieutenant Colonel Raymond L. Murray, a veteran of World War II. Lieutenant Colonel Murray had graduated from Texas A&M in 1935 and entered the Marine Corps as a second lieutenant. During World War II, he had fought with distinction at Guadalcanal, Tarawa, and Saipan, and was awarded the Navy Cross, two Silver Stars, and the Purple Heart.

While the 1st Provisional Marine Brigade was still forming, the 3rd Battalion, 6th Marines, from Camp Lejeune, was deployed with the Navy's Sixth Fleet, somewhere in the Mediterranean. The fleet was given new orders to proceed through the Suez Canal and head directly for South Korea, where upon arrival the 3/6 was to report to the 7th Marines—to fill out the ranks of that regiment—and immediately redesignate itself the 3rd Battalion, 7th Marines.

On July 12, the time the 1st Provisional Marine Brigade was prepared to sail from San Diego, the strength of the Marine Corps was 74,279 on active duty, with 27,656 Marines in the Fleet Marine Force. The number of infantry regiments in a division had been cut from three to two, the number of battalions in a regiment from three to two, the number of companies in a battalion from three to two, etc., right on down the line. The 5th Marine Regiment numbered 132 officers and 2,452 enlisted men. Its battalions were made up of: 1st Battalion—companies A and B, weapons company, headquarters & service company; 2nd Battalion—companies D and E, weapons company, headquarters & service company; 3rd battalion—companies G and H, weapons company, and headquarters & service company.

As the Marine brigade sailed on toward Korea, Army General Walton J. Walker's Eighth Army had been pushed back to a small perimeter at the southern end of the Korean peninsula around the town of Pusan. It seemed as though the North Korean army could not be stopped and by the last week of July the defensive perimeter threatened to collapse. It was at this time that General MacArthur ordered the Marine brigade to Pusan as the last of his available reserves.

President Truman, remembering that it had been only five years since the end of World War II, refused to reinstate the draft, but faced with the imminent collapse of South Korea and thousands of Americans being killed, captured, or wounded, the President gave permission to mobilize the Reserve and National Guard units. On July 19, President Truman authorized the call-up of "citizen-Marines." Mobilization of the Organized Marine Corps Reserve brought in 33,528 well qualified officers and men, many of whom had seen extensive combat in World War II.

While the 1st Provisional Marine Brigade sailed toward Korea, Brigadier General Craig had gone on ahead by air with his advance party to meet with MacArthur on July 19. MacArthur explained that if the brigade could be assembled by early September, he would land at Inchon, march on to free Seoul, cut the North Korean lines of communication, and then isolate the North Korean People's Army (NKPA). General Walker's Eighth Army would then break out of the Pusan perimeter and the North Korean invasion would be crushed in a classic hammer-and-anvil fashion, just ninety days after it had begun.

The brigade arrived at the port of Kobe, Japan, and set about drawing new ammunition and supplies while the plans to put the first elements of the brigade ashore at Pusan on August 2 were finalized. Arriving on schedule on the 2nd, the 5th Marine Regiment was moved inland and west forty miles by truck and train to an assembly area near the town of Changwon, to attack the NKPA as part of the Army's 25th Infantry Division. The regiment stepped off in the attack on August 7 and by the 13th had entered the town of Sachong.

General Craig was ordered to disengage from his attack

on the NKPA and quickly move seventy-five miles north to engage the 4th NKPA Division near the Naktong River crossing at Obong-ni. It was here that Marines made their first acquaintance with the Russian-made T-34 tanks, and destroyed a number of them using M-26 tanks, 3.5-inch rocket launchers, and 75-millimeter recoilless rifles. Inflicting heavy casualties on the North Koreans and pushing the NKPA back six miles, the brigade went into reserve and prepared to load out for General MacArthur's surprise amphibious landing at Inchon.

The great success of the Marines' landing at Inchon is well documented, as are the continued Marine actions in fighting to secure the city of Seoul. By September 29, President Syngman Rhee, escorted by General MacArthur, was able to make his triumphal return into the capital.

Despite General MacArthur's overly optimistic prediction of a total victory within ninety days of landing at Inchon, the Korean War continued to rage on. The Marines of the 1st Division found themselves advancing steadily northward from Wonsan to Hamhung during October and November. After Communist China's entry into the conflict, the division covered the retreat south from the northern reaches of infamous "frozen Chosin" reservoir. By early spring of 1951, the Marines found themselves in the eastern coastal town of Pohang.

As the new year began Lieutenant General Matthew B. Ridgway had assumed command of the Eighth Army from General Walker, who had been killed in a vehicle accident. The Army had established a defensive line south of the city of Seoul, while the 1st Marines controlled a sector stretching from the coast, at Pohang, northwest to the town of Andong. It was during this period that new plans and new players came to Korea.

General Ridgway planned for a "buttoned-up, shoulder-to-shoulder" United Nations counteroffensive called Operation Killer. The 1st Marine Division began the attack from Wonju on February 21 and, with the 1st and 5th Regiments leading the assault, it took its objective, Hoengsong, eight miles to their north, within three days.

Operation Killer was succeeded by Operation Ripper, which began on March 7, with the main attack against the NPKA positions led by the 1st Marines, commanded by Colonel Francis M. McAlister, and the 7th Marine Regiment, commanded by Colonel Herman "The German" Nickerson. By the end of April, the Eighth Army's defensive line was north of the 38th Parallel.

The division was located at the Hwachon Reservoir when the Chinese began their spring offensive on April 21. In one night's fighting the 6th Republic of Korea (ROK) Division, located on the 1st Marine Division's right flank, was swept away and a gap opened in the line ten miles wide by ten miles deep. Colonel McAlister's 1st Marine Regiment, in reserve, was flung into action on the 22nd, battalion by battalion, to seal off the penetration. The 7th Marine Regiment was withdrawn from its initial positions and echeloned to the left. The division was joined by the British Commonwealth 27th Brigade and, by April 26, the situation was once again stabilized. On that day General O. P. Smith turned over command of the 1st Marine Division to Jerry Thomas, now a major general, and by April 30 the division was again in a defensive position near the town of Hongchon.

The Chinese began the second phase of their spring offensive in mid-May. With the 1st Marine Regiment, now commanded by Colonel William S. Brown, coming to the aid of the Army's 2nd Infantry Division, ground that had been lost by the Army and the one ROK division was retaken. General MacArthur, fired by President Truman, was replaced by General Ridgway as the Commander in Chief, Far East. By early June all three of the 1st Marine Division's regiments had taken up a linear position along a ridgeline that overlooked a deep circular valley known as the "Punchbowl." Believing that truce negotiations were about to begin, the United Nations forces held their positions along this defensive line. By June 25, with the Korean

War one year old, 1,250,000 men had been killed, wounded, or listed as missing in action. Two million civilians were dead and three million were homeless.

It was during this same time period—mid-1951—that I was assigned to the 6th Marine Regiment at Camp Lejeune.

From when I reported in for duty until the day that I left, four weeks later, the majority of my time was spent as one of the junior members of a working party whose job it was to move metal wall lockers and bunk beds from one barracks to another. With the tremendous increase in the numbers of Marine reservists arriving at Camp Lejeune, additional living space had to be created to billet the men. When all of the red-brick barracks had been prepared for the Marine reservists, World War II–surplus canvas tents were erected and canvas cots were put into use for the new arrivals.

Finally, at one morning formation we were told to return quickly to our billeting area, pack our uniforms and equipment, and stand ready to depart from Camp Lejeune for a flight to Camp Pendleton. This news of flying to California was viewed as a big event because in those days the standard method of travel was by train. None of us had looked forward to a five-day journey across the breadth of the States, living in the cramped conditions offered on a troop train. In California we were designated as 15th Replacement Draft Battalion to begin several weeks of intensive infantry training in preparation for further assignment with the 1st Marine Division in Korea.

At Camp Pendleton our group was taken first to Camp Del Mar, where we were issued our individual field equipment, known throughout the Marine Corps as 782 gear. Then we were taken by truck to our new home at Camp Pulgas, properly named Tent Camp 1. I was assigned to the second platoon of Company I. Within several days the strength of our battalion grew until each and every billet was filled, from our commanding officer to the most junior rifleman in one of our company's rifle squads.

This was when I first began to learn the many supplementary skills required of a Marine rifleman. At Parris Island our drill instructors had made many references to the war in Korea and the possibilities of our having to go there. They told us that once we left boot camp for duty with the Fleet Marine Force, the real learning process would begin for us and our lives would depend, not upon such things as close-order drill, barracks inspections, and physical training, but upon the skill and knowledge of the privates, corporals, and sergeants in a rifle company who would mold us into a Marine rifle squad. The many classes we now took on squad-, platoon-, and company-level tactics proved those veteran drill instructors right.

Our days at Camp Pendleton were taken up with a very busy training schedule that was designed to teach the fundamentals of infantry tactics to every Marine in the battalion. Reveille was sounded at 0430 each morning. After morning chow, we ran through a quick clean-up of our living spaces, then fell in and marched to one of the many outdoor classrooms or firing ranges located several miles away from camp. A lecture and a demonstration on a particular military subject were then followed by a period of practical application. At noon we were fed C-rations, then marched to a different and distant classroom for another period of instruction. This constant movement from classrooms to ranges, always outfitted with our packs, equipment, and rifles, insured that physical conditioning and endurance were parts of our training.

Of particular interest to me were the classes on scouting and patrolling because I thought that I could take what I had already learned from my many days spent tracking and hunting in the woods of Maine and apply it to being an infantryman. I still recall our introductory class, taught by a sergeant who had recently returned from combat in Korea.

"After your outfit goes into combat, there will be times when you'll be sent out as a scout or a member of a scouting patrol. Your platoon commander will need as much information as possible about the enemy, the terrain that you'll be moving through, and about the disposition of other Marine units near yours. The information that he needs must be detailed, accurate, and timely. When he selects his Marines for these scouting missions, he and the rest of the platoon are going to be depending upon them to bring back accurate information because it'll help to save lives. That's why these classes may just be the most important part of the instruction that you'll receive while you're here."

Our training began with classes that demonstrated cover and concealment, the difference being that "cover" offered us a means to protect ourselves from enemy fire, while "concealment" was the means of protection from being seen by the enemy. As a part of these classes we learned how to properly camouflage ourselves and our equipment while scouting. We learned that there were four points to successful camouflage: the ability to recognize and use all forms of natural concealment; how to use available vegetation, soil, and debris for camouflage; how to properly use artificial materials; and remembering camouflage discipline. We learned how to paint our faces using greasepaint, lampstick, burnt cork, or ashes to reduce the sheen of our skin. We learned how to cover our equipment to prevent a chance reflection of light from alerting the enemy to our presence. We also learned from the sergeant that "camouflage discipline" was more than a catchy phrase.

"When you Marines go out to patrol, you'll become tired. Patrolling or scouting is always mentally and physically exhausting work and when you become tired, you get careless. A lack of good camouflage because of fatigue will only get Marines killed. Think about what you've seen and learned here today, and apply it to your advantage."

The subject of our next class was movement. It taught us the proper ways to move from one concealed position to another and stressed the importance of learning how to remain motionless, how to move the arms and head slowly and steadily without making quick movements, and how to select the next place to halt, taking advantage of walls, ditches, vegetation, and terrain. Once the daytime applications of these scouting techniques were explained and rehearsed, we learned how to do the same things at night, all to the satisfaction of our veteran instructors.

"When you're sent out to scout a particular area, you're on an important mission to observe and to report. So far, we've shown you the proper ways to protect yourself and how to move around, but now we want to concentrate on the job itself."

We learned how to select an observation position, move to it, and how to leave the area by using a different route to prevent getting ambushed. We learned how important the job of a trained observer was.

"A good scout always remembers what he saw, in the order that it appeared to him. He can describe in certain detail the terrain that he's moved through, any noticeable landmarks, and he'll remember all indications of the enemy. He's learned that the enemy leaves telltale signs that'll show his strength, the character of his troops, their condition, and the direction of their movement. This is an important skill.

"The size of an enemy bivouac area usually indicates the number of enemy and a quick check of empty ration tins is a good clue as to the size of the enemy force. Footprints and vehicle tracks'll help show the direction of enemy travel. Food left uneaten'll probably mean that the enemy is well fed. If all scraps of food are gone, you can assume that the enemy is short on supplies. You can learn from a track how long ago it was made; a fresh track has sharp edges, while the old track's sharpness is dulled by time—it looks old. A running man digs his toes into the ground, but a walking man's footprint is usually even.

"You can improve your own powers of observation by watching your own unit, either on the move, in camp, or deployed. These good tips'll also help you to estimate the size of enemy forces: If a column of troops is so far away that you can't count it, estimate its size by the length of time it takes the column to pass a given point. Infantry on the march raises a slow thick cloud of dust; a broken cloud usually indicates vehicles on the move; tanks and trucks raise a heavy, fast-moving cloud of dust. Be aware that the enemy is just as capable of reading signs about us, too."

Our seemingly nonstop training did cause many of us to become tired and sleepy during the long classes, but the Marine Corps always has a solution to cure that type of problem. The instructors at Camp Pulgas were masters at devising methods that were certain to keep most of us alert while the classroom lectures were being conducted.

Near each regimental camp on Camp Pendleton is some high, steep hill, always referred to as "Ol' Smoky," and for those Marines careless enough to be found nodding off during class, one of the penalties was to be sent—on the double—carrying a large, heavy pole to the top of that hill. The offending Marine would then have to run downhill, back to where he had started his assault. Just to witness this event was reason enough to keep from falling asleep, but sometimes not everyone got the message. For those few who threw caution to the wind, several of our instructors had devised a sure-fire cure for sleepiness. They attached beaver-tailed cactus plants to the end of their swagger sticks and those Marines who dared to nap received a quick slap to their backsides. That was guaranteed to keep them awake for the rest of the class.

As our infantry training progressed from individual skills, through fire-team, squad, platoon, and company tactics, we began to function more as a unit than a class. The importance of our small-unit training can best be described by one incident that occurred.

During much of the time that we were training in the field, different officers came to observe our company. On one particular day we were "on line" practicing a live-fire assault on a fortified position. One squad had been ordered to set up a base of fire, while the two remaining squads were to assault the position. A colonel who was observing this event walked behind one of our squads, watching its progress. He noticed that one Marine was shooting in the direction of several silhouette targets, but had failed to hit any of them. He grabbed the Marine by the shoulder, stopped him, and yelled, "How many clicks of elevation have you got on that weapon, son?" The Marine, obviously scared at the very sight of the colonel, answered, "I don't know, sir." "You goddamned idiot, give me that weapon." Whereupon the colonel adjusted the rear sight to the proper elevation, fired the rifle at the targets, and then slammed the weapon back into the chest of its owner. "You couldn't hit a bull in the ass with a handful of popcorn, so you had damned well better remember what your battle sights are in combat, boy, or you'll be dead! Don't ever fail me again."

This seemingly small event, witnessed by only a few other Marines, left such an impression on me that I immediately checked my own sights and swore to myself that if proper rifle sights were that important to a full-bird colonel then they had better be important to me.

It was only when we had completed our infantry training that we learned of the final two phases of training that remained before we would leave for duty in Korea: dry net training and cold-weather combat operations.

Our battalion moved from Camp Pulgas to what was known as Area 16 of Camp Pendleton, where we received our introduction to dry nets. Great platforms of steel and wood simulating the sides of a ship had been constructed, complete with rope netting that hung from the top of the platform to the insides of old surplus Navy landing craft. We were taught how to properly construct our transport packs, move from the "deck" of the ship and over the side by placing our hands only on the vertical lengths of the rope, and climb down the swaying net into the waiting landing craft. Some men were initially terrified of the fifty-foot height of the platform, others who had their hands stepped on by some combat-laden Marine from above quickly learned the technique of using the dry nets. However, it was only through our complete trust in our training, our equipment, and our instructors that we became confident and skilled at this difficult method of transferring from ship to shore.

In early September, with our dry-net training completed, we left the comforts of Camp Pendleton, and boarded Greyhound buses for the twelve-hour journey to the final phase of combat training: the Marine Corps Cold Weather Training Center in the high Sierras near the town of Bridgeport, California.

4

Cold-Weather Training

Prior to Item Company's leaving Camp Pendleton, every Marine drew additional, brand-new cold-weather gear that included three pairs of thick-soled wool socks, two pairs of long johns, one pair of felt-lined shoe pacs, two green woolen shirts, two pairs of wool-lined leather gloves, one wool scarf, a full-length alpaca-lined overcoat/parka, an Army-issue rain suit, and a pile-lined, four-sided hat, jokingly called a "Mongolian piss cutter."

Each and every piece of this new clothing was tried on and modeled before the watchful eyes of our squad leaders, insuring not only that it fit properly, but also checking to make sure that each piece of equipment was serviceable well before any of it was needed. Once our platoon and squad leaders were satisfied with the fit of our new gear, they taught us how each piece was worn, used, and properly rolled into our field-transport packs. The average weight of our fully loaded packs tipped the scales at just over seventy pounds.

Our bus trip from Camp Pendleton to the training center began at 0300 and the journey along California's State Highway 395 was an eye-opening experience for me. As our Greyhound bus headed toward the first rest stop near the town of Bishop, the low desert terrain of southern California had slowly given way to the magnificent scenery of the great Sierra Mountains. I had never before seen anything as majestic as that first vista of the Sierras that was provided to me through my bus-seat window. What a grand sight! Those mountains, resplendent in their fall colors, looked as though a painting of a western landscape had suddenly come alive. As we passed through the hills I closed my eyes and tried to imagine the numbers of deer and other big-game animals that lived in those mountains.

At our rest stop near Bishop, several hours of down time were used to refuel and clean our buses and each of us was issued two C-ration meals for dinner and supper. While we ate our lunch we listened to classes taught by our veteran noncommissioned officers providing information that they thought would help in preparing us for what lay ahead.

The Mountain Cold Weather Training Center was designed to train Marines for combat duty in the winter weather and the mountainous terrain of Korea, with classes on basic and advanced rock climbing, mountaineering, alpine skiing, and escape, evasion, and survival training. Courses were taught year-round. Permanent Marine personnel running the center consisted of eighteen officers, two hundred and thirty-five enlisted men, one Navy doctor, one Navy dentist, and eight Navy corpsmen. Apart from the enlisted mountaineering instructors, there was also one aggressor platoon, a messmen section, a maintenance section, a motor transportation section, and a small communications section. All of these Marines had been fully trained in mountaineering techniques soon after arriving at the center. The physical boundaries of the sixty-four-thousand-acre property were formed by the northern rim of the Yosemite National Park to the south, the famous Sonora Pass to the west, Highway 395 to the east, and the little town of Markleeville to the north.

It was late in the afternoon when we finally arrived at the lower-elevation base camp known as Pickle Meadows and were met by several of the instructors who seemed eager to get our training underway. They told us that the purpose of the center was to teach each Marine how to survive and how to fight in the cold-weather conditions of high elevation and rugged terrain. We would begin with the basics—learning individual cold-weather survival techniques and then progressing steadily in our training, which would culminate in a five-day tactical problem.

In our first lesson, we learned how to conserve our body heat and not lose warmth into the ground by remembering the acronym COLD. *C* was a reminder to keep our clothing and our equipment clean, *O* meant avoiding overheating, *L* stood for loose layers of clothing, and *D* was a final reminder to keep ourselves dry.

We busied ourselves for the rest of that afternoon, each of us teaming up with another Marine from our four-man fire team and constructing tents by snapping together the canvas shelter halves that each of us carried as part of our field packs. With six tent pegs, two sections of stout wooden pole, and two lengths of rope, our two-man tents began to take shape. When assembled, though, they provided us with a degree of shelter that was only equal to the amount of skill used in putting them together. The body heat that two Marines generate was supposed to provide a fair degree of interior warmth to our tents or so we hoped.

As the afternoon grew long, I could not help but notice the steady gathering of large cumulus clouds to the west, but, deferring to the fact that I was only a private first class, I was not about to challenge one gunnery sergeant's proclamation that there was no possibility of snow.

Not giving much more thought to the oncoming cold wind, I finished off my C-ration supper and, very tired, settled into the warmth of my sleeping bag, anxious to learn more about cold-weather training.

The weather changed quickly that first night and it began to snow heavily. When morning came, we awoke to find dozens of shelter halves caved in, equipment and clothing hidden under a ten-inch blanket of new snow, and Marines stumbling around wet and cold, not knowing what to do about it. Those Marines who had grown up in the city seemed to me to be the ones who had fared the worst during the night. It was obvious that they had paid little or no attention to any of the classes we had received prior to coming to Pickle Meadows and, having left their clothes and boots outside of their shelter halves, they had no means of keeping themselves warm or dry.

We learned from their mistakes, and by the end of the miserable day our shelter halves were set up properly and our equipment was placed where it was protected and could be quickly found. After spending a few hours in several "warming tents," those Marines who had become wet and cold were a little drier, but a great deal wiser. The classes we received on individual survival techniques had instant credibility.

We spent long days learning the proper techniques of walking, climbing, and traversing mountainous terrain while conserving our upper-body strength. We progressed to rock-climbing classes and were taught the various handholds used during climbing, the proper use of climbing ropes, and how to make the many types of knots used to haul ourselves and our equipment. We became familiar with equipment such as snaplinks, pitons, and piton hammers and we learned how to "free climb" without the use of ropes and special equipment. We then climbed in parties of twos, threes, and fours using 120-foot lengths of rope. Next came the techniques of rappelling, how to belay—or slow—the descent of a climber, and how to lower equipment and injured men over sheer cliffs. We learned how to properly lubricate our weapons against the cold and to keep our equipment serviceable in the hostile environment.

We learned about the various types of cold weather equipment—tents and stoves—that we would use for prolonged periods in the field and how to prepare the special rations that were needed to support the amount of liquids and calories that our bodies would lose to the cold weather. Our C-ration boxes contained twelve meals in each case along with accessory packages of several popular brands of cigarettes, chewing gum, and much-wanted candy. We heated our rations using jellied fuel, chemical heating tablets, or cans of wood alcohol that provided enough heat for several C-ration meals.

Never had I been so physically exhausted as during this training, but the good feeling that came with accomplishing the difficult training was infectious, and we became more proficient at beating the cold. Our instructors knew what would be expected of us and many, having recently returned from combat in Korea, cut no corners in insuring that our field training was as tough and demanding as they could make it. They wanted us to learn not only how to survive in the cold, but how to be successful in cold-weather combat.

It was the final—tactical—portion of our cold-weather training that would drive the message home. A master sergeant instructor shared his views of combat in a cold environment with us the day before the company went to the field. He said that there was really little difference between tactics in the cold and those we would use in other climates, but that some tactics would be affected by conditions that were peculiar to the cold. He said that it was the aim of our tactics in cold weather to deprive the enemy of the essentials for his very existence. This was to be done by destroying the enemy's ability to communicate.

He explained that offensive Marine tactics that take place in mountainous country like Korea, where there are high ridges and plateaus cut by numerous deep valleys, are well-suited for small-unit operations. These small units must be highly mobile with a good combat power/size ratio, which was why Marine infantry needed to know how to maneuver in the snow in order to have greater mobility.

The master sergeant explained that enemy lines of communication had to be controlled to assure our success in cold-weather operations. He said that if we could combine severe weather with the disruption of enemy communications and supply lines, the enemy could be destroyed. However, it was the element of surprise that was our most important weapon. When we used bad weather to our advantage—by exploiting such things as falling snow, blizzards, fog, and dense cloud cover—we would have the opportunity for a surprise attack. By using terrain, concealment, and good security measures to our advantage, we could achieve the greater combat power/size ratio that we needed.

The night before our tactical "war" was to begin, we received another surprise snowfall, but our training had prepared us much better to deal with the elements. Shortly after daybreak we got the word to "pull poles," and we trudged away on snowshoes from our lower base camp, up toward the higher elevations of the distant hills, where we would begin our tactical problems.

The bad weather stayed with us during our next four days of company-level tactics and, as we patrolled through the changes in elevation and temperature, we experienced either constant snowfall or freezing rain, but we were prepared for it.

Late in the afternoon of our fourth day in the field, the poor weather finally broke and a vision of blue sky and the late afternoon sun gave some of us the impression that we would be able to relax from our miserable, wet, cold existence, and get some rest on our final night. But such thoughts proved to be a very costly mistake. The men in the company who had been assigned to guard duty that night fell sound asleep, and the Marines of the aggressor platoon crawled past them and into our bivouac site. As the aggressors moved quietly about, removing the firing mechanisms from dozens of M-1 rifles, they added insult to injury, using tubes of bright-red lipstick to paint the faces of those who had been dumb enough to fall asleep while on guard duty.

We woke to the sounds of M-1 rifle fire within our platoon area, and as sleepy Marines jumped up and grabbed for their weapons they were dumbfounded to discover that we had no way of firing back at the "enemy" within our camp. Shortly after the firing stopped, the aggressor team leader, a 1st lieutenant, along with our embarrassed platoon leaders and company commander, conducted a hasty critique for the benefit of all hands.

"Just take a good look around and see who has a rifle without a trigger group. Now, take a hard look at those Marines standing here with red stripes painted on their faces. My men put those red stripes there. These 'red-faced Marines' fell asleep on guard duty. They thought that the war was just about over and they let their guard down for a few selfish minutes of sleep. They let their buddies down, too. If that should happen to you in Korea, you'll wake up to find that your throat's been cut from ear to ear. Never, never, never let your guard down! If you get tired, tell someone. Don't take the chance that you won't get caught nodding off. If the Chinese or the North Koreans get their hands on you, then you'll wish you were dead."

Although many of us felt that we had finished the exercise on a sour note, we learned a great deal from our experiences in the field. We realized that while it was one thing to read about a particular skill or to watch another Marine perform it, the real lesson was always in each Marine's ability to do it on his own. That was always the way. We had come to know and trust in our noncommissioned officers and they, in turn, knew who among us they could depend upon and who required closer supervision.

We also learned how difficult it was to survive in the cold and to move steadily through snow carrying a heavy pack, whether we were a part of a column or as flankers (Marines who moved along the outer edges of the column, in much deeper snow, for the protection of the main body). As a team we had learned to overcome these difficulties, and this would help us through the most trying of times. These were the hard lessons that would now take us into combat.

Luck was finally with us when the 16th Draft Replacement Battalion arrived to begin its cold-weather training at Pickle Meadows. No surprise snowfall was to keep us from heading back to the warmth of Camp Pendleton. Crystal-clear skies and low temperatures came with the Greyhound buses that brought the newest batch of Marines to the Training Center. Those same buses would take us back to Camp Pendleton as quickly as the latest arrivals climbed down. A few greetings were exchanged, but no secrets were revealed and no pearls of wisdom were passed along from any of us to any of them. We were the latest veteran students of the center and these Marines would have to learn for themselves what we knew.

At Camp Pendleton we learned that we would sail for Korea within four days. The little Stateside time left to us was wisely used by our noncommissioned officers to continue preparing us for combat. Late one afternoon, our entire company was marched over to a training area that was located on what now is a portion of the base golf course. Once there, a corporal gave us one of the most interesting classes on the subjects of noise and light discipline that I can recall. When we were seated along a brush-covered ridgeline, he began his class.

"Good afternoon. My name is Corporal Best, and I've recently returned from a year of combat duty with a line company of the 5th Marines that is still in Korea. What you Marines are about to observe may help to save your lives. During the next several hours I want you to pay particular attention to the trail that runs directly between the ridgeline that we are on and the ridgeline that is to our direct front, just four hundred yards away. You'll see and hear certain things and then you'll be asked to describe what it is that you've seen or heard."

As the class began we watched as a Marine, partially hidden in the brush and not more than one hundred yards away, lit up a cigarette. He was followed by another Marine who did the same thing, but at a distance of three hundred yards. A final cigarette was lit by a Marine seated on the far ridgeline. The sight was unmistakable.

"If you can be seen at night, you *will* be shot at. The North Koreans have some pretty fair snipers who are only too anxious to blow the head off a Marine who is dumb enough to light up a butt at night. Think about the target that you make."

The next portion of the demonstration was provided by a Marine who came into view as he walked down the trail carrying his M-1 rifle at the ready, but allowing a belt of .30-caliber machine-gun ammunition, draped over his shoulder, to slap against the wooden stock of his rifle. Every one of us could hear the rhythmic sound of the metal links banging against his weapon and we nodded as the silent message became quite clear. As the final rays of the afternoon sun faded into darkness, it became evident that any noise above a whisper was amplified at night.

We watched and listened as Marines carrying canteens full of water ran along the darkened trail. Those aluminum canteens, with metal caps secured to the neck of the canteen by a metal chain, became a part of the next lesson.

"Your metal canteens are a constant and dangerous source of noise. They'll bang against your canteen cup when shoved back into the canteen pouch, the metal cup will bang against the canteen when handled carelessly, and the plastic cap will squeak when you unscrew it from the canteen. Now, multiply this noise by the number of thirsty men in your squad and you can imagine the racket that is picked up by a well-trained ear."

We then listened to the familiar sound of a Marine's dog tags rattling—metal against metal—and heard the common sounds of Marines positioned at various distances as they coughed, sneezed, belched, and made farting sounds.

"The different noises that just one careless Marine makes at night can get several Marines wounded or killed. I'm here to tell you that the North Koreans and the Chinese are extremely skillful at night infiltration. They're only too happy to toss a couple of grenades in the direction of any noise that they hear."

We listened to the sounds of several Marines whispering "passwords" to one another and were surprised to learn from Corporal Best that these men were at least one hundred yards apart and one hundred yards distant from where we sat. It sounded to most of us as though they could not possibly have been more than twenty feet away. As the class continued, we learned just how easy it was for us to spot the luminous dial of a wristwatch or of a compass, and to see the yellow beam from a poorly hidden flashlight.

Again, Corporal Best centered himself in front of the class. "Now I want you to listen and tell me what you hear."

We leaned forward and strained to hear the faint *chop, chop, chop* sound of metal entrenching tools as they cut into the dry ground.

"Can anyone tell me how many men are digging? The North Koreans will dig in and they'll try and hold any ground that they've taken. You'll need to be able to know the difference between one, two, or even three men digging. What you are listening to is the sound made by three men digging a fighting hole, two hundred yards away." Best allowed the digging to continue for several minutes so that the sound might become etched into our memories.

The final portion of our night class was on flare discipline. We not only learned how to recognize the sound of a flare being fired into the sky, but realized the short amount of time we had to respond—either hitting the deck before the flare ignited, or freezing in place should we be caught out on open ground by surprise illumination.

The last lesson of the night was to learn not to look up at any burning flare, the quickest way possible for us to lose night vision and become temporarily blinded, becoming useless, good only as targets.

As we marched back toward our camp, Corporal Best and his assistants drove the lesson home as they fired off dozens of flares while we demonstrated our new talents of properly responding to them. The corporal's class was the topic of conversation for many days to come, and his prediction that what we had learned might prove to be lifesaving was validated within a few short weeks.

While our last days at Camp Pendleton were mainly spent in preparation for embarkation, we also received several short classes designed to educate us in the complexities of shipboard life and naval customs. By the time the battalion boarded the merchant transport *General Pope*, named in honor of the Civil War Union commander, we knew the difference between the bow and the stern and how to tell the time of day according to the eight-bell system that is used aboard all naval vessels.

Our senior noncommissioned officers, those older gentlemen who had spent a majority of their careers at sea, had also seen fit to teach us younger men the difference between Marines and sailors. On land we saw ourselves as "Leathernecks" or "Devil Dogs." We were the defenders of the nation and the blood and guts of our Corps. On board ship we soon learned that we were regarded by our merchant-sailor crew as not much more than excess baggage.

We sailed for Korea on November 1, 1951.

Voyage to Korea

We left behind our previous identity as the Marines of Item Company, 3rd Infantry Training Command, at Camp Pendleton, and with all of our clothing and equipment carried in our field-transport packs or stuffed into seabags, our battalion, numbering 38 officers and 2,278 men, was moved by truck convoy down to the port of San Diego. There, we assembled on a long wooden pier alongside the *General Pope*, were formed into thirty-man platoons according to alphabetical order, and boarded the transport.

After being escorted down to our platoon berthing spaces, we found our living accommodations to be much more confining than those we had enjoyed back at Camp Pendleton. Our racks were constructed of individual sections of thick canvas, which were laced to rigid steel frames and stacked eight bunks high. It was pointed out to us by our smiling sailor escorts that anyone who chose the convenience of sleeping on one of the lower level bunks also ran the unfortunate risk of possibly being on the receiving end of seven seasick Marines who would live above him. That was all the encouragement I needed to grab a top-level rack. Once we had put away our seabags and secured our rifles to our racks we were ordered back topside to learn our individual work assignments for the sixteen days it would take the *General Pope* to sail across the Pacific to our first stop, the port of Kobe, Japan.

It was not too long before I found out exactly what my new work assignment entailed.

"Habbard, Hamblen, Hunt, George, and Gillis, you're assigned to duty in the ship's butcher shop located next to the officers' galley. Get on down below and report to the chief butcher, named Robinson."

We initially considered our assignment to be pretty fair duty, considering the alternatives. Many other junior Marines were chipping paint, scrubbing decks, or standing daily personnel and equipment inspections.

We reported to Chief Robinson, a huge black man with a thick Southern accent, who wasted no time in letting us know who ran the officers' mess.

"You boys are now my assistants and you'll do exactly as I tell you to do. I'll take the time to teach you how to butcher these chickens, sides o' beef, and quarter sections o' pork and, by the time we all get to Kobe, you'll be qualified as butchers. This butchering area will be kept spotless. You'll make it shine like a diamond in a goat's ass. Do I make myself clear to y'all? Now, let's get busy and see what meat has to be cut up for today's and tomorrow's menus."

As we settled into our normal twelve-hour workday we learned that our unique duty assignment provided us with the luxury of getting to use a "head-of-the-line" pass for every meal and for the movie shown on the mess decks each night. Chief Robinson took care of his boys, but every time we headed for chow and filed past fellow Marines who stood waiting in line, we were the target of many unflattering comments aimed squarely in our direction.

During the first week of duty in the butcher shop we learned that the captain of the *General Pope* had a particular fondness for ground top-sirloin steak. Each day, as part of the noontime ritual, several pounds of beef were selected by the chief to be run through his new electrical meat grinder. It became my job to clean the meat grinder after the chief was done with it. I used a scrub brush, hot soapy water, and even a toothbrush to remove any visual signs of usage until it dawned on me to try to run a clean rag through the electric grinder, as if it was a piece of sirloin. After all, I had seen my mother use a clean rag on her hand-cranked meat grinder many times, so why wouldn't it work now? I took a white cotton napkin from the linen locker and began to feed it slowly into the machine when the teeth of the grinder suddenly took hold and devoured the napkin. The grinder stopped, jammed tight, the electrical motor began to smoke, fuses began to blow, and the angry chief had his massive hands on me in an instant. The look on his face told me that if he could have gotten away with substituting me for the captain's ground beef, he certainly would have tried.

"Hamblen, what in hell's name do you think you're doing? Now, shut off that damned meat grinder and replace those blown fuses. Now you're gonna learn how to take apart that grinder, clean it, and have it back in shipshape order, all before the skipper wants his next meal."

Fortunately for me, the chief had a great deal of patience, but true to his word and under his constant eye, I did learn more about the inner workings of that meat grinder than I had ever cared to know—with no one the wiser, it was reassembled and in good working order before the captain called for his next ration of ground sirloin.

The days at sea passed quickly. When we finally arrived in the port of Kobe it was reassuring to feel the firmness of Mother Earth beneath our feet once again as our battalion marched to a giant warehouse where we left the excess uniforms that we had packed into our seabags. We kept only our utilities, a pair of green wool trousers, three long-sleeved shirts, and our cold-weather gear. We would not see our personal belongings again until leaving for home, one year later. We remained at Kobe only long enough to store our extra gear and to load the *General Pope* with food and ammunition.

The majority of our remaining time aboard ship was spent listening to the latest combat information briefings, receiving additional classes on first aid, and test-firing our individual and crew-served weapons. We lined the ship's rails and watched as other platoons were routinely called out to report to the stern of the ship where, using empty oil barrels that had been set adrift as targets, they sunk them with rifle and machine-gun fire. The warming winds of the Pacific Ocean had given way to the colder temperatures that blew down the straits of the Sea of Japan, and we needed very little encouragement to wear our cold-weather clothing when we walked the decks of the ship.

It took four days for the *General Pope* to steam from Kobe to the shallow anchoring point off the eastern coast of Korea. Late in the afternoon of November 27, 1951, we received the long-awaited order to disembark from the ship and climbed down into landing craft known as Mike boats, which would take us from the warmth of the ship to coldness ashore. Rather than utilize the landing nets that we had trained on, we exited the ship from a side compartment, making our transfer into the waiting landing craft a much easier and safer event.

I believe that it is honest for me to say that although I had been eager to volunteer for duty with the Marine Corps, had enjoyed learning the basic infantry skills that were taught at Parris Island, and felt confident in my ability to survive in a combat environment, no reading of war stories, no Hollywood movies, and not even the most up-to-date combat briefings aboard ship had prepared me, mentally, for what I was about to experience.

As quickly as we disembarked from our landing craft our platoons were marched to an ammunition-supply point, where each Marine was handed several clips of new rifle ammunition and then escorted to a convoy of waiting Marine Corps trucks. Under black-out conditions we began a slow journey along a dirt road through several heavily guarded checkpoints to our final destination, a large staging and training area known as Camp Sharp, located in the 1st Marine Division's zone of action. As soon as we arrived at the camp, we re-formed into the same alphabetical platoons we had been assigned to aboard ship, and the administrative process that would ultimately take us to our new assignments with one of the rifle regiments began again. While waiting for assignment, our battalion was ordered to occupy new living quarters. dozens of reinforced-canvas "strong-back" tents, each one heated by two oil-burning stoves. Our encampment was less than one hundred yards away from a Marine 105-millimeter howitzer battery. Only a narrow, muddy stream divided our tents from those nine artillery pieces.

It had taken only several hours from the time we landed on Korean soil until we moved into the tents at Camp Sharp, but because of the constant, hurried pace and the unfulfilled anticipation of possibly being involved in night combat, an undeniable fatigue settled over most of the new arrivals. By the time we had settled in, taken off our field-transport packs, and crawled into our sleeping bags, we were totally exhausted. The unannounced firing of the nearby artillery battery sometime close to midnight changed this total exhaustion into total pandemonium.

We could not help but notice the battery when we first arrived at Camp Sharp—its howitzer barrels were pointed straight up at the night sky. But because we hadn't heard a single shot of gunfire since we landed, nor heard any warning about the possibility of the howitzers having to fire a mission, we felt we'd be able to get a good night's sleep.

At first, we weren't sure whether the sudden crash of the nearby explosions was from incoming rounds or from our own outgoing artillery. Wherever it was coming from, though, every sleepy Marine in our tent tried desperately to scramble out of his sleeping bag and grab for his helmet, boots, and rifle. The howitzer's muzzle blasts contributed to our confusion by causing the canvas sides of our tent to flap like loose sails and making the tent's heavy support poles sway dangerously back and forth. Before we could get our combat boots laced up. a corporal stuck his head in our tent and shouted at us. "Just relax, Marines. It's only our neighbors from the 11th Marines firing from the other side of the stream. Believe me. you new guys'll get used to it, just like we all did. We're too far away from that battery to hear their warning order to fire, so once in a while they'll catch us by surprise. Welcome to the war."

Further sleep was impossible because the howitzers continued to fire sporadically throughout the night. Since I was already wide awake and fully dressed, I sat down outside of my tent and watched in fascination as the Marine gun crews went about their business. From the high angle of fire, I could only imagine that the target was some enemy-held ridgeline or perhaps the reverse slope of a distant frozen hill mass.

Our next two days at Camp Sharp were spent in getting adjusted to the cold and to the sounds of outgoing artillery fire. We listened to a series of briefings that described the previous month's combat that had taken place within the 1st Marine Division's area and again test-fired our individual weapons. On the morning of my third day in Korea came the orders that took me, along with many other Marines, into the ranks of the 5th Marine Regiment. As our names were read aloud, we climbed aboard trucks and departed the relative safety of Camp Sharp to be taken several miles west. Arriving at Camp Tripoli, where the 5th Marine Regiment was headquartered, we were welcomed by our regimental commander, Colonel Frank P. Hager, Jr., and by the commanding officer of his 2nd Battalion, Lieutenant Colonel Houston Stiff.

Departing from the regimental commander's formation we donned our packs again and marched several miles to the 2nd Battalion's command post. There we received assignments to letter companies, mine being to 2nd Battalion's D (Dog) Company, commanded by 1st Lieutenant Tom F. Fagles.

We were taken by our platoon sergeant, Sergeant D. L. Miller, to the fighting positions that were held by our platoon and to the exact positions of the other two platoons within our company's area. When we returned from our tour, I took up residence as a member of a three-man fire team that occupied one of the fortified bunkers dug into our ridgeline on Hill 812. With only time enough to meet my squad leader—a corporal named Davis—and drop my pack and pick up a shovel, I joined in with the other Marines of my squad to "winterize" our sandbagged bunkers.

The frozen, rocky ground overlooking the Punchbowl that our company occupied had been taken from the North Koreans only several weeks earlier and the bunkers that we worked on had been built by them. We used everything we could scrounge to reinforce and insulate our home. Cloth sandbags were our primary means of reinforcing the walls, but empty ammunition cans filled with earth, small logs, and empty cardboard C-ration sleeves were combined to serve as our protection from both incoming enemy mortar rounds and from the cold Korean wind.

Our platoon sergeant reasoned that by having his new replacements work on improving the platoon's positions, he would get us accustomed to our bunker and trench-line environment as quickly as possible and we would work hard to protect ourselves. He was right. We made the interior of the bunker as comfortable as we could. An area was dug out that allowed two rubber air mattresses to be placed inside and ventilation was improved by raising the roof with logs. A small stove was "acquired" from somewhere back in the battalion area and produced a modest amount of heat as it dripped flaming fuel into a sand-filled ammunition can positioned on the floor of the bunker.

By the end of the afternoon of my first day with the squad, my willingness to work hard and do as I was told must have seemed evident to Sergeant Miller. He had been observing us throughout much of the day, but said nothing.

"PFC Hamblen, knock off workin' on that bunker and follow me."

M-1 in hand, I followed Sergeant Miller over to his position on the reverse slope of our hill and sat down in the presence of several squad leaders and a handful of other Marines, also new replacements in our platoon. All eyes turned toward him when Sergeant Miller spoke. "I want you new men to know what life is like up here on the line.

You have to learn quick up here and I haven't got the time to teach you all about it. That's what your squad leaders will do, but while I have you here I want you to pay attention to what I'm about to say."

He picked up a thin piece of metal rod and pointed to a small terrain model he had made.

"Our company is located here, along this ridgeline. It took us nine days, back in mid-September, to take this hill away from the North Koreans and it was done by the Marines you replaced today. It cost thirty-three Marines their lives and two hundred thirty-five more were wounded during the fight. We killed several hundred North Korean soldiers so we could sit on top of this hill. I want to keep this ground and I have to depend upon you new men to help me do that. Study this sand table and remember where our closest friendly units are located. From left to right, the 5th ROK Division's boundary is on our division's left flank. The 1st Marine Regiment is located on our regimental left flank and the 11th Marines are in general support and located here. Our company boundaries were shown to you this morning, but this sand table will help you to visualize all of the prominent terrain features. E Company is located on our company's left flank, and F Company on our right flank.

"The current scuttlebutt is that the armistice talks have put any big offensive operations temporarily on hold, but don't you believe it. I want you to believe that ten thousand North Koreans are headed in our direction tonight. Don't let your guard down and be ready for those sneaky bastards to try to get up here. They know the ground as well as we do—after all, they used to own it. Listen to your squad leaders. They know what they're doing up here. Don't get careless on me and skyline yourselves on the ridgeline. The NKPA has a 'duty' sniper who comes to shoot at us from that far ridgeline just about every afternoon at sixteen hundred. So far, he's shown us that he's not much of a shot, but all it takes is for him to get off one lucky round.

"This'll be your first night up on the line, so I know that

you'll be a little nervous. Pay attention to what's going on around you. We're linked to the other platoons with communication wire, but don't rely on it as your primary source of communications. The North Koreans have been known to tap in on our lines. We depend on runners to get any new word up to us from the company commander. The runners bring up the nighttime challenge and password each afternoon. Tonight's challenge is 'Brooklyn' and the password is 'Bridge.' Don't forget it, 'cause if you do, it'll get you killed. We'll be at a hundred-percent alert until nineteen hundred and then we'll stand down to fifty-percent alert until oh-four hundred. When you're on duty you'll be out in the cold for one hour at a time. We'll go back to a hundred-percent alert at oh-four hundred until oh-seven hundred. Keep your weapons close by, cleaned and lubricated, especially the BARs. I hope you learn to like C-rations, 'cause that's all we get to eat up here on the line. Any questions?"

Seeing that we had no questions, Sergeant Miller added, "Now, follow your squad leaders and get yourselves ready for tonight. You'll be fine."

Just as we were leaving, Sergeant Miller stopped my squad leader.

"Corporal Davis, tomorrow I'm sending your squad out to set up a listening post and conduct a night ambush. Come and see me about all the details first thing in the morning."

Night Patrol

Just as we were finishing with noon chow, one of the company's runners came up to our position and told us to report to our platoon sergeant for a patrol briefing at 1300. We used our remaining time to check the mechanisms of our rifles and then crawled from the warmth of our bunker into the bitterly cold air.

"We're going out tonight to set up a duck blind and then see if we can't ambush some North Koreans while we're at it."

With this ominous greeting, our squad leader, Corporal Davis, began the briefing for my first combat patrol. We had joined him close to the center of our platoon's sector on the reverse slope of the snowcapped ridgeline and listened as he began to describe his plan, using our platoon sergeant's terrain model to help orient us in the proposed routes of our patrol. Removing his K-Bar from its worn leather sheath, he pointed the fighting knife at the ground.

"We'll leave from right here at nineteen hundred and move down to our first stop near the second platoon's right flank. Once we pass through their lines we'll stay close to the left side of the long finger that slopes forward of their positions, toward 'Luke's Castle.' Our first checkpoint outside of the wire will be here, at the end of the finger. This is known as 'Benchmark One.' Once we arrive at this point we'll set in and listen for a little while and then move forward to our second checkpoint, here, by this small hill, known as 'Benchmark Two.' This is where we'll set up our LP. We'll tap into our comm lines that run back to the company CP and let them know where we are.

"We'll stay at our second checkpoint until twenty-two hundred and then move out to our ambush position, just two hundred yards forward, where we'll stay until twenty-three hundred. We'll put two men on each end of the ambush for local security and set up our killing zone here, where the trail narrows. Our sixty-millimeter mortars will be in direct support and they'll have illumination rounds on call in case we need them. If we don't make any contact with the gooks, we'll come back up the opposite side of that finger and reenter the second platoon's lines, here, on their left flank. Dress loose, but warm, 'cause it gets pretty damned cold waiting in the snow for an hour. If there're no questions then head back to your areas and get your gear ready for tonight. We'll test-fire our weapons at fifteen hundred and I'll be around to see each of you later."

The nine of us who made up the third squad assembled for our final inspection just before 1900. Our squad leader, the tenth member of the patrol, carried a lightweight .30-caliber carbine and a .45 automatic, three Marines carried heavy .30-caliber Browning Automatic Rifles, and the rest of us were armed with M-1 Garands. Dressed in our heavy cold-weather gear we were each required to carry not only our helmets, but our cartridge belts, with ten eight-shot clips of ammunition, two hand grenades, a bayonet, our small first aid pouch, one canteen full of water, and two cans of blood plasma kept next to our skin to prevent them from freezing. We had checked one another's equipment to make sure that we were each as silent as possible. After being inspected by our squad leader we set off in a column toward the second platoon's area. My position was next to last in the column of ten Marines and my job was to provide flank security during the times that the patrol halted. Our squad leader's final comment to the squad was, "Make sure you walk in tracks made by the man in front of you and you'll avoid stepping on mines."

As we passed through the strands of barbed wire that were a part of the second platoon's defensive positions, the only sound to be heard was the crunching of snow beneath our boots. The crystal-clear night provided us with good visibility and made it easy to see the progress being made by our point man as we moved slowly forward.

Corporal Davis had done his best to insure that this patrol would be well prepared. When he had visited with each fire team during the afternoon, he had asked us questions to make certain that we understood the purpose of the patrol, had studied the routes to be followed and the areas to be avoided, and that we each knew the locations of the closest friendly troops. His attention to detail was sharp. We had rehearsed how we would set up and conduct the ambush to his satisfaction. Even the weather seemed to be cooperative though the night temperature had dropped well below zero. The only thing that we did not know was what the enemy was doing while we moved into his territory.

When we came to our first rest stop we remained frozen in place, listening for enemy activity and carefully observing the surrounding frozen terrain. When the hand signal was given for us to sit down in the snow and wait, I became very much aware of how visible we really were. I guess that my days spent hunting in the Maine woods had provided me with this subconscious feeling, but in Korea those past experiences were now being applied in combat. During our training the element of surprise was always stressed as the key to any successful ambush, but to me being able to remain hidden while hunting deer was no different. Even as a child, when I played cowboys and Indians with my brothers and sister, we always tried to surprise each other, sneaking up on the other side, and jumping out from a hidden position when they least expected it. The lessons of those past moments were now going to be applied in a very short period of time. Surprise, shock, focus, and our patrol invisiblity would help us in setting up our ambush.

After checking in with our platoon leader to inform him of our progress, we moved forward to the position that the squad leader had selected for our listening post. We remained at the LP in silence for nearly an hour as the cold winter winds bit at our faces. Then, as the thumbs-up signal was passed from man to man, we rose slowly from the snow, unhooked the communication wire, and moved forward another two hundred yards to the ambush site, which overlooked a narrow trail. The squad moved quickly into position—just as we had rehearsed—and we again tried to remain motionless while we sat in the snow and waited.

The rugged new position provided concealment from enemy observation; the rocks and small boulders that littered the snow-covered ground not only helped in making it defendable, but added to the natural camouflage as well. Once we were in place, the squad leader moved about silently, rechecking our positions, insuring that both flanks were protected by two-man teams, and finally positioning himself behind the center of the patrol from where he could control the ambush. With the area sealed off at both ends by our two security teams, all that we could do was watch, listen, and shiver. Seconds grew into minutes, and the time started to drag on. In trying to control my thoughts as I sat, I briefly closed my eyes and thought of home, when the quiet calm of the winter night was suddenly ripped apart with automatic-rifle fire.

The short bursts of firing, coming from our two-man security team, were not farther than thirty yards to my extreme left, but from where we were positioned, on ground slightly higher than those Marines on our left side, I could only hear the shooting and wasn't able to see what was happening. However, my job was not to worry about what was happening on our left flank, but to be aware of what could happen on our right. As my security partner shifted his body in the knee-deep snow, I heard the muffled sounds of someone running toward us from behind. Turning to face our unknown assailant we were relieved to see the familiar figure of Corporal Davis as he came into view.

"Just sit tight. I've called for some illumination and we'll see if there are any more gooks out there. They sent a six-man patrol down that trail and they surprised the hell out of our right side. When the security team opened up, the gooks returned fire and then ran back in the direction they came from, but they may still be moving through the snow. I'm not sure if we hit any of them, but this bit of high ground may help us to find out. Keep your eyes open."

The distant sound of mortars firing was heard behind us. In thirty seconds the ground in front of us was illuminated as bright as day by three flares. Suspended beneath small white parachutes, they emitted a faint hissing sound as they burned, descending slowly to earth. Eyes straining to catch any movement, we studied the snow-covered ground to our front. We saw nothing. The mortar illumination lasted less than a minute, and as soon as the last flare burned itself out above the snow we were ordered to move out and away from our ambush position.

As we moved along our preplanned route, back toward our company's lines, the hills behind us were suddenly illuminated by a great bluish-white light. The entire squad dropped quietly onto the snow in one quick motion, and we stared back at the area now illuminated by moving searchlights.

The searchlight was manned by soldiers of the first platoon of the Army's 92nd Searchlight Company, a unit that had been attached to the 1st Marine Division earlier in the month. They were positioned on a ridgeline close to our company, but this was our first experience witnessing just how effective the searchlights were. As the great white beam scanned the distant enemy hillside we could detect no movement; as soon as the light was turned off we continued to move back toward our lines.

Just as we had rehearsed prior to our departure, the patrol moved into a concealed position and waited while our squad leader and one other Marine rifleman moved up toward the platoon's lines to make physical contact before we were allowed to reenter the safety of our company's position. The movement back through the defensive barbed wire went smoothly as our squad leader tapped each of us on the shoulder, making sure that he had returned with exactly the same number of Marines he had started with. Our patrol was not considered to be over until our squad leader had gathered all of us into a group on the reverse side of our platoon's position and began to unravel the finer details of what had happened to our left-flank security team.

This was the first time that all of us had actually spoken since we had begun the patrol. As one of the two Marines assigned to that flank security team began his report, our squad leader wrote down what he heard.

"Those six gooks were all dressed in white parkas and carrying burp guns and they were almost on top of us before we knew it. I thought that if I yelled out a warning to the rest of the patrol it would alert the gooks to where we were. I don't think that they had even spotted us, but I didn't want to take the chance. That's why I started shooting."

Our corporal squad leader listened to each of us in turn, as we described what we had seen and done during the six hours that it had taken us to run the patrol. He wasn't angry that our ambush was not as successful as it might have been, but was, in fact, pleased, not only with how well we had handled ourselves under fire, but to have returned to the company without having suffered any casualties. His acknowledgment of our efforts was short and sweet. "You men did real good out there. Now go back and get some rest."

I returned to our bunker feeling relieved, if only for the fact that I hadn't panicked when the firing had started. I had confidence in my squad leader and in my fellow Marines and this brief patrol, full of things to remember, confirmed that feeling. What had been preached to us since our first days at boot camp was true—the strength of the team would give us confidence in combat. This lesson was to be repeated time and time again before my tour of duty in Korea was over.

7

Life on the Lines

Our bunker was primary position and home for the three
Marines who made up one of our squad's three fire teams.
It was readily apparent to us that when the North Koreans
had constructed it some months before, comfort and defen-
sibility were made equal parts of the fortification's design
function. Not much more than eight feet square and six feet
high, our bunker was built primarily of frozen cloth sandbags, small pine logs, and pieces of scrap cardboard and
metal. Its L-shaped rear entrance was designed to make direct access impossible and the connecting four-foot-deep
trench provided us with a fair degree of cover and concealment as we came and went. Positioned close to the top of
a snowcapped ridgeline, we enjoyed a commanding view of
the rugged, enemy-held terrain. Two apertures, one at the
front and the other on the left side of the bunker, provided
us with firing ports. A raised earthen platform, in the center
of the bunker, allowed any two of us to sleep side by side
while the third member of our fire team was on guard duty
outside in a fighting hole. The interior platform also served
as a seat while we peered out from either aperture. Two
deep grenade sumps were dug in the forward corners of the
bunker, designed to provide us with an immediate solution
for enemy hand grenades that might be shoved inside. Of
course, incoming grenades would have to be picked up and
quickly thrown down into the sump holes, which would ab-

sorb most of the blast. The rest of it would be directed upward. Since our narrow dirt floor was sloped toward the sump holes, they also aided water drainage.

Directly in front of our bunker was a two-man fighting hole that we had improved upon during our first day on the line. To meet with the approval of our veteran squad leader, our bunker's fighting hole had been dug wide enough to accommodate two men, shoulder to shoulder and armpit deep. A firing step was constructed in the center of the hole to enable one of us to stand and fire his weapon. This platform acted as a seat as well.

The advantages of this type of emplacement over a one-man fighting hole were better continuous observation, mutual assistance and reassurance, and ease at redistribution of ammunition between occupants. Moreover, it could be manned for longer periods of time. The disadvantages were that a two-man fighting hole offered us less protection against enemy tanks, machine-gun strafing, and shell fragments. And, in case of a direct hit, two of us would become casualties instead of just one. However, with our rifle company positioned in a linear defense—defending a wide area with little threat of enemy activity from our flanks or rear—the use of deep, connecting trench lines gave us mutual support throughout the platoon and the company area.

To help illustrate our day-to-day life on the lines, an explanation in laymen's terms of our defensive organization and the basic tactics that we normally employed may prove helpful.

Simply stated, our mission during defensive combat was to stop the enemy by using both organic weapons normally assigned to the company and supporting-weapons fire forward of the edge of the main line of resistance (MLR) and to repel the enemy's assault by fire and close combat if he succeeded in penetrating our positions. All available supporting arms—mortars, machine guns, artillery, and even air support—are used to aid the defense. For our rifle squads this mission was divided into three parts:

(1) To take the enemy under fire once he comes into small-arms range of the squad's fighting position; the enemy is to be destroyed as far forward of the position as is possible. Obviously, the closer the enemy comes to the squad's position, the more friendly casualties he can inflict.

(2) If the enemy continues to press his attack to the point where he launches an assault, the rifle squad's mission is to repel the attack by continuing to deliver fire as part of the unit's final protective fires and, if necessary, by using hand-to-hand combat.

(3) If the enemy succeeds in penetrating the platoon's position, the rifle squads hold their positions and deliver fire on the intruding enemy and participate in counterattacks to destroy the enemy and restore the battle position.

There are two reasons for assuming a defensive posture: to gain time while waiting for more favorable conditions for the offense, or to occupy choice key terrain features—high ground, chokepoints, or good fields of fire.

There are several advantages of being in a defense posture:

(1) The use of field fortifications
(2) Fewer losses of men and matériel
(3) Effective use of preplanned fires such as mortars, artillery, and naval gunfire
(4) Choice of key terrain features
(5) Better coordination and control between friendly units.

There are also several disadvantages to being in a defensive posture: the attacker has the initiative, can mass his forces, and has the element of surprise, while the defender's morale will drop the longer he remains in his defensive position.

There are two types of defense—perimeter and linear—and they are parts of the main line of resistance. The MLR is, quite simply, the front line. A perimeter defense is where the outline of the MLR is circular. It is used when a unit must be prepared to meet an attack from any given direction. When frontiersmen circled their wagons for protection, they formed a hasty perimeter defense. In combat, a perimeter defense would be the forward edge of the fighting position. The linear defense is one where the outline of the MLR generally runs in a straight line. It is used when defending a wide area of terrain, with little threat of the enemy attacking from the unit's flanks or rear areas.

With Dog Company positioned in a linear defensive position we knew we gave the North Koreans the advantage of mobility. Thus, our area security was always a critical factor in our day-to-day lives. To constantly insure the unit's safety, our company's security forces were always posted—alert and watching and waiting for any sign of enemy movement. Our security teams would help prevent a surprise attack while we improved our platoon's positions. To accomplish this, three defensive security measures were available: observation posts, listening posts, and security patrols.

The purpose of the observation post (OP) was to provide daylight observation forward of the MLR. Its mission was to immediately report any enemy activity that is observed. These observation posts were usually located on the first key terrain three hundred to five hundred yards to our front, allowing for good observation. This advantage added a degree of depth to our defensive positions. Observation posts were placed in covered and concealed positions so that we could observe the most likely enemy avenues of approach. Manned by at least two Marines, they were assigned specific sectors of observation to the front and maintained at least on 50 percent alert. The primary means of communication for the observation post was communication (comm) wire, laid either to the platoon or to the company command post. Our observation posts were established just before dawn with those Marines assigned to OP duty returning to the company lines just after dark. Routes in and out of the observation post were made known to everyone, as were the exact locations of all of the OPs. The observation posts also had prescribed times for checking in and reporting enemy activity, accomplishing two things: showing that the communications lines were in good working order and helping to keep those Marines on duty alert.

The second security measure that we used was the listening post (LP), which provided security during darkness and during periods of reduced visibility caused by snow, fog, or rain. The men assigned to the LPs used their ears rather than their eyes, making absolute silence mandatory. Because they were used during periods of reduced visibility, listening posts were usually located closer to the MLR (one hundred to three hundred yards) than observation posts, and were normally placed in open areas or along the flanks of the avenues of approach that we thought the enemy might use for his night movements. Like the OP, the LP was usually manned by two Marines, with their primary means of communication—again—being wire. The LPs were established just after dark and typically were withdrawn just before dawn. Routes to and from the LPs were also known to everyone who would man them, and their locations were known to everyone along the MLR. The frequency of relief for the listening posts was affected by the physical condition of the men, the cold weather, and anticipated future combat operations.

The third security measure, and by far the most dangerous, was the daily security patrol. Our patrols were sent forward of the MLR looking for signs of enemy activity to our front. The patrols were to detect infiltration by the enemy, kill the infiltrators or take them prisoner, and to protect the company against surprise attack or possible ambush. They were also used to bring relief teams out to our listening posts at night. The range of our security patrols was normally within five hundred yards of the company's lines and the patrols—conducted at irregular intervals—were planned to move along enemy avenues of approach that could not be adequately covered by security posts. The size of these security patrols varied depending upon the enemy situation and the distance from the MLR, and were prescribed by the company commander. Radio was the primary means of communication, but many times we had to depend upon comm wire carried along with the security patrol.

We learned that while in our defensive position we had to be extremely conscious of anything suspicious around our area. Consequently, movement of any kind was likely to cause the platoon to become alert to a possible attack by the North Koreans. In order to prevent mistaking a security patrol, LP, or OP team for the enemy, set procedures were always used for immediate identification while moving through defensive lines. Challenge-and-response passwords were established to identify "friendly" Marines. Known by all members of the unit, they included two-word types (Brooklyn/Bridge) and number combinations—"the challenge and password number *must* total eleven" (if the challenge was six, the password was five).

One of the more difficult procedures that we learned was the passage of one friendly unit through another's lines. Although the explanation of this procedure sounds rather simple, the actual execution was always dangerous. Before exiting the lines, the patrol would make a brief stop inside the friendly lines while the patrol leader would meet with the Marines on duty requesting to leave. Then the patrol was guided through the lines. To reenter, a brief halt was made outside of the friendly lines in a well-covered position, while the patrol leader, messenger, or the patrol's radio operator would make liaison with the friendly lines. The challenges and passwords were used for recognition, a member of the patrol would be assigned to bring the group forward, and they would be guided back through the lines. The assistant patrol leader was the last man to pass through the lines, while the patrol leader counted and identified each member of his patrol, making sure that no enemy "tag-alongs" had joined his group. The final step in the process was to bring the patrol safely back to a designated area within friendly lines for a security patrol debrief. The opportunities for a variety of things to go wrong, especially during nighttime, are obvious.

Noise, light, and camouflage discipline were always considered very important aspects of our life on the lines. We had learned the fundamentals during basic training; they'd been reinforced at Camp Pendleton and during cold-weather training at Pickle Meadows, but in Korea they were viewed as matters of life or death. The company as a whole and the individual Marine were constantly reminded to maintain strict camouflage discipline. That meant avoiding any activity that could change the appearance of an area or reveal the presence of our positions and our equipment. "Camouflage is continuous" was the phrase used daily, and by having our OP and LP positions observe our defensive line to see what they looked like from a distance, we tried to keep our positions looking as natural—and unchanged—as possible.

Blackout rules were always observed on the line. Fires were only used well behind the lines, eliminating the possibility of detection due to smoke and light. All flashlights were fitted with red lenses and, on the rare occasions they were used, were turned on underneath the protection of a poncho. Smoking was forbidden on the lines.

Noise, particularly noise made at night, was a constant problem. Our dog tags were taped together, canteens were silenced, and electrical tape was always in great demand to help silence noise-producing equipment. We learned quickly that even the simplest of sounds could become the most fatal of mistakes.

8

Sniper School

After several weeks in our defensive positions with D Company up on Hill 812, a unique opportunity presented itself. It began with a visit to our bunker by our company gunnery sergeant, just about two weeks before Christmas 1951.

"PFC Hamblen, I was lookin' at your service record book yesterday and it shows me that you shot expert back at boot camp with a score of 224 points out of 250. The company is looking for six Marines to send to the division's sniper school over at Camp Tripoli, and I want to know if you are willing to go. I can't tell you too much about the school, other than that it'll improve your shooting, but I *do* know that once you finish there you'll come back to your platoon and be used along our lines as we need you. So, what d'ya say, Hamblen? Are you in or out?"

I didn't hesitate. The rifle being used by our two-man sniper teams was the '03 Springfield. Having used that old but reliable rifle during many deer seasons in Maine, I was more than familiar with its capabilities and fine reputation for accuracy. I saw the gunny's offer as a great opportunity.

"Okay, Gunny, you can count me in."

The following day I joined the five other Marines from the company who had also been selected. As we rode back toward Camp Tripoli in the bed of a covered supply truck, I introduced myself to a crusty old corporal who was soon to become my sniping-team partner. As he patted down his dirty field jacket, looking for matches to light his cigarette, he caught me staring.

"My name's Hamblen, corporal, and I was wondering what you thought about this sniper-school business. Do you think it's a good deal or not?"

"Yeah, I think that it's probably a pretty good deal 'cause it'll get us off the front lines for a little while. They say that the living conditions down at Camp Tripoli are pretty good and the chow is hot. I smell like I could do with a shower and I know that I could handle some hot chow. It's been three weeks since I've even felt clean. How about you?"

"I came in with the 15th Draft Replacement Battalion and have been with third platoon ever since we arrived. What platoon are you with?"

"I was a squad leader in first platoon, but the gunny said he was lookin' for snipers more than squad leaders, so I volunteered for this."

"How long have you been in, corporal?"

"Carico's the name. I've managed to keep these corporal chevrons sewn on my sleeve for the last nine months, but I've been in the Corps for thirteen years. I was a rifle-team shooter for about three years after the war. Shooting has always been a big part of my life, but it ain't too easy being a thirty-five-year-old corporal and back with the grunts. Every time I make corporal, I get too close to the ol' jug and get myself in trouble. I still have shirts with different sets of stripes sewn on the sleeves, but maybe this war will change all of that. I figure that if I can get enough points, I'll be able to leave here in just four more months, so becoming a sniper may just help me to get back home. I think I'd like that."

I took an immediate liking to Corporal Carico and thought that his many years spent with the infantry and his past shooting experiences in the Corps would help me to become a better shooter and a better grunt. His personal experiences, spanning the days before World War II, five years in the Pacific, and now this war, were to help me understand just why it was that some men stayed on in the

Corps, while others left it to pursue an easier civilian life. To Corporal Carico, the Corps was his home.

The ten-day sniper school was designed to first teach us the finer points of rifle marksmanship and then show us how to apply as snipers what we had learned, to be used by our company commander to kill any NKPA or Chinese Communists that we could locate using binoculars or our 20X field spotting scope. Our instructors worked on the assumption that we would practice the techniques of stealth required of a sniper by virtue of the fact that when we were on the lines to be seen was to be shot. So the emphasis at sniper school was geared toward enhancing our proficiency as riflemen rather than improving our use of cover and concealment.

We began our schooling, as always, by listening to one of our shooting coaches describe the weapon we would be using.

"The standard U.S. Model 1903 Springfield rifle, caliber .30-06, is a five-shot, bolt-action, shoulder-fired weapon. This rifle has a weight of eight point-seven pounds, has a twenty-four-inch barrel and is forty-three point two inches in length. It fires a flat-based, one hundred and fifty–grain bullet, with a muzzle velocity of twenty-seven hundred feet per second. The full-length, one-piece stock has a straight grip with finger grooves in the fore-end. Its steel buttplate contains a hinged trapdoor that gives access to the hole within that contains cleaning accessories. The rear sight, adjustable for windage and elevation, is attached to the breech end of the barrel. The one-piece wooden handguard extends forward to the end of the fore-end. The barrel has a groove diameter of point three oh eight inches, with four-groove rifling having a pitch of one turn in ten inches.

"However, the rifle that you Marines will be issued, once you complete this course of instruction, will be a modified version of the '03. The M1903A-4 is equipped with a better barrel, a better stock, and with a Unertl eight-power telescopic sight. The field of view provided by this high-quality rifle scope is eight feet and the accuracy of this modified '03, combined with the magnification of the Unertl scope and the training that you'll receive during this course, will allow you to hit your target at ranges in excess of a thousand yards."

For those next ten days we learned how to shoot the '03, beginning at a range of two hundred yards, and lengthening the distance to our targets to one thousand yards. Our targets were empty white fifty-five-gallon oil barrels, with a man-size silhouette painted on each barrel.

While one of us was designated as the "shooter" the other member of the team became the "spotter" and, using a pair of 7 × 50 binoculars or a spotting scope, he would observe the strike of bullet on the designated target. If the shooter missed his target, the observer would immediately give his partner the elevation and lateral sighting corrections enabling him to hit the target with a second shot. It was always this two-man effort that allowed us to get our shots on target. We practiced each day, despite the bitter cold, and worked at being a team.

I think that it was the combination of Corporal Carico's abilities as a trained rifleman and my desire to learn that made us a good team. When we finished the course at Camp Tripoli, we returned to D Company eager to show off our new talents. We didn't have to wait long.

Once a day, usually in the morning, South Korean laborers known as "chigger bears" carried containers of hot chow, soup, and coffee up to a secure area that was located on the reverse slope of our company's position. While Marines on the line took turns moving out of their positions to where the hot meal was being served, those men who remained behind provided security. This pattern of movement had foolishly been established on a daily basis and after being noticed by the NKPA, we became targets for their snipers. Thus, Corporal Carico and I were told to report to the company gunnery sergeant as soon as we returned from Camp Tripoli.

"I'm glad to see you made it back. Since you've been gone we've had our hands full with a bunch of gook snip-

ers who have taken a fancy to shooting at us when we try
to get to chow. I've sent the other two teams back to their
platoons and I want you two to set up near the right flank
of the company and get a bead on whoever is doing the
sniping. Most of the firing is coming from over near that
area. Now you can show us what you learned while you
were vacationing over at Camp Tripoli."

Corporal Carico and I scouted out the best position we
could find to give us an advantage over the enemy sniper.
We waited until just before sunrise before we moved into
our firing position.

Right on schedule, the chigger bears, moving at a dogtrot
along with their Marine escorts, came toward our company
position and set up their serving area about three hundred
yards behind the center of the company's lines. On this
morning it was the third platoon's turn to eat first, making
Corporal Carico and me even more intent to get a shot at
the gook sniper. While Corporal Carico used the spotting
scope to scan the hills to our front, I used our binoculars to
overlap the same area that he was viewing. A cloud of dust
gave the North Korean sniper away.

"Corporal, do you see that white-faced boulder, two fingers to the right of that hilltop? Keep your scope zeroed in
on the base of that boulder and tell me what you see."

"Well, I'll be. It looks like Luke the Gook is working on
diggin' himself a better hole. Do you see his rifle?"

"I'm not sure, but I think that I can see the barrel of a
rifle right next to him."

"How far away do you think he is, Ham?"

"He looks to be about four hundred yards out, at the
most."

We continued to study this North Korean soldier as he
popped up and down from his position, emptying the contents of an apron he was wearing over the edge of his fighting hole.

"He just might be makin' that hole bigger, for another
pal of his. Let's just keep an eye on him, Ham, and we'll
see if he stops diggin' and makes a grab for that rifle."

We waited for at least ten minutes, watching that enemy soldier's every move, when he suddenly stopped digging, looked down at his wristwatch, and made a move for his rifle. It had a scope attached to it—all the indication I needed to put him into the crosshairs of the Unertl scope and, with one shot, end his sniping career.

After reporting in to the company gunnery sergeant and telling him of our success, Corporal Carico and I were sent down to where the hot breakfast was being served to the company. After passing through the chow line and filling up our mess kits with hot scrambled eggs, bacon, and slices of toast, we filled our canteen cups with hot coffee and found a place to sit along a wall made of sandbags. My sniper-team partner wanted to talk.

"Ham, I'm not sure how you feel after you shot that North Korean, but having gotten to know you during these last couple of weeks and knowing that you were raised as a Quaker, I don't want you to feel badly about having to take another man's life. The same thing happened to me in the beginning of World War II. I was a young kid, eager to join the Corps and fight. It all seemed pretty glorious until the shooting started. I saw more killing than I ever wanted to. Then you change. You learn to do what you have to, and that's it. I want you to understand that I know what's going through your mind, 'cause I probably felt the same way back then as you do now. I was glad to see that you didn't enjoy doing it. This is war and the enemy will kill you any time he gets the chance. I don't care if it's a trained soldier, an old woman, or even a little kid; you can't take a chance on what they'll do. Just use your instincts and trust in the Marines in your squad, and you'll be okay. That's all I want to tell you."

For the first time since I had joined the Marine Corps, someone had actually taken the time to tell me that he, too, had been scared and that I was not alone in my thoughts on whether or not it was right to take another man's life. This old corporal's concerns for my feelings were genuine and his insight helped to relieve my initial feelings of guilt. To him, I had passed the test and that was all that mattered.

D Company spent the month of January occupying the same defensive positions we had been introduced to since our arrival. During that time our daily routine varied little. OP and LP patrols were conducted every day as were our nighttime security patrols. When I wasn't up on the line with my fire team in the third platoon, I was teamed up with Corporal Carico moving within company's boundaries and trading shots with the NKPA.

After having spent nearly three weeks on the line, Corporal Carico, a PFC Gordon, and I were given permission to go to Camp Tripoli and use the hot-shower facility. It was welcome news to be taken off the line and being granted the better part of a day to get clean, and we took every opportunity to savor this moment. Using our haversacks as a "ditty bag," each of us placed one clean bar of Ivory soap, a new tube of toothpaste and toothbrush, one fresh razor, a face cloth, and our cleanest dirty towels inside. Then, armed with our M-1s and canvas-web fighting equipment, we hitched a ride back to Camp Tripoli in one of our company's supply trucks.

The shower system at Camp Tripoli was an infantry-man's delight and a logistician's nightmare. As we dirty Marines entered the canvas tents, we stacked our rifles, stripped off our equipment and cold-weather clothing, placing it in a tagged bin, and then tossed our dirty uniforms and long johns onto a growing pile of filthy clothing, destined for the camp's laundry.

Entering the shower, we stood under the warm-water spray, closed our eyes, and became lost in our dreams of home, family, and loved ones. In scrubbing ourselves clean of the dirt and stink of Korea and removing the layers of soot acquired from many hours spent within our bunkers, we also cleansed ourselves of the war. No matter how brief the time, it was the closest thing to total contentment we would know while we were up on the line.

By the time the bar of Ivory had become nothing more

than a thin sliver, held in a wet and wrinkled hand, reality crept back and we shuffled off toward a huge drying room on the other side of the showers. Here, each of us was handed a fresh pair of long johns and one set of clean but used utilities that had once belonged to some other dirty Marine. Young privates would suddenly find themselves wearing utility shirts that bore the black chevrons of a staff sergeant, while a gunnery sergeant might find himself wearing the clean uniform of some second class hospital corpsman, complete with the medical caduceus stenciled on the sleeve. But no one seemed to care; the uniforms were clean, dry, and they fitted, which was all that really mattered.

After getting dressed, we found our way to one of the camp's mess halls and took our time eating a hot meal before having to go out in the cold and hitch a ride back to D Company. After Corporal Carico had finished smoking one last cigarette, he looked over at Gordon and me and motioned with his thumb. We knew it was time to hit the road. Still having several hours of daylight remaining before the sun would set behind the western hills, we walked along the frozen road and listened for the sound of an approaching vehicle. An Army supply truck happened to be passing and we waved to the driver, signaling for him to stop.

"How far are you jarheads going?"

"We're headed up to the 5th Marines area. Can we catch a ride?"

"Sure, hop in the back, and I'll have you there in half an hour."

"Thanks, bub. We sure do appreciate this."

As we rode along in the back of the truck Corporal Carico's curiosity took the better of him and he began to quietly investigate the contents of several wooden crates that were centered in the bed of the truck.

"Hey, Ham, would you look at this! This guy is carrying smoked hams and fresh eggs. Wouldn't we make some kind of hit with the guys back at the platoon if we showed up with eggs and ham?"

"What about the driver?" Gordon asked.

"The hell with him, Gordon. He's Army and we're Marines. He should have known better than to pick up three Marines and put them in the back of a truck loaded with food. Besides, by the time anyone finds out that a few items are missing, we'll be gone and so will the evidence. Just stuff a couple of these big hams in your haversacks and I'll keep the driver busy when we get near our drop-off point."

As Corporal Carico watched the progress of the truck and kept the driver occupied in conversation, PFC Gordon and I pulled four hams and several dozen eggs out of the crates and tucked them inside of our haversacks. The driver never saw a thing.

"Okay, bub, you can let us out just up ahead. We sure do thank you for the ride."

When the supply truck stopped, Gordon and I jumped out and remained directly behind the truck so that the driver wouldn't be able to see us in either of his two large side mirrors. Corporal Carico walked up to the driver's door and again thanked the soldier for the lift, while Gordon and I moved away from the truck and from the attention of the unsuspecting driver. With black smoke pouring from the truck's twin stacks, the driver shifted gears and continued down the road toward his original destination. As we laughed and congratulated ourselves for liberating the food from the hands of the U.S. Army, Corporal Carico took charge.

"We need to hide that stuff before we go back to the company area. We'll tell the company gunny what we've 'found' and he can send a jeep down here and bring these goodies back to the CP. That way it won't look like we stole this stuff."

There was no doubt in either my mind or Gordon's as to why Carico had been a corporal half a dozen times, but if he wasn't worried about being caught for theft, than neither were we. He rationalized his actions by saying that he was doing this not for himself, but for the Marines in the company.

The next day, Corporal Carico walked over to where PFC Gordon and I were standing duty and said, "You guys won't believe this, but there's an Army captain, a supply sergeant, and a truck driver down at the company CP trying to find out if any Marines from this company came back to camp yesterday in the back of one of their supply trucks. The Army is accusing them of stealing food from the back of one of their trucks. Can you believe the nerve of those guys? The company gunny says he's going to take care of it, but the CO was really lucky, 'cause he and the first sergeant had just finished eating their scrambled eggs and sliced smoked ham when that doggie captain and his pals showed up."

9

Winter Operations

The use of helicopters in combat, whether for battalion troop lifts or in resupplying frontline units, had been viewed as something of a novelty only a year earlier, but during the second week of January 1952, Operation Mousetrap began as a real test of the ability of Marine Corps Sikorsky HRS-1 helicopters to launch antiguerrilla attacks on very short notice. Marines from D Company were a part of that operation. On the morning of January 14, at 1000, two Marine rifle companies—more than five hundred men—were airlifted into a landing site that had been cleared by the division's air delivery platoon. Given specific areas of responsibility, the letter companies fanned out and we began looking for signs of North Korean soldiers.

Third platoon occupied positions on a ridgeline overlooking a very small village to watch for enemy infiltrators. This tiny village had been considered secure for several weeks, but small groups of North Korean soldiers had somehow managed to infiltrate the MLR in an attempt to attack U.S. Army and Marine positions from the rear. Our high command was apprehensive of them being able to mass their forces and attack.

On the second day of the operation several Marines within my squad noticed a faint plume of white smoke rising from one of three thatch-roofed hooches down in the abandoned village, so we were given the mission to take a closer look. As we prepared to move off our ridgeline, we were joined by two Korean Marine Corps (KMC) interpreters who had just been assigned to travel with the company.

With the order of march established by our squad leader, Corporal Davis, those Marines who had been issued skis moved along our squad's flanks, while the rest of us trudged through the knee-deep snow wearing snowshoes. The second platoon of D Company watched our progress and covered our approach to the village. The better part of an hour passed before our squad was in position. The Korean Marine interpreters were given the opportunity to try and contact whoever was inside the little hooch, and while the interpreters shouted the equivalent of "come outside with your hands held high," we took up firing positions just in case anyone decided to ignore the opportunity to surrender. It paid off.

After waiting several minutes for any sign of activity from within the three hooches, Corporal Davis directed one of our Marines to fire a burst from his BAR into the roof of the hooch that had the smoke coming from its chimney. Within seconds the wooden door was flung open and four North Korean soldiers, each clad in a white jacket and wearing white tennis shoes, ran out into the snow with their hands waving wildly above their heads. On command from our interpreters, they stopped running and suddenly started bowing up and down in the direction of our rifle squad.

"Keep your eyes on those other two hooches. This may be some trick those gooks have thought up. Gordon, fire another magazine into that hooch and see if it helps persuade any more of their pals to come outside."

As twenty .30-caliber rounds ripped into the roof of the first hooch the rest of us kept our rifles trained on the other two shacks and on the four frightened prisoners. They were still standing thirty-some yards away in knee-deep snow, undoubtedly convinced that they were about to be executed.

The barrel of a rifle began to inch its way over a window sill on the far hooch and, seeing the movement, two Marines fired M-1s through the opened window. Screams came from within the hooch, followed by silence. We watched as the door to that hooch slowly opened and, to our surprise, four more North Korean soldiers ran out into the snow. Again, Corporal Davis had Gordon fire another twenty-round magazine into all three of the hooches, and again we watched and waited.

When no one else appeared and our squad leader was satisfied that it was safe to move in, he signaled to one of our fire teams to physically search the buildings as we covered their every move.

The first group of prisoners was told by our KMC interpreters to join their four friends and then to walk forward, one at a time, arms above their heads, to a position closer to our squad. With protection provided by Private Hopkins, one of the KMC interpreters and another Marine rifleman searched the eight North Koreans.

The bodies of three dead North Korean soldiers were dragged outside and thoroughly searched. To our surprise, the enemy soldiers had been armed with just two U.S.-made .30-caliber carbines and had carried less than ten rounds of carbine ammunition among them. Their captured weapons were tagged and would ultimately be sent up the chain of command to find out where they had come from. The location of the three dead NKPA soldiers was also recorded.

Corporal Davis had radioed back to our platoon leader, 1st Lieutenant Hill, and explained exactly what had taken place. Then, leaving his radio operator standing beside the dead North Koreans, he came to where the rest of the squad stood and told us that we would soon be joined by the rest of our platoon. First platoon was also coming down to see the results of our brief firefight and to help escort our prisoners.

As we waited, Corporal Davis said, "Take a real good look at these gooks. They can't be any more than eighteen or nineteen years old and they sure don't give 'em very much to wear. How they can survive with so little gear is beyond me, but I don't feel sorry for 'em. I just wonder where they got those two carbines."

The dead North Koreans appeared to be about the same age as our prisoners. The white-colored clothing that was common to all of them was a lightweight linen material that provided very little protection from the bitter cold. Even worse was the quality of their footwear. We had been given a new insulated black-rubber combat boot—we called it the "Mickey Mouse boot"—which replaced the old shoe pac; our enemy wore only a lightweight, white tennis shoe that offered absolutely no protection from frostbite. They looked like ballet slippers.

Our interpreters apparently were not being answered to their satisfaction and as each new question was asked, it was followed by a vicious slap to the side of a North Korean's head. The South Korean Marines' contempt for, and hatred of, the North Korean soldiers was something that we had heard of but had not witnessed before. Fortunately for the prisoners, the interpreters realized that eight live prisoners would be a much better source of intelligence than eight dead ones, and accordingly restrained themselves.

Shortly after we were joined by the rest of the Marines in our platoon, 1st platoon arrived and we prepared the prisoners for the cross-country march back to our company's main position. They were placed in a column with their gloveless hands tied behind their backs and empty sandbags placed over their heads. A length of black communication wire connected them from neck to neck.

When we arrived back at the company command post, we learned that two Marine HRS-1 helicopters had been requested to transport the prisoners to a more secure area in the rear for debriefings and interrogations. Though they must have been terrified by the flight and by fears of execution, we knew that they would obviously be treated far better by their foreign enemies than they were treated by their own countrymen.

In early February, a deception plan known as Operation Clam-Up was put into effect across the entire front of the

MLR. For the Marines in D Company, the results of this operation were barely short of a disaster. The purpose of this large-scale operation was to fake a withdrawal and lure the enemy into sending out patrols that would, it was hoped, yield prisoners to units of the U.S. Eighth Army. A message sent from the 1st Marine Division headquarters directed the 1st, 5th, and 7th regiments to "attempt to decoy the enemy into dispatching patrols against our lines and ambush and capture such patrols."

With the 11th Marines' artillery firing twelve thousand rounds of harassing and interdiction missions as if to cover a large-scale withdrawal, the three Marine regiments on the MLR—from left to right the Korean Marine Corps (KMC), 1st Marines, and 7th Marines—did their part to fool the enemy. Those units that were held in reserve executed daylight marches on foot to the rear and then returned to their original positions after dark by means of truck convoys. Our regiment, the 5th Marines, was sent back to Camp Tripoli and was also required to participate in the feigned withdrawal.

After our artillery units had completed their covering fire, the entire length of the front line was plunged into an eerie silence. It was during the second day of this five-day operation that our platoon, as part of a company move, was sent to reoccupy our old positions along the defensive line. We had been instructed to observe very strict noise and light discipline—no Marine was allowed to smoke a cigarette within several hundred yards of the lines during the daytime, and absolutely no smoking was permitted at night. The use of all flashlights was prohibited and adherence to our challenge and password security plan was in effect for all Marines moving within our platoon sector. We slipped back into our former positions, which had been protected during the day by one of our platoons, and waited.

The quiet of the winter night was broken when a North Korean loudspeaker system unexpectedly blared, "Marines, Marines, you will die tonight. We know who you are,

Number two battalion, 5th Marines. We are coming to kill you."

Corporal Carico was sitting beside me when the voice on the loudspeaker began.

"Ya know, Ham, the Japanese used that same tactic in the Pacific. They want to get on our nerves and see if they can draw our fire. They'll keep that crap up all night long, so get used to it."

Somewhere close to midnight the sounds of rifle fire close by brought everyone to their feet. We saw the muzzle flashes from North Korean rifles as they tried to get the Marines along the line to shoot back and give away their positions. Suddenly, off to our left flank, one Marine platoon opened fire on an unseen enemy and briefly illuminated the area with white phosphorous grenades. The screams of men being burned could be heard and we could only imagine what was happening out in front of Hill 812.

Word came the next morning that a North Korean patrol had crept up toward the company's lines until it was moving through our barbed wire. Not until one of them had almost stepped on a Marine had that platoon opened fire. Surprisingly, the white phosphorous grenades hadn't been thrown by our men, but had been used by the North Koreans in their attempt to get away from the deadly fire of the Marines. The enemy left behind ten dead and two wounded.

That small—but important—action alerted the North Koreans to the fact that not all of the Marines had left the area, so on February 13 our battalion was on the receiving end of the heaviest concentration of enemy artillery and mortar fire that we had experienced since our arrival. Three hundred and forty-four artillery rounds and 1,469 mortar rounds were fired at us during that next day and night.*

*The number of enemy rounds that landed in or near our positions was not an estimate: The amount of incoming rounds was the subject of daily reports sent by each squad leader to his respective platoon leader, and then up the chain of command.

Our surviving that incoming fire without suffering any casualties within the company is testimony to just how well
our trench-line system, fighting holes, and bunkers were
constructed.

For the next two days, the tactics of the North Koreans
remained the same—they sent out probing patrols to determine if our regiment had actually given up its positions. By
not patrolling out beyond our front lines, we suckered them
in and then shot the hell out of them when they got too curious.

Overall, Operation Clam-Up fell far short of its goal.
During the time that the Marines were pulled back from
their positions, the NKPA wasted no time in resupplying
their units with food, water, and most important, ammunition. The NKPA did lose a number of men to small-arms
fire—fifty-six dead and fifty-four wounded, but during the
same five days of "immunity" from our artillery fire, they
more than made up for their losses in manpower. It was reported that five deserters from the mortar company of the
1st Battalion, 91st Regiment, 45th NKPA Division revealed
that advantage had been taken of Operation Clam-Up by
detailing mortar personnel and men from the rifle companies to carry ammunition up to the line. During the five-
day lull, according to these prisoners, 2,600 rounds were
brought up for the company's nine mortars.

It was shortly after Operation Clam-Up that Corporal Davis departed Korea for the States. I was given his position
as the third-squad leader of the third platoon, Dog Company, 2/5. His boots would be hard to fill. Though I hadn't
known of his plans to recommend me to our platoon leader
as his replacement, he had been grooming me for the position and I would try my best not to let him down. He had
been fair, honest, and demanding of the Marines in his
squad, and he had gotten to know our strengths and weak-
nesses. He had never asked any of us to do something that
he wouldn't do and I thought that if I used his good example as my guide I would do a pretty fair job of it. Although
I was still a private first class, I alone was now held re-

sponsible for the welfare, training, and discipline of the
Marines in three fire teams—nine men—and for their tactical employment and fire discipline in combat.

In support of Operation Clam-Up, several tanks from our
1st Tank Battalion had been assigned to cover Dog Company's sector of fire area. It was during the time that they
were positioned with our company that I learned how to
use a tank effectively against the NKPA. Behind our
squad's position was a rocky slope that allowed a single
tank to move close enough to the front lines—remaining
hidden in a "hull-defilade" position—and able to fire its
90-millimeter gun at enemy targets of opportunity several
thousand yards away. To us, the tank was our "long-range"
sniper and we established a symbiotic relationship with the
three Marines who lived inside it. If we could find a suit-
able target and the tank was nearby, they would answer our
call.

There were some obvious advantages in having the tank
around. By using an external telephone line that was located
at the right rear of the tank, we could talk directly to the
tank's commander. Using a clock system of reference, we
could designate enemy targets over the tank-infantry telephone. The forty-foot phone-extension line was long enough
to permit us to take cover on either side of the tank and, in
some circumstances, underneath it, while the tank was firing.
While we provided close protection for the tank, it provided
us with high-velocity direct fire. We also learned that there
was one very big disadvantage in having a tank around—it
drew a considerable amount of the enemy's fire.

One morning, while Corporal Carico and I had been
busy using our spotter scope and binoculars to watch for
enemy movement, we heard the unmistakable rumble of the
approaching tank. I left the bunker to request the tanker's
help and to guide the tank into a newly dug-out firing position close to our bunker. Corporal Carico remained inside
and continued to scan the far hills for targets. The tank's
new firing position had been improved by our squad, which
had spent several hours digging out a trench line that al-

lowed for one Marine to position himself, lying beneath the belly of the tank, with enough clearance to peer out in the direction of the enemy and direct the tank's fire using the internal telephone line. I was to be the first one to try out the new position.

As squad leader I was assigned several walkie-talkie radios that enabled me to communicate with my fire-team leaders, my platoon leader, or even with our company commander simply by switching frequencies. By giving Corporal Carico one of these extra radios I could communicate with both him and the tank commander whenever we spotted a good target.

Standing beside the trench line, I motioned to the tank driver to drive forward at a creep until his tank straddled the trench line. Giving the forty-ton tracked vehicle a few minutes to stress-test the sides of my dugout, I ducked underneath the tank with my rifle, binoculars, radio, and the telephone. The wait was not long.

"Ham, can you read me?"

"Yeah, go ahead."

"I've got three Chinks out at your tank's two o'clock, up near Hill 854, at a range of about a thousand yards. It looks like they may be setting up a mortar tube. I can observe the tank's fire. Let's give it a try."

Now it was my turn to talk to the tank.

"Tank, this is infantry."

"Go ahead."

"My partner is in the bunker on your right side and says he's got a good target for you: three gooks settin' up a mortar tube."

"Go ahead."

After passing on Corporal Carico's information to the tank commander, I focused my binoculars on the hillside where the NKPA mortar position was thought to be and listened to the grinding of the tank's machinery as the gunner loaded the 90-millimeter gun and swung the turret in the target's direction. Eyes glued to my binoculars, I waited for the tank to fire. The loud blast and recoil from that

90-millimeter gun shook the earth and rocked the tank,
shaking free mud and dirt from beneath its chassis, covering my head and face. I couldn't see the impact of the
round, but as I spit and wiped the dirt from mouth and face
I could hear the familiar voice of Corporal Carico coming
in over my walkie-talkie.

"Tell 'em too short, Ham. Too short. The direction is
good, but they're about two hundred yards too short."

I relayed Corporal Carico's request for additional range
back to the tank and a second round was fired off within a
few seconds. Again, dirt and dust fell down around my
head, but not as much as the first time and I was able to
watch the round strike the side of Hill 854.

"Ham, tell 'em to fire two more rounds in the same
place. I think that they covered our target real good, 'cause
there ain't no one movin' out there anymore."

Two more 90-millimeter rounds slammed into the spot
that Corporal Carico had identified. As I continued to watch
the area, the tank shifted gears and rolled back and away
from the forward slope of the hill. I heard Corporal
Carico's warning shouted over the roar of the tank's engine.

"Come back inside of the bunker, Ham. That tanker's no
fool. He's played this game before."

In less than a minute, our ridgeline became the concentrated impact area for a barrage of at least a dozen
82-millimeter mortar rounds that the NKPA delivered in obvious retribution for our tank's appearance on the line.

It was simply a matter of tit for tat, and this same tank-
infantry procedure was repeated on a daily basis. The only
change in our strategy was when we used the tanks at
night. The U.S. Army's 92nd Searchlight Company was
still attached to the 1st Marine Division, and their illumination was used in two ways: The first was to directly light
up a suspected area. This would temporarily blind the enemy while they were being fired upon by our tanks, artillery, and organic weapons. The second method was to
"bounce" the brilliant rays of the searchlight off of low
cloud cover, illuminating larger areas of terrain, but in a

more subdued light. This indirect approach was not as effective as the direct method, but it kept the NKPA from patrolling into the lighted areas.

We remained in our defensive posture around the area of the Punchbowl and on Hill 812 until March 1952. It was the last full month that the 5th Marines would spend on the eastern side of Korea. Marine casualties for February were 23 KIA, 102 WIA, and 1 MIA. Enemy losses were reported as 174 confirmed and 381 estimated KIAs, 606 WIAs, and 63 prisoners taken.

10

The Move West

In the spring of 1952, when the United Nations and Communist forces were facing each other from static positions and fighting local engagements, Operation Mixmaster took place. Mixmaster was a complicated rearrangement of U.N. divisions across the entire Korean front during March, and involved the shuffling of about 200,000 men and their equipment over distances from 25 to 180 miles. The 1st Marine Division's Operation Order 8-52, dated March 18, directed the 1st Marine Division to proceed from the divisional reserve area at Camp Tripoli to the new division area east of Munsan-ni, and from there to move into frontline positions. The 7th Marines, after being relieved on the 20th by elements of the 8th ROK Division, assembled at Camp Tripoli and moved by truck to western Korea.

When we got the word that we would be leaving our positions, the wheels were set in motion to prepare ourselves for the long ride. We had been told by our new company commander, Captain William A. Harper, to strip the line clean of all materials that would help us when we set up in our company's new position. Much of our spare time prior to moving out was put to use stacking up second-hand building materials along with anything else that would make our lives just a little more tolerable during the remaining months of winter.

Every effort had been made to insure that all Marines

were outfitted with the new Mickey Mouse boots. The comfort and protection that this one piece of equipment brought to combat operations was viewed by all as nothing short of a godsend. The new boots could be worn with only one pair of heavy cushioned socks and they were guaranteed to keep our feet dry and warm. Our old shoe pacs didn't offer us the same degree of protection—in them it seemed that the more our feet perspired, the more they subsequently froze. The only disadvantage to this new insulated boot was in its innovative design. A pressurized air space between the inner and outer layers of wool-pile insulation was sealed off by a layer of latex, creating a "vapor barrier" that would not allow any body heat to escape. If that air seal was broken by a piece of shrapnel or was punctured by barbed wire a "flat-tire" effect caused the wearer to have one cold foot and one warm foot until the damaged boot was replaced or patched.

As warmth was always a factor of survival in the Korean winter, our endless attempts to find it could be quite novel. Some Marines took extra Sterno-type fuel cans designed to heat C-rations and positioned themselves, wrapped up in their ponchos, over the lit heat cans. While this did provide some degree of relief from the cold, occasionally individuals inhaled too much of the Sterno's noxious fumes, causing them to become violently ill, while others became unconscious.

A few Marines took experimentation with the use of wood alcohol a bit too far. They tried to separate the wood-grain alcohol from the Sterno by chopping up the jellylike fuel and straining the liquid alcohol through a T-shirt for use as the primary ingredient in home brew. The few Marines desperate enough to sample such drinks risked immediate hospitalization or a violent, convulsive death from the effects of wood-alcohol poisoning. This was by no means a common practice, but it happened enough times to convince us not to allow any more of our men to try the deadly concoction. We reasoned that it was bad enough to lose one of our own to combat without adding to the growing evacuation list by drinking wood-grain alcohol to stay warm. The practice came to an abrupt halt when the Marine Corps replaced its Sterno with a new type of fuel bar made with a core of alcohol-impregnated felt.

Just prior to our move west, Dog Company lost a Marine from our first platoon under unusual and tragic circumstances. Small groups of North Korean soldiers had continued to probe our lines during early March, and to counter their patrols our platoon security teams began throwing hand grenades above the heads of the enemy, hoping to create an air-burst effect without having the deadly blast of the grenade smothered in the waist-deep snow. One night, a Marine who had been seen warming his gloved hands with his breath heard the sounds of an approaching North Korean patrol. He removed one hand grenade from his fighting harness, pulled the pin, and let the spoon fly, still holding the grenade tight and counting to three before attempting to throw it in the direction of the North Koreans. But the subzero temperature had caused the condensation from his breath to freeze the hand grenade to his glove, where it exploded, killing him instantly.

Our company's move west began with my squad being assigned to occupy and protect two "six-by" trucks that were part of our motorized convoy. This winter road trip was a continuous stop-and-go affair that covered more than 140 miles of rocky, mud-slick, mountainous roads. During this trip our company's officers demonstrated their concern for the welfare of the Marines in the company with one small but heartfelt gesture.

We had begun our move under cold, dark skies that produced a steady freezing rain, and as our trucks crept along the muddy road all that we could do was to rock back and forth with their movement and stare out from beneath our canvas roofs, feeling wet, cold, and genuinely miserable. Early on the second morning out, our convoy came upon an American Red Cross unit set up at a roadside rest area that was offering hot coffee and stale doughnuts. Perhaps "offering" is not the correct word—they were actually *selling* coffee and doughnuts. Since most of us carried no money, Captain Harper and our platoon leaders pooled their financial resources and bought coffee and doughnuts for every Marine in the company as well as for our drivers. Though this event may seem insignificant, it was considered by every tired, hungry, and sleepless Marine in D Company to be the very best belated Christmas gift imaginable. We would not soon forget our officers' example of thoughtfulness, nor would we forgive the American Red Cross for lining its pockets at the expense of a hungry Marine convoy.

Before our departure, we had been briefed that our regiment would be held in reserve on the Kimpo Peninsula, to be trained for future amphibious landings. These orders were changed during our trans-Korea move, because the division's new battlefield lines had been extended to cover more than thirty miles of hostile terrain. That required the immediate emplacement of our regiment along the new MLR. The 1st Marine Division now numbered 1,364 officers, 24,846 enlisted Marines, 1,100 naval personnel, and 4,400 Koreans from the 1st Korean Marine Corps Regiment. The 5th Marines' mission was to occupy and defend the new defensive positions along the center section of the MLR, with the 1st Marine Regiment on our right flank and the 25th Canadian Infantry Brigade of the Commonwealth Division holding on our left flank. Our battalion, commanded by Lieutenant Colonel William H. Cushing, was placed in reserve and stood ready to relieve either of our regiment's other two battalions on the line, or as an immediate counterattack force. It was not until the following day, March 24, that we received an enemy-situation briefing from our platoon leader and began to realize the size of the enemy opposing us.

"We're facing a new enemy. The Chinese Communist Forces, the CCF, have two armies, the 63rd and 65th, positioned several miles away, and our best intelligence estimates give them a total strength of about fifty thousand men. The 195th Division of the 65th CCF Army is dug in to our direct front. The Chinese have fifteen infantry battalions, supported by ten artillery battalions with one hundred and six field guns aimed at us. And in addition to those units already identified, one more armored division and one airborne brigade are both headed this way."

With orders to dig in and wait near the rear of the 5th Marine Regiment's sector, we returned to our platoons to supervise the hasty construction of our new positions. However, the Chinese didn't allow us the luxury of time; they launched their first attacks along our lines early on the morning of the 25th, firing a concentrated mortar and artillery barrage of 189 rounds, wounding ten of our Marines. Day and night probing attacks—testing our regiment's defenses across the center section of the line—increased as the dance for control of the ground between us and the enemy was joined. Our company spent the next two weeks in regimental reserve, constantly improving the reserve positions behind the MLR for the battalion whose frontline place we would assume. On the morning of April 10 we got the word that we were moving up on the line to replace 1/5.

After we had moved into the 1st Battalion's positions, our platoon leader called for a meeting of his squad leaders and began his brief on what he expected.

"Fox Company is on our left flank and Able Company, One-Five, is on our right flank. The key piece of terrain, a mile out in front of our company's lines, is Hill 67, which is flanked, as we look at it, by Outpost Number Two to the left and Outpost Number Three on the right. Just half a mile from Outpost Number Two is Panmunjom, where the peace talks are going on.

"Our company's job is to send out security patrols between us and Outpost Number Three and to keep that area clear of any Chinks who get between us and that outpost. We'll rotate between the other platoons for these day and night patrols; that schedule is being set up by the CO right now. In the meantime, get your men to improve on the positions we have, 'cause the Chinks' artillery is zeroed in on our lines. The deeper we dig, the better off we'll be."

On April 12, I was assigned to take my squad out toward Outpost 3 on a security patrol. With the welcome addition of three .30-caliber machine-gun teams to reinforce the squad, we left our lines early in the morning, scheduled to return later in the day. However, the Chinese had made other plans for us, which began with their firing off a bright green flare high above the Marines out on Outpost 3.

The first rounds of incoming artillery impacted on the right and left sides of 3, as the Chinese bracketed their target and enemy machine-gun fire began to stitch the ground in front of it, kicking up dirt and splitting rocks between our position and the outpost. I moved my squad behind a low dirt wall. From where we sat we looked toward the north as the enemy artillery fire was joined by mortar rounds that inched their way up the eastern slope of Hill 67. The Chinese had planned the use of their artillery well: first softening up both Hill 67 and Outpost 3, and then shifting their artillery and heavy machine guns to the ground between our lines and the two outposts. As long as they could continue to pound the area that divided us from the outposts, their ground assault would be opposed only by the handful of Marines manning the two hilltops. As we watched for enemy targets, my radioman crawled over to me.

"Ham, the lieutenant says to get back on the double. He says that some Chinks are moving up on the company's right flank and he needs our machine guns back there. *Now!*"

Our platoon leader's orders were not open to any discussion. After alerting my fire-team leaders and machine-gun teams to the change in plans, we left the protection of the dirt wall and headed back toward the company lines at a dogtrot while the enemy artillery and mortar fire continued to pepper the two outposts.

At the company position, we were met by our company gunnery sergeant, Staff Sergeant Miller. "You machine-gunners, get over to first platoon's area and find the lieutenant. He knows where he wants you. Hamblen, get your squad back in on the lines and then try to get some rest, 'cause you'll be taking your reinforced squad out again tomorrow to help set up on OP Number Three. I'll be going along too, just for the walk."

We spent most of that night catnapping and watching our long-range artillery rounds impact far to the north of Hill 67. The occasional sight and sound of some distant secondary explosion would raise a faint cheer from our company lines, but we knew that our next day's assignment would put us closer to the Chinese than we had ever been before. That was nothing for any of us to cheer about. Early the next morning, we would leave our lines and move off in the direction of OP #3.

The enemy artillery and mortar fire had been a rehearsal for an attack on Hill 67 and, realizing the potential danger in defending against their next assault, we made some plans of our own. The following morning the reinforced third platoon, no more than forty Marines, departed Dog Company's lines and moved out quickly to relieve Outpost 3. The Marines who had been on the OP during the night had managed to survive the previous day's artillery and mortar barrage only because of the deep trench line and the heavily fortified bunkers they had constructed. They welcomed our arrival and wasted no time in returning to the safety of their own company's lines.

As part of our defensive plan to counter any frontal assault by the Chinese, our platoon had carried along five empty fifty-five-gallon drums that were later filled with napalm, designed to help us in discouraging the enemy. Staff Sergeant Miller explained his plan for the napalm to the squad leaders.

"We've lugged these barrels of napalm all the way out here to use in front of the OP. We've got enough picks, comm wire, batteries, and TNT to help make it all work. The first and second squads will cover the third squad while we get these barrels out in place. I want you two squad leaders to get busy stringin' barbed wire in front of your positions. Hamblen, gather up your squad and come with me."

Under the direction of Miller and the protection of two rifle squads, we rolled the five barrels of napalm into a shallow trench that ran forward of and parallel to our lines. Then we watched as our enterprising staff sergeant rigged each of the barrels with two one-pound blocks of TNT, complete with electrical firing devices and connected to the communication wire that was run from the barrels back to the center of the OP. We camouflaged the barrels and returned to our positions, knowing that if the Chinese did come at us from the front, our hidden explosive surprise—if it worked—would make life for them more than just a little unpleasant.

The Chinese began to register their artillery and mortars late in the afternoon and then signaled their real intentions when another green flare ignited high above Hill 67.

Our own artillery responded quickly to the Chinese fire and illumination rounds began exploding in the sky forward of our regiment's lines to bring muted daylight to different sections of the battlefield. The brilliance of the burning illumination rounds allowed me to use my binoculars and, once focused, they revealed dozens of helmeted Chinese moving slowly toward our outposts. These small figures disappeared from view as our artillery and 4.2-inch mortars cut into their ranks.

As I moved to rejoin my squad, I was met by Corporal Carico.

"Jesus Christ, Ham, did you get a good look at all them gooks? I heard the Lieutenant say that they think it's just a Commie rehearsal for bigger things to come. What d'ya think about that?"

"If all of this is just a rehearsal, then we may be in very big trouble. That's what I think."

The artillery and mortar fire ceased and there was no more probing of our lines by the Chinese for the next two days, but our Lieutenant's grim prediction of "bigger things" came true on the 15th, when the quiet of the afternoon was suddenly shattered by Chinese Communist artillery rounds impacting on both Hill 67 and on outposts 2 and 3. This was no rehearsal, and as the enemy artillery rounds impacted closer and closer to our company lines, we heard the faint sound of bugles being blown, gradually sounding closer. The enemy's bugles were replaced by the thunder and roar of their mortar rounds impacting all around our outpost. When the barrage lifted, the Chinese came at us from the north, east, and west. While illuminated Marine artillery and mortar fire began to impact among the columns of attacking Chinese, our .30-caliber air-cooled machine guns began to find their mark. Still the Chinese waves moved forward.

Their organization for battle was something we had not seen before. The first ranks of Chinese infantry that came into range carried automatic weapons and Soviet-model burp guns. They were closely followed by rows of grenadiers wearing cloth aprons filled with hand grenades and stick grenades. Behind the grenadiers came men carrying sections of bangalore torpedoes, which are used to breach barbed wire. Behind the demolition men came several ranks of Chinese soldiers carrying wooden ladders and straw mats above their heads, waiting only for the moment when they could be thrown across any remaining barbed wire. The last of the ranks of Chinese infantrymen were unarmed, waiting to retrieve the weapons dropped by dead or dying comrades to use them in continuing the momentum of the ground attack.

Our machine-gun teams did their best at keeping the Chinese from getting close enough to penetrate the defensive barbed wire. While their heavy volume of automatic fire cut into the screaming enemy columns, turning patches of ground red with Chinese blood, small groups of Chinese soldiers managed to continue their charge toward the base of our hill, only to be cut down by our rifle fire.

Our only avenue of escape was to the south, and our signal to pull back was supposed to be the simultaneous detonation of our hidden drums of napalm. Nothing happened.

Staff Sergeant Miller had maintained his position near the center of the hilltop, staying close to the radio and directing the fire of our second squad, until an explosion from an enemy bangalore torpedo opened up a gap near him. He decided it was time to blow the napalm, but his first attempt to use the electrical firing system failed because enemy mortar fire had managed to cut the wiring. Without a moment's hesitation, Miller called for a BAR man to join him on the line and from their vantage point they began to pour automatic-rifle fire into one of the barrels of napalm, hitting a bag of blasting caps that had been taped to the blocks of TNT on the back of the drum. The resulting explosion, sending jellied gasoline and shrapnel flying across the shallow trenchline, created the desired effect and the Chinese infantry began to fall back.

"VT on me. VT on me." Staff Sergeant Miller's request for our battalion's 81-millimeter mortar crews to have their high explosive rounds explode directly above our hilltop was sent over his radio. It was followed by his warning to us, "Rounds on the way. Take cover."

The 81-millimeter mortar is capable of firing a ten-pound high-explosive round to a maximum distance of 4,500 yards. Miller's request for "VT" indicated a barrage of variable time–fused rounds that would explode above the ground at varying heights. With a bursting radius of twenty to thirty yards, each explosion will rain downward, covering a wide area with hot, ripping shrapnel.

Once Miller had received word that the mortar rounds were "on the way" it was only a wait of about thirty seconds before the air above us was filled with steel splinters. As the 81-millimeter mortar rounds exploded over Outpost 3, third platoon found protection in the trenchlines and inside the bunkers on the hill. Those Chinese who had remained standing up in the vicinity of the hill were cut down by the fire, which lasted no more than a minute. The Chinese ground assault on Outpost 3 was stopped just after 0300.

When artillery illumination rounds brought artificial daylight over the outpost, we could see some of the results of the mortar fire, but it would not be until dawn, when we were joined by Marines from second platoon, that we would realize the extent of the carnage. More than sixty Chinese soldiers lay dead, fifty more lay wounded, and a dozen were captured, still wandering around, shell-shocked. Six Marines died during that night on the hill, and twenty-five were evacuated to field hospitals in the rear. We considered ourselves fortunate—only three of the ten Marines assigned to my squad were wounded during the night attack, none too seriously, and all three returned to duty with the platoon after a brief stay in the battalion aid station.

11

Corporal Carico

For several weeks following the night attack on Hill 67 and outposts 2 and 3, the Chinese kept their distance, continuing to probe and test our lines in small numbers but not again daring to send human-wave assaults in our direction. The warmer spring weather had replaced winter snowfall with a continuous heavy downpour, and the company settled into the mundane routine of infantry in the defense— improving on our fixed, watery positions and constantly patrolling along our muddy sector of the MLR, known on our tactical maps as the Jamestown Line.

It was not unusual for Marine battalions to rotate their rifle companies off the front lines, replacing one rifle company with another that had benefited from the luxury of seven days' rest and relaxation at a training camp in the rear of the division's area of responsibility. D Company had been relieved from duty on the front lines in late April, but after enjoying only five days of hot chow, dry uniforms, and some needed rest, we got the word that we would be moving out again, taking over defensive positions that had previously been manned by the Marines of E Company, 2nd Battalion, 5th Marines.

As we made the hasty move into our new positions, we were given a thorough briefing by one of the platoon sergeants from E Company. "We've been up here for about a month now, and it's pretty quiet. We've sent our security patrols out every day, but the Chinese bastards know the ground out there just as good as we do. Our lines are spread real thin, and those gooks can see us move as well as we can spot them. You can see that there ain't a whole hell of a lot of cover on any of those hills to our front. I'd just make damn sure that you always have your security patrols covered by another squad, all ready to go, each time you go out through the wire. The gooks will hit you with mortar fire every chance they get. Good luck."

That tired platoon sergeant was certainly not exaggerating about the distance that our rifle company had been given to cover with only three platoons. After I got my squad set in along our lines, all squad leaders were summoned to meet with the company gunnery sergeant to walk the lines starting from where our first platoon was positioned to the last two-man fighting hole that was occupied by Marines of third platoon. The distance we covered during that walk was almost half a mile long—nearly twice the textbook distance allotted to a rifle company in the defensive!

Late in the afternoon of our fourth day on the lines, I was told to report with Corporal Carico to the company command post to meet with Staff Sergeant Miller for a new assignment.

"Corporal, the CO wants you and Hamblen to take your sniper rifle and see if you can go out and take care of one gook soldier who has been raising hell with the Marines over near first platoon. This guy showed up only two days ago and has made a habit out of firing a couple of eighty-seven-millimeter antitank rounds at our lines. Before sunrise tomorrow, I want the two of you to go out through third platoon's lines and see if you can't get a good bead on that gook."

Our map study showed us the folds and draws that the Chinese soldier had probably used to cover his approach over the rolling ground that lay forward of the first platoon's area, so Corporal Carico and I selected the best route to take us within range of his last-known firing position.

The rest of the day was spent in preparing for the business of sniping. While I cleaned the '03 Springfield and the Unertl scope, Corporal Carico put some time in on cleaning the .30-caliber carbine that he would carry. We would travel light, wearing our normal fighting harnesses and carrying only our rifles, the 20X spotting scope, and two signaling flares to be used in the event of trouble.

I turned my duties as squad leader over to my senior fire-team leader and met up with Corporal Carico to begin our slow walk out through the company lines. By the first light of dawn we had moved up into a finger that provided us with an unobstructed view of the area from where the last enemy antitank rounds had been fired. With Corporal Carico positioned only twenty feet away from me to my left, we began to search the open ground for signs of movement. Carico, using his spotting scope, saw him first, and he whispered his discovery to me. "Ham, I can see him. He's about three hundred yards away to our left front and he's in a trench line. He's fooling around with an anti-tank launcher. Let's just wait and see what he does."

The Chinese soldier had really planned well for shooting at our positions from the safety of his emplacement. It was reported that he had used not just one, but at least four antitank rocket launchers, positioned at various intervals along the trench line. I sighted in and waited only for the moment when he would shoulder his rocket launcher and provide me with enough of himself so that I could not miss from a range of three hundred yards. The shot was not going to be easy. Complicating the situation was the reduced amount of daylight that I had to work with. The 8X Unertl scope was the best there was, but it would have been better to have had the morning sun behind me, casting more light on my target. The early-morning clouds obscured the sun, and I was trying to place him in the crosshairs of my scope when he suddenly moved to the right. The muzzle of the 87-millimeter launcher burned bright white as he fired a rocket in the direction of our company. Then he vanished from my view, only to reappear about thirty yards further down the trench line to the right. Popping up from this new position, he fired off a second rocket.

Corporal Carico kept his spotting scope zeroed in on our target.

"Okay, Ham, you know where he's headed next. Just move to the right about thirty yards and when that little bastard pops up again, let him have it." That Chinese soldier had committed the cardinal sin that gives every rifleman the chance for one well-aimed shot on a moving target—he had established a pattern. When the top of his black hair slowly inched above the rim of the trench line, I lowered the crosshairs of my scope to a point several inches below his chin and fired.

The recoil from the '03 caused the rifle to jump, making me lose my telescopic view of him, but Corporal Carico had not moved at all. He just turned his head toward me and said, "Good shot, Hamblen. Now, let's go home."

His words had not even registered in my mind when the first enemy 60-millimeter mortar round slammed into the side of the hill where Corporal Carico and I were lying.

"Let's go!" I shouted and, as I turned to watch Corporal Carico get up, a second 60-millimeter round exploded directly between his feet.

He vanished for an instant, engulfed in a cloud of orange-white flame and gray smoke, and when the smoke cleared I saw the outline of his shattered body on the ground.

I knew that he was dead before I reached him.

The air around us was filled with the sickening-sweet stench of blood and the foul odor from his ruptured bowels. I knelt beside him and gently turned his body toward me, cradling his head in my left hand. It felt like a sack of beans. He never spoke; his eyes were fixed open in a sleepy skyward-stare.

My friend was gone.

Grabbing for his carbine and the spotting scope, I placed them on his chest and dragged his broken body away from the exposure of the hillside to a place that offered better cover. The enemy mortar team had done its job.

The firing of my white star-cluster flare got the immediate attention of one of our squads, and a short time later I was joined by Marines from our platoon. A stretcher team of two cooks and two truck drivers had come along with the squad. Without much ceremony they lifted the broken body of Corporal Carico onto their green-canvas litter and carried him back through our company lines.

I returned to my bunker alone and wept.

After I had cleaned the Springfield and wrapped it in a towel, I hung it above the bunker's doorway. The spotting scope that Corporal Carico had carried with him did not require any work; it was now useless, shattered by shrapnel.

12

Wounded

We remained in our defensive positions, patrolling and defending our muddy territory along the Jamestown Line until the end of April 1952, when new orders came down from regimental headquarters directing our battalion to move and occupy a sector of the lines that had been previously held by 2nd Battalion, 7th Marines. As a part of this battalion relocation process, our company relieved C Company, 2/7, and a briefing presented by one of the outgoing company's platoon sergeants indicated that the Marines of C Company had spent much of their time patrolling well forward of their lines. Unfortunately, the sequence of events that began on the morning of May 8 told a much different story.

A new regimental operational order had been developed that called for the 1st Battalion, 5th Marines, "to seize and occupy a series of three intermediate objectives en route to OP 3." While the three letter companies of 1st Battalion—A, B, and C—were committed to the raid on suspected Chinese enemy positions, our battalion was to remain in place and deny the Chinese Communists any avenue of escape.

For our company commander to have the best possible picture of what lay before him, one platoon was to conduct a combat patrol to occupy a hilltop less than four hundred yards forward of the company's lines. From this small but key piece of terrain a platoon would be able to carry out multiple tasks acting as the eyes and ears of the company commander. However, the success of the mission would depend on the platoon's ability to communicate. With a telephone line from the hilltop back to the company's command post, any requests for supporting-arms fire could be answered quickly, the enemy terrain could be described, and any enemy activity could be immediately reported. But most important, the Chinese would be denied ownership of that hill.

The third platoon, reinforced by three .30-caliber machine-gun teams, was given this mission, and my third squad was assigned to bring up the rear of the platoon. We were positioned on the reverse slope of a small rise when the first squad began to move out. Our plan called for the second and third squads to follow in trace of the first squad rather than committing the entire platoon to the open and unfamiliar ground between our frontline positions and the objective. First squad had barely made it halfway to the base of the objective when mortar rounds began to fall around them.

We watched as our platoon sergeant, positioned with the second squad, gave his hand-and-arm signals calling for the next squad to move forward. As those Marines went on toward the hill, Navy hospital corpsmen and several groups of litter teams, made up of Marines from the division's band and from our headquarters and service battalion, ran past us to aid the wounded.

As the second squad moved through the area where the first squad had been hit, it shifted direction to the right and found cover in a shallow draw, which would have protected some of the Marines of the first squad had they been able to make it that far. The call for us to move out came from our platoon sergeant and, as we scrambled in an echelon formation to the right of where the second squad had disappeared into the draw, great clouds of white smoke, fired by a Marine artillery battery, began to drift across the ground, obscuring the battlefield. The movement of my squad toward the right side of the hill had been at a quick, nonstop pace, and as we ran on toward the base of the hill, we heard the distant sounds of mortars being fired.

The first enemy mortar rounds impacted to the left of my squad and as I moved forward to where I thought I could direct my fire teams, another barrage of 60-millimeter mortar rounds landed all around us. Instinctively, I turned my body away from the direction of the nearest explosion, but I was too late: The blast knocked me completely off my feet. When the dust and dirt settled, I looked around. Four of the Marines in my squad lay nearby, flat on the ground.

Before I could move, another cluster of 60-millimeter rounds slammed into the ground close by, spraying the air with shrapnel. The concussion from this series of explosions knocked the wind out of me and caused my ears to ring. I rolled over and tried to get up on my feet, but when I bent my left leg a wave of searing pain, unlike anything I had ever experienced, swept up from below and seemed to cover my body. I reached for the place where it hurt the most, between my left ankle and knee; when I pulled my hand away from my trousers my fingers were red with blood. The screams of "Corpsman, Corpsman!" echoed across the backside of the hill, and within what seemed to be only seconds one of our company corpsmen was kneeling by my side.

"Where're you hit, Ham?"

"My left leg, Doc. Christ, it burns, but how does it look?"

"You'll be okay. You picked up two nice chunks of shrapnel and they've gone down to the bone, but I'd guess that you'll be fine."

The calm control in the corpsman's voice made me relax just a little. Since I could do nothing but lie there, I watched as he used his knife to slit open my trouser leg, exposing my wounds. His work was fast but gentle: He emptied a pouch of yellow sulfa onto my leg, removed the one battle dressing from the first-aid pouch attached to my cartridge belt, and then wrapped the bandage around the bloody portion of my leg. From out of his field-jacket pocket came a small box of morphine Syrettes and he injected one of them in my leg. A small, gray cardboard tag, describing my wounds and the field-expedient treatment I had received, was attached to my jacket through a buttonhole, and then I saw him stand up over me.

"Hamblen, I can't do any more for you now. That shot of morphine will kick in soon and you won't feel a thing. Just lay still 'til a litter team gets over here." He looked around for the next-closest patient and he was gone.

When the litter team came to where I was lying, the first Marine who reached me bent down and read the tag that the Doc had left tied to my buttonhole.

"Okay, Hamblen, just keep still and we'll get you back to the company. Do you think you can stand the trip?"

"Yeah, I don't feel too bad. Just don't forget my rifle."

With their own weapons slung over their shoulders, the four Marines lifted me onto their stretcher, and with my M-1 tucked in beside me we started back. Unfortunately, the litter team, unfamiliar with the area, had selected a roundabout route that began to take us by several flooded rice paddies. As they began to walk out onto one of the earthen dikes, a squad of seven Chinese soldiers, hiding behind the dike's far wall, stood up and began to rake us with automatic-rifle fire.

My mind instantly focused on the shouts of "Ambush, Ambush!" and I tried to raise my head up high enough from my litter to locate the direction of the enemy fire. However, the unanimous decision had already been made, and I was dropped on the ground like a sack of potatoes when the four Marines abandoned me for the safety of the distant rice-paddy wall. As I lay on my stretcher, feeling as though I was the highest point of elevation directly between the Chinese and the men of the litter team, the enemy squad charged straight at us.

There was not the slightest doubt in my mind that I was going to die. I was helpless; my rifle was still beside me but I was unable to lift it in the direction of the attacking Chinese. All that I could do was watch them as they came running with spike bayonets fixed to their rifles, shouting back and forth to one another as they continued to fire.

Within seconds they had closed the gap between us. When one of the running soldiers came to within several yards of me, he aimed his rifle at my head and fired. The bullet tore through my field jacket, hitting me at the top of my right shoulder and knocking me half off the stretcher. For whatever reason he didn't fire at me again, but continued running past me, firing in the direction of the Marines behind the paddy wall. I turned my head slowly, watching him pass by and then falling backward as he was shot dead.

The firing and shouting of the Chinese continued as they followed through on their assault. Knowing that I was nothing more than a fish out of water and could be shot or bayoneted at any moment, I lay motionless, praying that the Chinese soldiers would think I was dead and pass me by.

A short time later I felt the tug of a hand as it grasped the collar of my field jacket and began to lift me up.

"You still alive, Ham?"

It was one of the Marines from our company who, as part of a rescue team, had come out to help.

"Looks like you got a few problems."

I was carried back through company lines and brought to a staging area, where the wounded were placed aboard jeeps for a half-hour ride to the battalion's aid station. It was during the next seven days—spent inside a recovery tent—that I learned more about what had happened on May 8.

Because the 1st Battalion was attacking, the artillery support that we had requested prior to our moving out toward our objective had been delayed. Radioed requests for smoke rounds to cover our approach had been denied, resulting in our exposure to the Chinese. To help complicate the situation, we had been led to believe that the ground between our company's lines and the hill had been secured by the patrolling efforts of the previous tenants; it hadn't, and our movement toward the hilltop, which was still occupied by the Chinese, was stopped by their murderous mortar fire.*

Of the four Marines who had made up my first litter team, two had been bayoneted to death, the third was badly wounded, and the fourth survived the ordeal. Three of the four Marines in my squad who had been hit by the mortar fire that day—Privates First Class Gordon, Hale, and Harmon—returned to duty with the company.

Two pieces of shrapnel were removed from my left leg and a Chinese bullet was removed from my shoulder. No bones had been broken and the Navy surgeon who removed the Chinese round from my shoulder later enlightened me as to why I had been spared further damage.

"It's a good thing for you that the Chinese make cheap weapons. The slug that I took out of your shoulder came from a Chicom burp gun. The Chinks use a piece of rubber tire as part of their recoil system and we've learned that they have had to reduce the amount of gunpower in their bullets. If you had been hit with a fully loaded seven-six-two round it probably would have killed you."

I returned to D Company still a little tender, but also a great deal wiser, and resumed my duties as third squad leader of the third platoon only a week after having entered the battalion aid station. I also received a Purple Heart during a formation nearly one month later, and I sent the medal back to my mother and father, who were still living on our farm in Winthrop.

*Records later revealed that the Chinese Communists fired more than four hundred mortar rounds during one five-minute period that day.

13

Bunker Hill

"Bunker Hill" was the name given to a key piece of terrain located a thousand yards forward of the 1st Marine Regiment's center sector of the Jamestown Line. Though a great deal has been written about the terrible battle that took place from August 8 through the 13th between us and the Chinese, two violent incidents occurred that will remain with me forever.

In early August our company had moved in to occupy a section of the MLR that had been previously manned by Marines of the 7th Marine Regiment. As part of our night defensive plans my squad was slated to go several hundred yards forward of our company lines and set up an ambush/listening-post position along the banks of a narrow river that ran parallel to the MLR. We referred to this shallow river in front of us as a viaduct and considered the near side of the waterway to be "ours" and the far side "theirs."

Led by a corporal nicknamed Whitey, one machine-gun team was attached to my eight-man squad for added fire support. I was tasked to run a long section of communication wire out to our ambush site, which gave us a constant link with the company command post. We had been told that past security patrolling had kept the area cleared of creeping Chinese Communist soldiers and that we should have "no trouble" moving down near the viaduct. Just prior to our departure I was given new instructions from the company CO to extend my advance, crossing the river and setting up the LP on the far hillside.

After 2000, under a drizzling rain, we left the company lines. When we reached the viaduct I told Whitey that it would be the best place for him to set up his gun team so that he would be able to protect the squad with machine-gun fire when we crossed the river and when we made our trip back. While the squad waited for Whitey's team to get into position, I called back to the company and informed them of our progress. Once the gun team signaled they were ready we started across the river, trailing out our roll of communication wire, reaching the other side undetected. I moved my squad up onto a finger that came down from the left side of a small rolling hill and there we sat, trying to watch and listen for sounds of the Chinese through the pouring rain. By midnight we had heard nothing except the increased drumming of heavier showers, which caused me to worry about our ability to recross the now-swollen river. I called back to the company explaining the situation and was given permission to return.

It took the better part of an hour for the squad to move through the thick mud that had developed because of the heavy rains. When we reached the edge of the viaduct my previous suspicions were confirmed—the slow-moving water that had been ankle deep when we had crossed earlier had become a fast-moving obstacle.

We were halfway across the viaduct, struggling through the waist-deep water with our rifles held high, and working to keep our communication wire above the stream, when all hell broke loose. The Chinese began firing at us from covered positions on the right side of the hill. As soon as they opened up on us, Whitey's machine-gun team went into action, giving us good covering fire as we continued on across the river.

As soon as the Marines who had been at the front of the squad reached the other side of the viaduct, they took cover wherever they could find it and began to fire back at the yellow muzzle flashes of the Chinese, covering the rest of us and supplying the precious time we needed to get onto solid ground and alert the company to what was happening. I worried that our communications line would not work because of the water but, for the time being, luck was with us and my request for illumination rounds was immediately answered by both mortar and artillery support. The first illumination rounds revealed dozens of Chinese spread out before us. I fired off two white star flares, the preplanned signal to let the company know of the seriousness of our problem.

Before they tried to cross the river, the Chinese soldiers concentrated their rifle fire on Corporal Whitey's machine-gun team to eliminate the automatic weapon that was capable of spitting five hundred rounds per minute in their direction. While we waited for the company's reaction squad to come and give us a hand, we continued to shoot into the groups of Chinese soldiers running toward the edge of the viaduct. The situation intensified as the Chinese managed to cross the viaduct, well to the right of Whitey's machine-gun position, making it all the more difficult for my two fire teams to concentrate our fire on any particular area. A break in the shooting allowed us only a little time to move away from the open ground along the river, but our new positions did provide us with better cover. There we remained until finally joined by a reinforced rifle squad from second platoon. With the addition of twelve riflemen and two more machine-gun teams, combined with the continuous fire support from our mortars and artillery, we managed to force the attacking Chinese away from us and back across the river.

The gray light of dawn presented the grisly picture of just how close we had come to being overrun by the Chinese—Corporal Whitey was dead, bayoneted, stripped of his uniform, and dragged from his machine-gun position to the bank of the river. Three Marines from the reaction squad also lay dead in the mud and two Marines from my squad had been wounded.

After carrying the dead and wounded back to the company aid station, I reported directly to the company commander and described the events of the night. I told him that the information we had been given indicating that the area was free of Chinese was obviously false. The Chinese had fired on us from numerous well-constructed positions on the forward slope of the hill. Any previous security patrols should have known this and warned us about it. The captain agreed with me, but before I could continue to describe more of what had happened, our session was interrupted by the arrival of a colonel from the division's operations staff, who wanted to meet the squad leader who had taken out the previous night's patrol. I was introduced and after the colonel sat down I continued to describe the events of the night. The captain was satisfied with my report and he commended me and the Marines in my squad for the way we had conducted ourselves during the long firefight. I was told to rejoin my platoon and dismissed, but had hardly cleared the captain's bunker when I heard the colonel's voice begin to rise.

"What the hell are you doing, captain, sending a young private first class out to lead a reinforced squad on a night-ambush patrol? Where the hell are the NCOs in this company? It's a damn miracle that any of those Marines got back here at all! In the future you will make sure that you have sergeants and staff sergeants leading such patrols. I hope that I have made myself very clear. Good day."

Of course the colonel was not aware of just how short our company was of noncommissioned officers. We had PFC squad leaders, senior corporals were platoon sergeants, and senior sergeants were often used as platoon leaders, a billet normally filled by a commissioned officer. There were just not a lot of Marine NCOs to select as qualified squad leaders. The thinking at the time was that because every Marine was an infantryman, those with the most experience could get the job done. I learned that day that a staff officer's view of the battlefield was much different from that of the Marine standing in the trench line.

As the seven-day battle for Bunker Hill continued, we

were given orders to seize, occupy, and defend a series of three small hills that were forward of the company's new position. The order of movement called for our first platoon to move under the protection of a base of fire provided by second platoon and supported by our 60-millimeter mortars and other crew-served weapons. The third platoon was held in reserve, to be assigned as needed. As we prepared for the attack a steady rain began to fall.

To help control the company's movement toward the objectives, our company gunnery sergeant, Technical Sergeant J. J. Nixon, was assigned, along with one radio operator, to move out with the second platoon. Gunny Nixon, a native of Daly City, California, was a highly respected World War II veteran who had brought his many years of infantry experience to the company. From the day he joined us, in the spring of 1952, his presence was felt.

He moved along the lines learning our names, asking us questions, testing our knowledge, and always lending his expertise wherever it was needed. But on this particular day all of his past experience had not prepared him for what was to happen.

The situation turned bad as soon as the first platoon moved out into the attack. The Chinese put their mortars to use and began to bracket the hills with a heavy concentration of 60- and 82-millimeter mortars as our Marines moved forward. We answered with counterbattery fire and smoke, but the cries of "Corpsman, Corpsman" were echoed back to the rear. Not wanting to lose the momentum of the attack, the second platoon was committed and Gunny Nixon moved forward through the mud and the rain with his radio operator by his side.

Within an hour the casualties from first platoon's efforts to take the hill began to come back through our front lines. With them came the word that Gunny Nixon had moved the second platoon onto the hill. However, heavy casualties were also experienced by the second platoon so third platoon was to join them.

The requests for additional smoke rounds to mask our

movement were answered and when we finally reached the base of the first hill we found a small gathering of Marines who had been wounded and were waiting for the litter teams to take them to the rear. Among those wounded Marines was Gunny Nixon's radio operator. Our platoon sergeant asked him where Gunny Nixon was; those of us who were close by heard his startling reply.

"The gunny told me to drop my radio and help him pull some of the wounded to the back side of the hill. Then he grabbed his carbine and said, 'I'm gonna kill all of those Chink bastards' and he moved off in the direction of the first platoon. That was the last I saw of him."

Our platoon moved past the casualty-staging area and set up a hasty defensive line along the crest of the hill. That was when we discovered what had happened to Gunny Nixon. A Marine sniper and his assistant spotter, assigned to the third platoon, had been scanning the area looking for targets, when they saw movement about three hundred yards to the front—a group of several Chinese soldiers. As the sniper team prepared to shoot, they saw Gunny Nixon, too. The Chinese had captured him and, after stripping him of his uniform, had him spread-eagled on the side of a hill. It appeared that he was still alive.

Several attempts were made by individual Marines to reach Nixon, but each met with enemy sniper fire and mortar barrages. The closest that anyone got was two hundred yards away, but Marines still left the safety of their cover and tried desperately to move through open, muddy ground. The Chinese had the best bait they could find and they used it to lure our men within range. Unfortunately it was obvious that the gunny could not be helped. The horrible ordeal ended when a request was finally made for a flight of Marine F4U Corsairs to come in and strafe the enemy hillside with their rockets and then drop bomb loads onto the enemy position.

More than a dozen Marines had been wounded in futile attempts to save Gunny Nixon. His body was never recovered, and he was listed as missing in action.

The fact that the Chinese Communists demonstrated absolutely no regard for the value of their own lives had become obvious to us after we witnessed their repeated use of human-wave attacks. They also knew how much we valued the life of every single Marine and the extent to which we would go in trying to preserve it.

The measure of the results of the Bunker Hill fighting is seen in the price paid. Chinese losses were estimated by 1st Marine Division reports at approximately 3,200 casualties, including more than 400 known dead. Marine casualties were 48 killed and 313 seriously wounded. Several hundred additional wounded Marines were treated at the divisional medical facilities and returned to duty shortly thereafter.

14

Back to Stateside Duty

In September 1952, I received a field meritorious promotion to the rank of corporal and, wearing the two stripes of a Marine noncommissioned officer, I returned to my assigned duties, remaining as a squad leader in the third platoon. Our company still maintained its position along the MLR. While the months of September and October slipped by, we conducted numerous day- and nighttime ambush and security patrols to keep the "creeping" tactics of the Chinese Communists in check. During the first week of November we received the long-awaited word that Marines of D Company who had joined its ranks a year earlier were to report to a huge logistical center known as Ascom City, to begin processing for our return to the States. The 26th Draft Replacement Battalion had come to Korea; it was our turn to rotate home.

As part of the requirements for being deemed ready for embarkation every Marine received a fresh haircut, a new set of utility uniforms, new boots, and was given a thorough physical examination, which included a trip to the delousing area. Here, each of us was told to stand at attention in front of a Navy hospital corpsman while he pumped an ample dose of powdered DDT into our sleeves and into the tops of our loose-fitting trousers. Each Marine was required to present a urine and a stool sample to the medical laboratory as part of our physical examination. We were happy to learn that the majority of those Marines who had been stationed in the rear areas and who had access to local Korean food needed to be treated for intestinal worms; those of us who had spent the better part of the year up on the lines eating a steady diet of C-rations were found to be surprisingly worm-free.

The S.S. *Weagle*, sister ship to the *General Pope*, the merchant vessel that had taken us to Korea, was scheduled to return us to San Francisco, by way of Kobe, Japan, in late November. Sadly, less than 50 percent of those who had sailed for Korea with D Company were to make the return trip. We were told that our voyage would be a luxury cruise compared to our trip over. The difference was evident with our being served meals unlike anything we had seen in a very long time. The Navy had left no stone unturned in trying to accommodate our desires as far as chow was concerned, and as we passed along the serving lines of the mess decks, we helped ourselves to hot soup, fresh salads, baked potatoes with sour cream, a wide assortment of mixed vegetables, thick, grilled steaks, and dessert choices of ice cream, cakes, or apple pie à la mode. Unfortunately, our cravings for the types of food we had only been able to dream about caused nearly every Marine to fill his tray high with choices and the resulting sudden shock of the rich food also caused the majority of us to become sick. Still, the Navy cooks continued to serve us steak during the breakfast meal and at the evening meal, too. In fact, the ship's mess decks remained open to anyone who wanted to eat, and there was always plenty of Lipton's chicken noodle soup and saltine crackers for those who wanted more of a bland diet.

Our trip home was fairly uneventful. We stopped at the port of Kobe and took on board a large number of U.S. Army personnel who were also scheduled to rotate back to the States, but their numbers did not fill our ship to capacity, and we were not as cramped in the sleeping compartments as before. We departed Japan on November 20, and enjoyed two Thanksgiving meals, one before and one after crossing the International Dateline.

Our arrival at San Francisco was even more memorable as we sailed under the Golden Gate Bridge, a sight that many on board had once thought they would never live to see again. Within several hours of our arrival we were to step onto the soil of the United States for the first time in more than a year.

Greeting our ship was a military band and, of course, several representatives of the Red Cross. As each Marine tossed his seabag over his shoulder and headed for the ship's gangway he was approached by a local reporter, a photographer, and a Red Cross volunteer. Questions like, "What are you going to do now that you're home?" were usually met with a quick response, such as, "I'm gonna make like a Christmas tree and get lit." Those who smoked received a carton of cigarettes from the Red Cross volunteers and then a photograph was taken of the smiling Marine. But when that individual reached the end of the gangway, the carton was taken back and just two packs of cigarettes were handed to him. The carton was then refilled and made its way back to the top of the gangway to repeat the process for the press. It was just viewed as another Red Cross stunt.

I had been granted thirty days of leave prior to having to report to my next duty station, Camp Lejeune, North Carolina, and I flew home to Winthrop to be united with my family and friends over the holidays.

In reviewing the Marine actions during this period, the Secretary of the Navy commented:

Marines in Korea have established an enviable record of success in carrying out their assigned missions. The First Marine Division began its third year in Korea holding an active sector of the United Nations front guarding the enemy's invasion route to Seoul. It was frequently subjected to fanatical Chinese attacks supported by intensive artillery fire. Some of the heaviest fighting during the year took place along the front line held by this Division. Enemy attacks were well coordinated and numerically strong. Continued patrol activity to keep the enemy off balance resulted in bitter hand-to-hand fighting with numerous casualties on both sides.

This type of prolonged static warfare gave little real satisfaction to Marines accustomed to waging a war of movement and attaining a more tangible "mission accomplished." The year of positional warfare in western Korea was costly, too. Total U.S. casualties in the Korean War numbered approximately 137,000 men killed, missing, or wounded. The Marine Corps toll was 30,544. Of this number 4,262 were killed, an additional 244 were listed as nonbattle deaths, and 26,038 were wounded. During the last part of the war, Marine casualties (both air and ground) totaled 13,087 plus an additional 2,529 for the attached 1st Korean Marine Corps. Amazingly, 1,586 Marines, or 39.6 percent of the infantry Marines killed in the entire war, were victims of the static outpost warfare in western Korea. Another 11,244 were listed as wounded in action during this period, representing 43.9 percent of the total number of ground Marines wounded during three years of war.

In January 1953, I reported in at Camp Lejeune, North Carolina, home of the 2nd Marine Division, and was assigned as a squad leader in B Company, 1st Battalion, 8th Marine Regiment. The regiment had a well-organized annual training program that allowed for its three infantry battalions to leave Camp Lejeune and practice amphibious warfare skills in different parts of the free world. Typically, the months of January through June were spent conducting joint amphibious operations with the Navy in the Mediterranean Sea. Upon returning to North Carolina, the month of July was reserved for annual requalification with the service rifle and pistol. August through October was scheduled to be spent aboard ship in the Caribbean, and late November and December were considered slow months, divided by the holiday season. The "Med cruises" were always looked upon as time well spent while deployed and as an opportunity to travel and see the world. I had just missed my chance to visit the Mediterranean with 2nd Battalion; they sailed for the Med only several days before I had reported in, and since the 1st Battalion had just returned to Lejeune, I became a new member of that unit's rebuilding process.

The opportunity for me to leave Camp Lejeune finally came with our battalion's deployment to the island of Vieques, located only ten miles east of Puerto Rico, but 1,070 miles southeast of Florida. Consisting of forty-eight square miles of land used primarily as cattle country, only sixteen miles of the island were owned by civilians; the rest of it was taken up by military installations that could accommodate up to seven thousand Marines.

We sailed south from Morehead City, North Carolina, and spent several months learning the intricacies of naval gunfire, ship-to-shore movement, and practicing how to attack and defend the terrain along Vieques's fifty-five-mile coastline. We knew that the island could not compare to the worldly splendors offered in the Mediterranean—the dirty little town of Isabella Segunda, with its population of nine thousand, offered no more than warm beer, a few gambling joints, and was off limits, as well. However, even time in the field on Vieques was better than the mundane duties of a Marine rifle battalion in garrison or in training in the flat, humid pine forests of the Camp Lejeune reservation.

Our training time at the squad level consisted primarily of teaching junior Marines how a rifle squad was organized, the techniques of employment, combat formations, and the different types of signalling. During offensive training we concentrated on the squad's mission—to attack. To do this, our offensive combat training was divided into three phases: preparation, conduct, and exploitation. Each phase was subdivided according to the mission of the platoon.

During the preparation phase we practiced how to move to an assembly area, how to conduct reconnaissance patrols to the objective, and how to rehearse for those patrols. We finished the preparation phase by practicing movement to the line of departure.

During the conduct phase of offensive training, we practiced squad and platoon movement, how to advance using fire and maneuver, and how to assault through our assigned objective. The result was a well-trained platoon that knew how to consolidate and reorganize once the training objective had been taken. The final phase, exploitation, was either a continuation of the initial attack or pursuit of the enemy using organic or supporting weapons.

Defensive combat training centered on organizing the rifle squad for holding territory. Simply stated, the platoon leader organizes his squads in the defense by specifying a sector of fire and primary fighting positions. He selects terrain features to indicate the lateral and forward limits of each squad's sector of fire. He also designates the general fighting positions and principal directions of fire for specific automatic rifles, which are critical to the defense of the platoon. Included in our defensive training were the following tasks: posting of security, listening posts, observation posts, and conducting our security patrols. We practiced how to position automatic weapons, how to clear fields of fire for them, how to properly construct fighting holes and obstacles, and how to camouflage our positions.

When I think of training on Vieques, one particular event still sticks in my mind. A Marine reservist, a young captain, had recently been assigned to our battalion's intelligence (S-2) section and was given the job of conducting a class on the proper use of cover and concealment. When he arrived at our bivouac site he found the men of the company seated and ready. He opened a folder containing his lesson plan and began, "I believe that any Marine who has been awarded the Purple Heart obviously did not do a good job of using proper cover and concealment."

This opening remark brought looks of bewilderment to the faces of the many combat veterans seated in the class, but they did not interrupt.

"My name is Captain Reed, and although I have not yet

been in combat, I think that you men will agree with my reasons for believing this. If proper cover and concealment was practiced by every Marine, then it would be almost impossible for any of us to become wounded or killed."

The captain regaled us until I could not stand to listen to his battlefield philosophy any longer. I stood up and raised my hand.

"Yes, Corporal. Do you have a question?"

"Yes, sir. I have several questions, sir. What about Marines moving out in the attack? What happens when they come under artillery and mortar fire? What're they supposed to do then, sir? Where is the cover and concealment for Marines moving across open ground?"

The reflective look on the captain's face told us that he had never considered the fact that at times Marines had no way of protecting themselves when crossing hostile open ground.

"Have you been in combat, Corporal?"

"Yes, sir. I have."

"Then what would you tell this class if you were me, Corporal?"

"Sir, I would say 'class dismissed,' if I were you, sir."

I was not trying to be a wise guy, but the words just came out and all remaining seriousness of his class was lost.

The captain must have thought that the use of an attention getter at the start of his class would help him establish some rapport with the Marines in the company, but it hadn't. He had alienated himself from the veterans in the company and lost credibility. I had made my point, but the cost of embarrassing the captain was a trip to see the company 1st sergeant. My explanation was understood and I was cautioned not to let my sensitivity override good judgment. It was a lesson learned by both the captain and me.

For me, the most enjoyable portion of this training program was always patrolling, and the many hours that were spent teaching new Marines how to conduct the various types of patrols—security, reconnaissance, and combat—

were the most beneficial. By studying the mission and then organizing the men for the patrol, each Marine became more familiar with his importance in the squad and with his responsibility to his fellow Marines.

These were the situations that made our squads, platoons, and the company come together as a team. Those of us who were veterans of Korea knew how important such training could become later on. We returned to Camp Lejeune as a tight, combat-ready company. However, typical of the way things were run, each returning battalion was expected to transfer a number of men to augment the service unit running the Marine Corps Base at Camp Lejeune. As a part of this requirement, I received orders to report to the base rifle range for assignment as a primary marksmanship instructor and rifle coach.

My new assignment was to last for six months and I decided it was time to buy my first automobile. I took leave and returned to Winthrop in hope of getting a good deal from the local Ford dealer. My father told me that the Ford dealer in Winthrop was the best place to purchase tractors or trucks, but the better place to go and buy a car would be Augusta, where the Ford dealership had an impressive car lot to choose from.

I had saved the majority of my combat pay from the previous year in Korea, and with the princely sum of $1,000 cash in my pocket, I drove to Augusta in my father's truck, dressed in my Marine uniform. I walked around the Ford lot, looking for the best buy, and decided on a two-door green 1952 Ford with a sticker price of $1,300. I went inside the dealership to make my offer thinking that having cash in hand would allow me to purchase the car for a price lower than the one advertised on the car's window. However, the salesman wasn't interested in talking to me.

A Chevrolet dealership was directly across the street from the Ford dealer and, displeased at the way I was being treated, I marched out of the Ford showroom and crossed the street to do business with the competition. A 1952 Chevrolet, a Businessman's Coupe, caught my fancy and I asked the dealer if he would allow a discount on his asking price if I could pay for the car in cash. He agreed to my offer and I, in turn, offered him an additional $50.00 if he would open the large glass doors of his showroom and back the Coupe into his service area to prepare the car for my trip back to North Carolina. This was done in full view of the Ford salesman and I have remained a Chevy man ever since.

At the time, only Marines in the grades of corporal or above were given permission to own an automobile and to drive it aboard the base. Upon registration at the base, small, metal identification tags were attached to the front and rear license plates, identifying the owner of the vehicle as either an officer, a noncommissioned officer, or civilian employee. Permission to have a car was just one of the privileges that set the noncommissioned officer apart from the "non-rates." Those Marines of lesser grade than corporal who arrived at the base's main gate were simply pointed in the direction of their assigned regiment and told, "Your unit is located seven miles down that road, Marine, and there's no hitchhiking allowed aboard this base."

In April 1954, I made the decision to reenlist in the Marine Corps for four more years. I had worked hard at becoming a Marine and I could think of no other demanding job that would give me the personal satisfaction, the responsibility, or the enjoyment of being a corporal of Marines. It was shortly after I had reenlisted that I was promoted meritoriously to the rank of sergeant. My platoon commander, a 1st Lieutenant named Adams, asked me to stop by his office for a talk. As I stood centered before his desk, I was surprised by what he had to say.

"Sergeant Hamblen, I've been reviewing your service record book and I think that it's time for a change in your life. Your record is commendatory and I was wondering if you had ever given any consideration to becoming a Marine officer?"

"Sir, my service record book must show you that I wasn't the best student who ever came out of the state of

Maine, and I don't think that I pack the smarts to become an officer. It wasn't until my physical examination, down at Parris Island, that they discovered I had a vision problem. The doctors at P.I. told me that my vision was probably the biggest reason that I didn't do too well in school. I'm far-sighted, sir. I can see a rabbit at two hundred yards, but as a student I couldn't make out the printed words on the pages of a textbook. Reading glasses have helped me to correct the situation, but my high school grades will always remain the same. Ya see, sir, a kid growing up on a farm didn't get taken into town to see a doctor unless it was a matter of life or death. I think that I might be wasting your time, sir."

First Lieutenant Adams thought about what I had said, and then spoke. "The Marine Corps prides itself on finding its very best officers from within its enlisted ranks, Sergeant Hamblen. Your combat record is impressive. You have been an outstanding squad leader from the time you were a private first class until you came here. You have done a fine job as one of our best rifle coaches and you were field meritoriously promoted to corporal. I think that you're wasting your time here as a sergeant. So why don't you listen to what I have to say before you make any decisions?"

"I'm sorry, Lieutenant. You talk, and I'll listen, sir."

"That's better. Please sit down. Home for me is Hartford, Connecticut, and not too far from Hartford is the Marine Barracks at New London. A good friend of mine is stationed up there, and he's looking for a reliable sergeant of guard. Duty at the barracks is considered to be great, and you'd have time to take college courses while you're there. Let me see if I can arrange for you to transfer up to New London, and then the rest of it will be up to you. The worst that can happen is that you'll get to be at a good duty station for three years, and you won't be too far from your home in Maine. You have nothing to lose, Sergeant Hamblen, and this is my way of saying Thank you for doing a good job."

15

Marine Barracks, New London, Connecticut

In 1955, the United States Naval Submarine Base, New London, Connecticut, was the largest sub base in the world and the only submarine base in the United States. From its early history as a coaling station for the Atlantic Fleet during World War I the base continued to grow, becoming the home of the "silent service." Submariners who were trained at New London accounted for more than half of all Japanese tonnage sunk during World War II. The New London base was the home of the U.S. Naval Submarine School and the U.S. Naval Medical Research Laboratory. The Submarine School was divided into two specific divisions, the Basic Submarine School and the Nuclear Power School. Courses at the Basic School were the equivalent to a post–high school technical institution, while the curriculum at the Nuclear Power School was, in many respects, more advanced than most college-level courses.

The submarine base and related naval industry contributed to the economic success of the small cities of New London and Groton, Connecticut, with more than eight thousand military personnel—counting those assigned to ships home-ported there—twenty-seven thousand dependents, and nine hundred civilian workers pouring an estimated 90 percent of the annual $31 million payroll into the local businesses. Electric Boat, the engineering corporation that produced the Navy's fleet of diesel and nuclear-powered submarines, was situated nearby, on the Thames River. The security required for the base was in the hands of the two Marine officers and the sixty-four enlisted men who made up the ranks of Marine Barracks, New London.

In addition to the normal duties of the commanding officer of the barracks, our CO, Captain Barnes, was assigned as the security officer on the staff of the submarine base commander, the base safety officer, the highway patrol officer, and the fiscal and supply officer of the Marine Barracks. His executive officer, 1st Lieutenant J. O. Harrington, was assigned to handle all other duties as our Marine exchange officer, special services officer, and barracks guard officer.

The following points dictated the operation of Marine Barracks, New London: (1) The maintenance of sentries, patrol escort, messenger, and orderly posts on the submarine base; (2) the maintenance of an armed, trained, and mobile force available for answering any emergency calls that might arise in the locality; (3) the identification and control of personnel and vehicles entering and leaving the limits of the base; (4) control and issue of base identification cards; (5) registration and issuance of base decals; (6) the enforcement of parking and traffic rules; and (7) designation and control of parking areas and signs.

When I arrived at New London I was assigned as one of the sergeants of the guard and quickly learned what was required of the guard force to provide the security for the base. The guard was divided into two twenty-seven-man sections. Our daily "port and starboard" routine began with our posting at 0700 each morning and ended at 1630 each afternoon when the second section of the guard was posted until 0700 the following morning. Our weekend duty lasted until Monday morning, when the weekly process was repeated. Between standing duty, personnel inspections, military subjects training, physical training, and the cleaning of the barracks, we had a full schedule. Four posts comprised our guard. Post No. 1 placed two Marines on the base main gate; Post No. 2 was one Marine guarding the back gate;

Post No. 3 required one Marine to be assigned as a roving patrol for traffic and parking offenses, driving new reliefs to their posts, and to inspect cars for decals; Post No. 4 was that of the barracks duty man—a guard, phone watch, messenger, fire watch, and master-at-arms.

Sergeant James O. Tchakirides was the platoon sergeant for the second section of our guard force and became a trusted friend who helped teach me the finer points of being a sergeant of Marines. Our friendship began one morning over a friendly conversation.

"Ham, it's about time that you and I had a talk. I've been here for a couple of years and I want to pass on all of the good scoop before I get my orders out of here. This tour at the barracks should be your best tour of duty while you're in the Corps. You'll never find another place that offers so much. Pull up a footlocker and let me tell you what a good deal we have going for us. The way I see it, the Marine Corps has *used* you for the last four years. Now, let the Marine Corps *help* you."

Sergeant Tchakirides spent the better part of that afternoon explaining the details of how the New London Marines had made their lives at the barracks a little more comfortable by using a self-help system. Our squad bays were located on the second deck of an H-shaped barracks that was built in 1942. By taking our meals in the Navy's mess hall we were spared the extra duties of having to work in the kitchen. Within our ranks we had our own barber who doubled as our uniform presser; weekly haircuts and sharp, pressed uniforms were accordingly free. We even had our own small Marine PX located within our barracks, and in the basement was our own indoor pistol range, where we competed regularly against state and local police force pistol teams. Our lounge was located on the first deck of the barracks and doubled as an off-duty reading room. Our barracks was a showplace and a fine place to live.

I learned from Sergeant Tchakirides that many of the Marine Barracks' local public commitments were great op-

portunities in disguise and he told me how I could benefit
from the many educational programs that were offered at
the submarine base. It was after this talk that I began to see
a plan for my future.

Back at Camp Lejeune, 1st Lieutenant Adams had helped
to change my life by suggesting that I "get educated" and
within my first year at New London I finished my remaining high school courses and "graduated." Next, I enrolled
in several courses taught aboard the base and completed
two years of college courses in the Nuclear, Biological,
Chemical Warfare School (NBC) and the Military Instructor's Course, taught by the Navy. Several Marine NCOs
convinced me to enroll with them in the Basic Submarine
Instructor's School Course and when we had completed the
course we were asked by the Navy to help during "Open
House" weekends. We were used to explain the complexities of the submarine to many visiting civilians amazed to
find United States Marines as knowledgeable as any sub-
mariner stationed at New London. Having found how enjoyable learning could be, I focused my attention on one
subject that had always intrigued me—flight.

One of the agencies that the Marine Barracks helped to
support was the Civil Air Patrol. The CAP worked in support of the local and state police and on many weekends,
Marines would be asked to fly with the local pilots as part
of the CAP program. When asked if I was interested in
helping out I all but jumped at the chance. I could not hide
my enthusiasm for flying and, at the cost of only $555, I
earned both my private and my commercial pilot's licenses,
flying a Piper Vagabond and a J-3 Piper Cub from an old
airfield located in the town of Salem, Connecticut. When
my section of the guard force had an off-duty weekend, I
could usually be found somewhere high above the state of
Connecticut in a rented Piper Cub.

In 1957, while still the platoon sergeant for the first section of the guard, I was giving a tour of the sub base to a
Marine captain named Taylor and his platoon of twenty-
four Force Recon Marines who had come up from Camp

Lejeune. The purpose of their visit was to test Force Recon swimmers in the 120-foot diving tower used by Navy submariners to simulate emergency exits from submarines. The Force Recon Marines used the diving tower to practice an underwater technique known as "blow and go's," which simulated exiting a submarine from various depths and swimming to the surface as part of the reconnaissance platoon's mission of conducting hydrographic surveys on foreign beaches.

The tower had access chambers built at twenty-foot intervals that allowed the student swimmers to make their ascents from a maximum depth of 120 feet. This deep-water training was done without the help of any scuba equipment, and the closely spaced access chambers made it possible to retrieve any student who found himself in trouble underwater.

For several days I watched in fascination as the Marines practiced their skills in the tower and asked Captain Taylor how I might go about volunteering for duty with a Force Recon company. The captain told me that the Force Reconnaissance company was always on the lookout for qualified Marine NCOs and he advised me to get in the best physical condition possible and then request an interview with a Force Recon platoon commander the next time one came to New London to observe his unit's training. Taking the captain's advice to heart, I began to concentrate on building my upper-body strength so that I would be ready to take the Recon physical-fitness tests. In the meantime, it was back to duty at the barracks.

Until 1957, it had been the responsibility of the U.S. Navy to manage the base brig as a correctional facility for the drunks, thieves, malcontents, and assorted naval service personnel who had been sentenced to specified periods of confinement. But because of an investigation that had called for the immediate relief of the Navy chief petty officer in charge of the facility, the base commander assigned responsibility for the running of his brig to the Marine Barracks. As part of my duties as platoon sergeant I was assigned to help run this facility. None of the Marines assigned to the guard force was particularly happy about this added responsibility and it was decided that we, as Marines, should try our level best to change the attitude of those sailors who were "guests" in our brig and to insure they would not want to return. The key to achieving this goal was discipline.

As soon as a prisoner arrived at the brig he handed over his wallet to the senior brig guard and was handed back a receipt. Every new prisoner immediately received a free Marine haircut, was taken to the showers, and then handed a clean dungaree work uniform. Cigarettes and lighters were confiscated; smoking was a privilege, not a right. An indoctrination class was conducted and the rules of the brig were explained to all confinees and their daily work schedule was posted for all to see. Each morning began at 0430, with one hour of physical-fitness training conducted before breakfast. A daily detailed personnel inspection insured that all prisoners were clean and presentable before going to work. After their noon meal a one-hour period of close-order drill—shouldering dry swabs instead of rifles—was mandatory for every prisoner. Upon returning from their afternoon work details all prisoners received classes on current events and military subjects peculiar to Marines—map reading, judo, and even bayonet fighting. A second personnel inspection was conducted before the evening meal and following chow the entire population was used to field-day the brig from top to bottom before the call for "lights out" was sounded at 2200. The prisoners in our brig were treated with the respect they earned, but they were not given any time to enjoy their surroundings. We took care of their individual needs, purchasing items they requested from the PX and giving them receipts for the cost. We got them in good physical shape and for the first time in their lives they felt challenged. We wanted their experience in the brig to serve two purposes: They would learn subjects that were useful while they were in our charge, and they would not want to return to the brig, ever. We did such a good job of turning out model prisoners that our program almost back-fired: The Navy began to use almost any excuse to send marginal performers to the brig in the hope that Marines would correct what they could not.

A Navy warrant officer who had received orders for a tour of duty aboard ship had presented his aging pet bull-dog to the Marines at the brig and upon examining the dog we discovered that he had hardly any teeth remaining in his big, ugly head. We accepted the bulldog as our new mascot and appropriately changed his name to Snapper. It was Snapper who helped to reeducate some of the more reluctant soldiers sentenced to the brig. A corporal had taken an instant liking to ol' Snapper and over a period of time he'd taught the dog to bite, on command, at a blue rag. Soon, it became a game to get Snapper to growl and bark as a prelude to the fun of chasing after the rag, and it was by no means coincidence that the color blue had been selected for the game—every Navy confinee was required to wear blue dungarees and a blue shirt. If Snapper happened to be touring the area with his corporal handler and a new prisoner failed to move at a particular pace, the command of "Get the squid" usually changed that prisoner's attitude. It didn't happen too often, but just enough to petrify any confinee at the sight of the huge bulldog running around loose within the brig. Ol' Snapper thought it was a game, but the new prisoners feared for their lives. We kept them thinking that way.

It was not only Navy personnel who could find themselves sentenced to stay in the New London base brig. As part of our procedures for seeing to the health and comfort of the prisoners, scheduled trips to the base PX were arranged to meet their individual needs. Each prisoner's pay was brought to the brig and their money was kept in our safe. The cost for cigarettes, stationery, and magazines requested by the prisoners was deducted from their pay envelope and receipts for these items were kept to justify the purchases.

An inventory of all monies kept in our safe was conducted weekly and the results were sent to both the barracks and the base commanding officer. When one inventory revealed that two twenty-dollar bills were missing from a prisoner's envelope, an investigation was begun. We were given seventy-two hours by the barracks executive officer, Captain Harrington, to solve the problem. Initial questioning of all Marine guards assigned to duty in the brig indicated that they knew nothing about the disappearance of the money. In our attempt to solve the mystery, an amnesty program was announced. One room in the brig was opened for a period of twenty-four hours and in the room an open envelope was placed in the center of a small wooden table. In hopes of giving our thief one last opportunity to return the money without further action being taken, all of the brig personnel were directed to go into the room. But by the end of the amnesty period the open envelope remained empty. The very thought of having a thief within our midst was intolerable and, having given every Marine a chance to return the money without the desired results, the pace of the investigation quickened.

Our affiliation with the local and state police had created a very good working relationship, and when we asked that a lie-detector test be given to all hands, our request was granted. Based on those Marines having access to the safe and the probable time of day when the money was taken, we had our suspicions as to whom the culprit might be. But since no one had admitted to the crime, everyone remained suspect. The surprise announcement of the lie-detector test still did not produce our thief.

Two trips were required to transport the Marines from New London barracks to the New York City Federal Building, where the lie-detector test was administered. The first group of Marines was made up of those we believed had no possible connection to the theft. The second batch was the one we were most interested in. And in it was a Marine corporal, a unit newcomer, who finally cracked under the pressure. The lie-detector test was still administered to all of us even though the corporal confessed to stealing the money just before going into the testing room. The return trip from New York City to New London was made in complete silence.

The thieving corporal was found guilty at his subsequent court-martial, was reduced to the rank of private, forfeiting all of his pay and allowances, and was sentenced to confinement at the Portsmouth Naval Prison for a period of two years. He was a prisoner in his own brig for thirty days before being taken away to Portsmouth, all for a lousy forty dollars.

The only other incident to mar my three-year tour of duty at New London was the most tragic of all, and happened one night while I was posted as the noncommissioned officer of the guard. Because of a substantial increase in the amount of base traffic due to a growing submarine fleet, Post No. 2, our rear-gate security, had been upgraded to a two-man post, and on this particular evening one of the two Marines assigned to the post became bored. While his assistant left the comfort of the heated guard shack to allow a car to come aboard the base, the second Marine decided to remove his .45 Colt automatic from the lanyard that kept the pistol attached to his body, and practiced "quick-drawing" the pistol from his holster. When the Marine who had gone outside finally returned to the guard shack, he was confronted by his partner, who told him to sit down and watch how quickly he could pull the .45 from its leather holster—"just like on TV." The unsuspecting Marine sat down in a chair and watched as the private yanked the .45 from his holster, aimed it in his direction, and pulled the trigger. The .45-caliber bullet that had been loaded into the chamber of the pistol during the time the private had been fooling around with the weapon blew a neat little hole in the center of the seated Marine's chest, killing him instantly.

After responding to the telephone call for help at Post No. 2, the commander of the guard and I informed the barracks commanding officer of what had happened. The Marine who had accidentally killed his friend was a combat veteran of Korea and had been married for less than a month. At a general court-martial, he was found guilty of involuntary manslaughter.

In the spring of 1958, I received orders back to the infantry and was transferred to the Fleet Marine Force, joining the 2nd Battalion, 4th Marine Regiment headquartered at Kaneohe Bay, on the island of Oahu, Hawaii.

My dad preparing to cut ice on Lake Cobbosseecontee, Winthrop, Maine, 1930.

Me with the year's prize catch, 1938.

The first-grade class of Winthrop Grade School, 1939. I am fourth from the left in the top row.

Home from Korea with my mother, December, 1952.

Luke's Castle (Hill 812), Winter 1951. If you look carefully, you can see an AD approaching the right-hand peak from the right.

After the AD has dropped its gift and gone its way.

Ready to test parachutes at El Centro, CA, June 18, 1961. (Top row, left to right): Burhans, McAlister, Johnson, Eakin, me, (unidentified U.S. Navy), Schmidt, Lowless. (Bottom): Massaro, Goewey, (unidentified U.S. Navy), Coates, Duffy, (unidentified U.S. Navy).

This is my last jump with two legs, from GV-1 over the Tankpark Drop Zone, 1100, September 21, 1962.

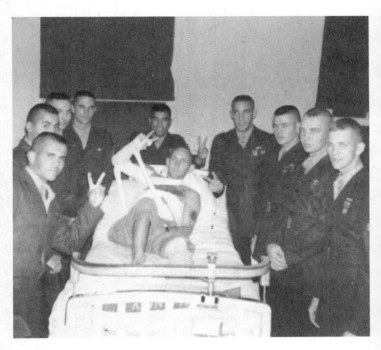

My pathfinder platoon comes to visit, early October 1962.

SAN DIEGO GAS & ELECTRIC COMPANY
P. O. BOX 4175
TELEPHONE BE 2-4252   SAN DIEGO 4, CALIFORNIA

ACCOUNT NO

REFER TO
INVOICE NO
INVOICE DATE
VENDOR'S NO
File No:
X-Ref:

SOLD
TO

U. S. Marine Corps.
Camp Pendleton
California

For damage to Company property on or about September 21, 1962, a approximately 11:05 a.m., Staff Sgt. Donald N. Hamblin, serial No. 1199883, a paratrooper for the above-named, blew into 69kv line, his feet in 12kv momentarily, causing three spans of 12kv to burn down an adjacent spans to slack back on utility pole 21155 east of Highway 10 near Aliso Canyon, south of the Tank Farm, California.

Our line crew responded and made the necessary repairs and replacements.

Material:

1	-	Insulator	$3.13
4	-	Sleeves	1.73
42#	-	#4 Wire	19.30

NET MATERIAL CHARGE:	$ 24.16
Labor Expense:	129.34
Transportation:	14.40
	$167.91
Supervision & Administrative Expense 12%:	20.15
Less Salvage:	- 8.74
TOTAL EXPENSE:	$179.32

KB:sa

The bill I was sent by San Diego Gas & Electric "for damage to Company property." I've always wondered what they salvaged that was worth $8.74.

(Left) Lieutenant, j.g., Mariann "Z" Zeweber, the nurse responsible for my physical therapy.

(Below) Exercising the stump.

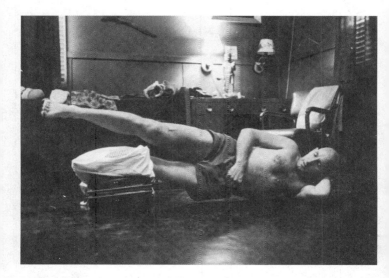

Descending into Lake O'Neill on my first jump after the accident, September 11, 1963.

Splashdown!

I am met by my friends from the press.

During my 1964 trip to advise The President's Committee on Employment of the Handicapped, I met Maine Senators Edmund Muskie and Margaret Chase Smith (above) and with Harold Russell (below), a former Army paratrooper who was a member of the committee.

(Above) Listening to President Johnson's opening remarks.

(Right) I also got a chance to visit with two fellow amputees and tried to recruit them for the Marines.

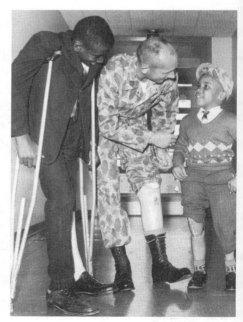

The Staff NCOs of First Force Reconnaissance Company in 1964.
(Top, from left) Staff sergeants Reidl, (unidentified), Henderson,
Freitas, Zwiener, me, Phebus, Dodge. (Bottom) Gunnery sergeants
Avery, Goewey, Massaro, Echols, Parrish, (unidentified NCO from
motor pool).

SOG Team Romulus, 1965.

A member of the team tries on one of my legs.

First Lieutenant Paull and I look over a terrain model.

This skull was Team Romulus's mascot, Ho Chi Minh.

"Before" shot of a beach house built so the team could practice a prisoner snatch.

After.

Here we are surveying the damage done by a VC night attack on My Khe in 1966.

Frenchy, one of the members of SOG Team Romulus.

Me in black VC pajamas, on a chow break while training for a mission.

March 1967. Wounded again. The small-caliber bullet is still in my arm.

Our SOG navy: SWIFT-class boats in foreground, NASTY-class in background.

Team Romulus preparing for a rehearsal. Not visible in this shot are the eyes painted in red on the bow of the IBS.

From the left, that's CWO-2 Dennis Zoerb and CWO-2 Ed Miller, me, and HM1 E. E. "Doc" Bliss at Captain Tom Gueney's wedding.

My wife Reiko and I.

16

Back to the Fleet

In February 1955, the 4th Marine Regiment and the required aircraft for Marine Air Group-13 (MAG-13) arrived for duty at the Marine Corps Air Station, Kaneohe Bay, Hawaii, with the 1st Provisional Marine Air Group Task Force. Marine Air Group-13, the brigade's air arm, was considered to be unique because it was the only aircraft group in the Marine Corps that contained squadrons of three types of combat aircraft—fighters, bombers, and helicopters. On May 1, 1956, this task force was redesignated the 1st Marine Brigade. My tour of duty with the brigade was another great learning experience.

I flew from Hartford, Connecticut, to California, and upon arriving at Travis Air Force Base, I became one of many passengers who boarded a huge, four-deck Air Force C-124 Globemaster, for the nonstop flight to Hawaii. My nine-month tour with the 1st Marine Brigade began with my assignment to the 4th Marine Regiment, where I was further assigned to the regiment's 2nd Battalion, and joined F (Fox) Company as the platoon sergeant of the company's second platoon.

Our reinforced brigade was made up of three infantry battalions and MAG-13, and was rounded out with artillery and logistical support units. These support units included elements of the 3rd Battalion, 12th Marine Artillery Regiment, a company of 106-millimeter recoilless rifles from the 3rd Antitank Battalion, and Marines from B Company, 3rd Reconnaissance Battalion. The 3rd Service Battalion and 3rd Force Service Regiment provided our overall supply, motor transport, and maintenance support. The brigade was completely air transportable—capable of conducting assaults from the sea and employing the Marine Corps' new doctrine in using helicopters for vertical envelopment.

It was during my time with Fox Company that I began to learn how a Marine air-ground team really operates. To insure that every Marine in the brigade understood the complexities of this air-ground concept, a cross-training program was instituted throughout the brigade. As part of this training schedule, infantrymen routinely visited aviation units, while the aviation Marines got an equal chance to see what those Marines assigned to rifle companies did for a living.

The diversity of terrain within the Hawaiian Islands played an important role in our training. There were beaches, jungles, and mountains on all of the islands, rolling countryside on Molokai, and areas of desert on the island of Hawaii. It was even possible to conduct cold-weather training, complete with snow, in some of our maneuver areas. But the biggest problem that we faced during our training was centered around our dispersion.

The Marine Corps Air Station consisted of only three thousand acres, and after subtracting the land needed for our barracks, hangars, and military housing, there wasn't too much room left for infantry training areas, and the brigade had to find its maneuver areas throughout the islands. Kaneohe Bay, on the windward side of the island of Oahu, offered seven hundred acres at a place called Kapaa, which was used for company bivouacs and mountain- and jungle-warfare training. Another thousand acres at Waikane was used for our live-fire ranges. On the northern end of the island of Oahu there were a number of training areas that belonged to both the Army and the Air Force, and they allowed us to share the use of them.

Twice during the year the brigade moved to Hawaii—the

Big Island—for a one-month training evolution at Pohakuloa, where the Army had sixty thousand acres of the best training areas in Hawaii. This training site was located between Mauna Kea, the highest mountain in the Hawaiian Islands, and Mauna Loa, the second highest peak, at an elevation of 6,500 feet. It was the only maneuver area large enough to allow all of the weapons in the brigade to be combined for combat fire-support missions. The great distances between these many training areas became apparent after a brief map study—two hundred miles separated Kaneohe Bay from Hilo, and Kauai was a hundred miles from "K-Bay," but in the opposite direction. Maui was seventy miles to the southwest of Kaneohe, and Molokai, which got the most use, was separated from our base by thirty-three miles of open water.

There were only two ways to reach these outer islands—by aircraft or by ship—and since the brigade did not own any ships, the job of transporting the Marines of the brigade fell to MAG-13's helicopters. The group's helicopters were always up to the task, but whenever possible our battalion still used the time-honored infantry method in getting from one place to another—we marched. It was not uncommon for our battalion to make the thirty-four-mile hump from Kaneohe to Kahuku, and then three days later make the return march home.

During these long endurance marches, new challenges were added to our training. The use of gas masks was becoming more and more popular, and it was not uncommon for Fox Company Marines to wear their gas masks during the hikes that covered more than ten miles, and make a game out of seeing which platoon could outdistance another.

The small size of our maneuver areas meant that most of our field-training time was concentrated at the company level. This was always considered the best type of training by the noncommissioned officers. Away from the mundane base requirements, working parties, and extra guard details, we spent our time concentrating on improving our small-unit tactics and fire-support coordination. Squad leaders and fire-team leaders learned the tricks of the trade from those of us who had been in combat. When we returned from the field, cleaned our weapons and equipment, and passed our personnel inspections, liberty call was placed in the hands of the platoon sergeants and squad leaders.

Kaneohe Bay, commonly referred to as K-Bay, housed nearly 9,000 military personnel and employed about 600 civilians. The brigade was considered to be an important part of the Pacific's force in readiness. In 1958, with a rapidly growing population of 585,000, the Hawaiian Islands were home to 58,000 military personnel and their dependents.

There were three different tour lengths—Marines assigned to duty with the brigade were stationed at K-Bay for only nine months; single Marines doing a "base" tour were assigned to duty for two years; married Marines accompanied by their dependents had three-year tours.

By those of us assigned to the brigade, Kaneohe Bay was considered a great place to be stationed for several reasons. The average daily temperature was seventy-two degrees, so, despite a rainy season, no one ever complained about the climate. Our liberty was equally enjoyable because the base offered such a wide variety of after-hours activities. There was an eighteen-hole championship golf course, an Olympic-size swimming pool, numerous tennis courts, an archery range, and a trap and skeet range. From time to time the base special services offered pig hunts, using crossbows for weapons, on some of the more remote islands. There were active skin-diving and sky-diving clubs, and sailboats and chartered fishing boats were available for everyone's use. A ham radio station located aboard the base enabled us to contact families on the mainland. Sightseeing was always popular, especially just before payday when money was always low.

For those Marines assigned to longer tours of duty in Hawaii, the government provided additional pay to offset the cost of living in paradise. Military quarters were at a minimum at Kaneohe Bay and Marines who arrived with their dependents were allowed temporary lodging allowances for their first sixty days of duty. That amounted to $15 per day for a Marine and two dependents, and $22.50 a day for a Marine with three or more dependents. After the initial sixty days, a Marine could apply for housing allowance. A corporal with over four years of service received a daily housing allowance of 70 cents; a sergeant 80 cents; a staff sergeant 95 cents, captains and majors $1.85. Those of us assigned to the brigade did not have to worry about the difficulty of surviving on the open economy; our days began and ended in the squad bay.

My time spent with Fox Company was certainly not as eventful as my tour of duty in Korea, but it was just as rewarding. Our training schedule always kept us busy learning and practicing the trade of the infantryman, and taught us the importance of helicopters more than ever before. Unlike my earlier tour of duty at Camp Lejeune, our battalion did not deploy for training far away, but we did spend more time in the field, which made my time with the brigade seem to fly by. So it was welcomed news when I received my next set of orders directing me to leave Hawaii, "for further transfer," to join the 7th Marine Regiment headquartered in the middle of Camp Pendleton at Camp Pulgas, for a three-year tour of duty.

Reporting in to the 7th Marine Regiment's 2nd Battalion, I was directed to the office of 1st Sergeant Holmes, the senior enlisted Marine of Echo Company. Before entering, I rapped loudly on his door frame three times and waited to hear the Top command me to enter. I then marched smartly into his office, centered myself six inches in front of his big oak desk, and stood motionless at the position of attention. He rose from behind his desk and took possession of my service record book and, without so much as an upward glance in my direction, sat back down and took several minutes to study my record entries. Then he focused his dark eyes on me, and slowly worked his stare from the top of my head, down to where the rest of me disappeared below the edge of his oak desk.

Apparently satisfied with what he saw before him, he leaned forward, extended his huge right hand toward me, and said, "Welcome aboard, Hamblen. Your record speaks for itself. This company can use you, and I think that you'll like it here. I'm assigning you as the platoon sergeant of weapons platoon. I'll arrange for you to meet the company commander and our battalion sergeant major later. Thank you. You're dismissed."

About face and out the door. Short and simple. I had been welcomed aboard and given my marching orders. That was how it was done in 1959.

As platoon sergeant of a forty-man weapons platoon it was my responsibility to be completely familiar with the employment of our .30-caliber machine guns, 60-millimeter mortars, 3.5-inch rocket launchers, and the one weapon most feared by all infantrymen in the defense, the flamethrower. These were our company's organic weapons and my knowledge of infantry tactics would be called upon to make certain that these crew-served weapons were always kept in good working order and would be properly utilized. I looked forward to the challenge.

Not long after I joined the ranks of Echo Company, I learned that our battalion was involved in the division's new training program, referred to as "Lock On." The infantry battalions of the 1st Marine Division that were routinely scheduled for six-month deployments to the island of Okinawa were given a period of time in which to prepare themselves both tactically and administratively before deployment. Those Marines who were physically fit and had enough time remaining to serve in the Corps were locked into a demanding one-month battalion training program, whereas those Marines from within the deploying battalions who were considered to be "nondeployable" were transferred to other companies, allowing for only qualified Marines to take their places. Because of this shifting of personnel, the battalions that were not scheduled to deploy often found themselves the recipients of "problem children" sent from other battalions. My first introduction to this new breed of cat came shortly after my assignment to weapons platoon.

One morning, I watched out of curiosity as seven individuals, none of whom had attained a rank higher than that of private first class, came to a rest in front of my platoon's Quonset hut. Not recognizing any of them, I went outside to see what they could possibly want. "What are you people doing here?" I demanded. "We were sent down here from Charlie Company, One-Seven, Staff Sergeant, to join up with your platoon. Ya see, we can't deploy because we're too short."

"Shut your face. Fall in and come with me."

I marched the group up to company headquarters and told them to stand at attention outside. Then I went to find the company 1st sergeant and took the risk of sticking my head inside his office. We had gotten to know one another, and I thought that I had begun to cultivate a pretty good working relationship with 1st Sergeant Holmes.

He was sitting behind his desk and caught me staring in at him. "What can I do for ya', Ham?"

"First Sergeant, I need seven G.I.-can lids and seven broomstick handles."

"What in the hell for?"

"So that I can arm those seven goddamned goons that you sent down to my weapons platoon for me to train! That's what for."

My poorly worded comments caught the immediate attention of the company commander, Captain T. C. Budd, who I had yet to meet but whose office was directly across the hall from the 1st sergeant's. Before the 1st sergeant could say a word to me, we heard the CO's voice. "First Sergeant, send whoever said that in here to see me, at once."

"You heard the man, Ham. Now's as good a time as any to meet the CO. I wish that it could be under better circumstances."

After trying to explain myself under the somber glare of the captain, I knew that I had made a foolish mistake and that the best place for me was as far away from him as possible. First Sergeant Holmes helped to make that a reality when he informed me, later that same day, that as the "new guy on the block" I had been nominated as the company's most eligible noncommissioned officer to go to the Marine Corps Cold Weather Training Center at Bridgeport, California, to attend the evasion, escape, and survival training course.

Of course, I later learned that the seven goofballs whose sudden appearance had caused me to overreact had been sent to join another platoon in the company, and had wandered into my area by mistake. But I had "skylined" myself with Captain Budd and only hoped that the incident would eventually be forgotten. In the meantime I packed my gear for Bridgeport.

Marines from every military occupational specialty (MOS) were selected to attend this training, but the majority of students were pilots and other air-crew personnel most likely to find themselves shot down in enemy territory. The other NCOs and I considered ourselves fortunate in having been selected from the Marines in the division to help fill the training quotas for this class. Thinking that the training would be reminiscent of my younger days spent in the woods of Maine, and recalling my training prior to leaving for Korea in 1951, I thought that twelve days in the field would now be a piece of cake. I was in for a great surprise that made the trip to Bridgeport one of the very best training exercises that I ever experienced.

After flying from Camp Pendleton to Reno, Nevada, we were taken to the Cold Weather Training Center by chartered buses. The place still looked vaguely familiar after eight years' time. There were fewer instructors than before; revisions in the Marine Corps' Table of Organization required that the staff at the school be reduced to 199 men and 17 officers. The senior officer-in-charge was a 1st lieutenant.

Our twelve-day course began with an extensive introduction to the fundamentals of survival and learning about survival psychology—how a desire to survive, combined with an ability to improvise, would play an important role in our overall success. Classes on emergency communications, signalling, and survival first aid came next. We learned how we could feed ourselves from the land, using traps, snares, and deadfalls, and how it was possible to catch the local trout using field-expedient methods. Detailed classes on the recognition of edible plants extended the menu of what we might find to eat, and many students were surprised to learn how to recognize and cook wild onions, watercress, pine nuts, and dandelions. We were taught how to tell the difference between edible and poisonous mushrooms, and what plants could be used for medicinal purposes. The most versatile piece of equipment was a parachute, and we learned how to fashion shoes, clothing, gloves, sleeping bags, and shelters from this single piece of gear. The proper design of camouflaged shelters was another portion of our classroom time and, after demonstrating our abilities to build them, a practical application test was administered.

For those of us who were infantrymen, many of these classes were a repetition of military subjects with which we were already familiar, but it was pointed out by our instructors at the beginning that our lives might be placed in the hands of those Marines who were learning these skills for the first time. This reasoning made a lot of sense to us who had been in combat because we knew that it was always the group effort that determined our successes or failures; it would be the same with this class, too.

The climax of the course came when all of our lessons were put to the final test. We were brought into a classroom, for what appeared on our training schedule as another lecture, but this time our class was interrupted when a group of menacing instructors, dressed as "foreign aggressors," stormed into the room, firing blanks into the air, throwing furniture around, and screaming at us in a made-up language. That was the signal for us to begin an exercise known as "Barbed-Wire City." Those few unfortunate students who were caught in the initial attack on our classroom were subjected to two days of brutal interrogation giving them more than just a sample of what World War II and Korean War POWs experienced. They were introduced to a casketlike device, the "black box," and those individuals who thought they could not be "broken" found out just how quickly a real interrogation became productive. They were placed in the box in a half-crouched, half-kneeling position with a length of two-by-four placed under their knees. This prevented them from becoming too comfortable. The lid of the black box was shut and they were lowered into the ground. No matter how much they later pleaded and begged to "confess" to crimes, they were not released.

The majority of E&E students who managed to get away from the initial attack began the 130-hour field exercise, which was divided into two phases. The first portion of the exercise lasted eighty-five hours, during which time all of our classes on individual survival were used to insure that we would be able to survive off the land. The second half of the exercise was devoted to our application of newly learned evasion techniques used against the training center's aggressor force.

Each of us had been issued a one-day survival ration for the six-day problem. In addition to this, we received one parachute, several sections of parachute shroud line, a poncho, a small survival axe, a few fishhooks, two needles, one compass, and a map of the area. We were divided into two-man teams, and knew that we would have to cover distances between twenty-five and fifty miles. In this phase of the exercise individual teams were sent out on compass marches from the school site to a static camp, where we stayed for two days, constructing shelters, improving equipment, building fires, and setting up our traps and snares.

On the morning of the third day we were required to navigate cross country in teams to a designated bivouac area, where we would spend more time demonstrating survival techniques. On the morning of the fourth day, all of

the teams moved to yet another bivouac site, still looking
for food and water. On the evening of the fourth day we received a briefing on the evasion portion of the exercise,
which explained how we were to successfully evade capture over rugged, unfamiliar terrain during both daylight
and darkness, ultimately reaching a checkpoint for which
we were given the coordinates. Each of the teams was
given a different route to follow.

Our field problem was made even more difficult by the
fact that "partisans" played by the Center's permanent personnel would make contact with us along the route, but
would speak either a foreign language or a made-up tongue
in playing their roles. There were, in fact, Marines assigned
to the center who spoke fluent French, German, Danish,
and Spanish, and we were expected to find a way to make
ourselves understood to them.

When the evasion portion of our course was finally over,
all students were taken to a classroom for a final debriefing
session and were given the opportunity to critique the
twelve-day course. The last scheduled event was a trip to
the center's mess hall for a welcome traditional meal of
grilled steak. Many of us had not eaten during our last three
days in the field.

The consensus was that the demanding course allowed us
to use our initiative and ingenuity in order to be successful.
It was made tough because that was how conditions would
be if we found ourselves moving behind enemy lines or trying to survive in a prisoner-of-war camp. The motto of the
evasion, escape, and survival course was "We replace fear
of the unknown with respect for the known!" Little did I realize how important this training credo would later become.

Within a year after my tour with the 7th Marines had begun, three opportunities presented themselves that served to
change my life forever. The first of these came when I decided to resume my interest in flying. I had missed the excitement of piloting an airplane since leaving the Marine
Barracks at New London, and my tour with the 1st Marine
Brigade on Hawaii did not allow me the time to continue

the hobby. Since the Oceanside Municipal Airport was located only a mile south of Camp Pendleton, I decided to take advantage of their aircraft-rental program and take to the skies once again.

Living with half a dozen other staff noncommissioned officers in one of the Quonset huts at Camp Pulgas, I learned from my discussions with several of them about the many local airports in southern California and that a sport-parachute club was starting up in the nearby town of San Marcos. I was invited to go with several of them to watch the club participate in a jump. That was my introduction to the jump-qualified Marines assigned to 1st Force Reconnaissance Company—and the second opportunity for change.

After standing alongside the San Marcos airport runway and feeling the adrenaline run high while members of the sky-diving club climbed into their jump plane and took off for a three thousand-foot jump, I was bitten by the bug and knew that I had to give this sport a try. The following weekend I signed up for their civilian jump course and made two jumps in two days. For me, this was pure excitement.

The third opportunity to come my way was the arrival of 1st Lieutenant Tom Powers, who was assigned as the platoon leader of weapons platoon. The lieutenant was a "mustang" officer, having attained the rank of gunnery sergeant before deciding to accept a commission. He, too, was anxious to get involved in the new sport of skydiving. We soon became good friends.

First Lieutenant Powers was a long-time friend of our battalion's supply officer. By using the latter's connections within the military supply system, it was arranged for the lieutenant and me to take a trip to March Air Force Base and obtain thirty Air Force parachutes that the Air Force considered to be unserviceable because they were older than seven years. The Marines, on the other hand, made it a policy to extend the shelf life of these surplus but otherwise serviceable parachutes to ten years to get the optimum use out of them. By using this standard, we supplied the fledgling San Marcos Skydiving Club with thirty new "old" parachutes. In acknowledgment of his hard work, the skydiving club elected 1st Lieutenant Powers its first president.

During the next several months the number of my parachute jumps increased to a point where I felt extremely comfortable in falling through the air to earth. I decided to see if it would be possible to request a transfer from the ranks of the 7th Marines and join 1st Force Reconnaissance Company, where my skills as a parachutist could also be put to use.

First Sergeant Holmes said that I would first need to interview with 1st Force Recon Company's 1st sergeant and that I would be required to take a physical fitness test immediately afterward. I prepared myself for the interview, studying the operations manual used by the reconnaissance company, and nearly doubled the amount of time I dedicated daily to my physical conditioning so that when I went to Camp Del Mar for my interview I would be ready.

When the day of the interview came, I had little difficulty explaining to the 1st sergeant my desire for wanting to join the company. I believed that I had been promoted over the years by seeking additional responsibility and for doing the best job that I could for the Marines whom I was privileged to lead. I told him that I was not a stranger to hard work and that I wanted to join the company to improve my knowledge of the many skills required of a reconnaissance Marine. My explanation was accepted and I was told to change for the physical readiness test.

The prescribed physical training (PT) uniform back then was a pair of combat boots, a clean white T-shirt, and a pair of tan shorts called "brownies." The test was designed to stress every prospective candidate's upper-body strength and endurance: maximum sit-ups within two minutes (I did ninety), maximum push-ups within two minutes (I did eighty), and a six-mile run along the Pacific Ocean at Camp Del Mar beach. My running time was thirty-nine minutes.

When the test was over I was told to return to Camp Pulgas. I was to hear from the 1st sergeant within a week.

One week later to the day, I was told by 1st Sergeant Holmes that my transfer had been arranged and that I would report to Camp Del Mar the following Monday morning for duty with 1st Force Reconnaissance Company.

17

1st Force Recon Company

I joined 1st Force Reconnaissance Company in October 1960, and after reporting in to be welcomed aboard by the company commander, Major R. G. Hunt, Jr., and the company 1st sergeant, "Top" Henry, I was assigned as the assistant platoon sergeant of the pathfinder platoon. The pathfinder platoon had a dual tactical mission—to perform pre-assault and distant post-assault reconnaissance and to conduct the terminal guidance of initial helicopter waves into landing zones. To accomplish these missions we would be inserted into a particular area—by parachute drop or by exiting a submerged submarine—then move inland to locate the best helicopter landing zones and the quickest routes into an objective area. It was essential that every Marine in the pathfinder platoon be extremely knowledgeable in land navigation techniques and in the use of the multichannel, high-frequency radio. To further understand the significance and complexity of our small but well-organized company, I will try to explain its organization, primary mission, and the concept of its employment.

In 1960, 1st Force Recon Company's Table of Organization (T/O) called for 12 officers, 148 enlisted Marines, and two Navy hospital corpsmen to man the three sections within the company: the headquarters section, consisting of 5 officers and 17 enlisted men who made up the operations and intelligence sections; the supply & service platoon, consisting of 1 officer and 27 enlisted men who made up the communications, supply, medical, and amphibious maintenance sections; and the main body of the company— the four reconnaissance platoons, each with 1 officer and 26 enlisted men.

The rank of the commanding officer, according to the T/O, was a major, his executive officer and his operations officer were both captains, and our platoon commanders were lieutenants. The majority of the Marines in the company had begun their assignment to 1st Force Recon Company as basic infantrymen.

The methods that we used to accomplish our primary mission are described in five short paragraphs:

a. The force reconnaissance company, as part of the task organization of a landing force, is employed to acquire information on the enemy, weather, and terrain for that force. It accomplishes these tasks by introducing small scout teams oriented on specific collection missions, or by establishing observation posts at selected vantage points.

b. The company has no offensive capability and is wholly concerned with the acquisition of military intelligence information.

c. Introduced by aircraft and dropped by parachute into a small unprepared drop zone or landed covertly from a submarine, each reconnaissance team, utilizing movement, observes and physically reconnoiters the area or object of intelligence interest, and reports by radio or via a relay station or relay aircraft directly to the landing force commander. Upon recovery, the team is debriefed and a detailed supplementary report prepared and forwarded together with any documentary, physical, or photographic data acquired.

d. The support performed by the force reconnaissance company is not in the form of a direct service or support to a subordinate element of the landing force. Rather, it consists of the acquisition of raw information for the landing force commander. The force reconnaissance company does not produce intelligence. The unit headquarters plans, coordinates, and supervises the introduction, communications with, and the recovery of its subordinate reconnaissance teams.

e. Force reconnaissance teams have the inherent capability to provide terminal guidance to initial helicopter waves in landing zones. This capability is equally possessed by force and division reconnaissance elements, differing only in the exclusive parachute entry available in the force unit. To a lesser degree, infantry and other ground units can provide terminal guidance commensurate with the less-complex routine helicopter operations conducted within the division's zone of action. Pathfinder missions are usually executed by reconnaissance teams assigned prelanding reconnaissance tasks within the general landing area. This pathfinder terminal guidance capability does not include landing-zone traffic-control functions.

Even though I was an active member of the San Marcos Skydiving Club and had completed twenty-eight jumps prior to joining the company, my time spent dropping out of the sky above San Diego County didn't amount to a hill of beans in the eyes of the Marine Corps. Civilian parachute jumping was a sport with the emphasis on the word civilian. To be jump-qualified, I needed to attend the U.S. Army's Basic Airborne Course, taught at Fort Benning, Georgia.

Normally, I would have been required to attend the prejump course, known throughout the Marine Corps reconnaissance world as Junior Jump School (or simply "JJ"), but I was spared because of the short amount of time before the scheduled beginning of the Army's next airborne class. The company routinely conducted a junior jump school because the quotas for Marines to attend the Airborne Course were so low and because the Corps would not waste a jump-school quota on any Marine who was not fully qualified to attend the Airborne Course. The prejump course was also used as a method of identifying and separating those not qualified to remain within the company. Nevertheless, within three weeks of joining the company I was given a set of orders to what was then known as the

Army's Airborne–Air Mobility Department. I was to complete the Army's Air Transportability and Aerial Delivery of Heavy Equipment Course, taught to all officers and to enlisted men in the grades of E-5, E-6, and E-7, and then attend the three-week-long basic parachutist course.

The Air Delivery Course was designed to teach Marine officers and staff NCO jumpers the many skills required to properly load the various types of aircraft we would use in parachuting men and their equipment. Aircraft nomenclature, methods of securing equipment, and load planning made up the bulk of the course, but during the entire week we never took to the sky. Instead, we used fuselage mock-ups to learn all of our lessons in the classroom. The Basic Airborne Course would prove to be a much different affair.

The Airborne Course at Fort Benning consisted of three weeks of ever-increasing training, culminating with five jumps for each student before graduation. Our course was divided into three weeks: Ground Week, Tower Week, and Jump Week. Upon arrival we were quickly formed into a three-hundred-man student company and billeted in three-story wooden barracks. Our first training week began as a combination of learning the fundamentals of basic jump techniques and the history of parachute operations, but seemed dedicated more to constant physical punishment. Marine students were particularly singled out by many of the school's 266 Army instructors, and the penalty for committing any infraction of their rules was push-ups. We were told that a sound body and a well-coordinated mind were essential traits of a paratrooper, and the countless push-ups demanded by our instructors were credited with producing better students.

As I've mentioned, the primary emphasis of our first week's training was centered on learning the basic jump techniques, of which there were five: (1) control of your body inside the aircraft and knowledge of the nine jump commands; (2) control of your body from the moment the aircraft is exited until the student feels the opening shock of the expanding parachute canopy; (3) control of the parachute during descent; (4) making proper contact with the ground; (5) control of the parachute after landing.

The use of mock-up aircraft fuselages gave each of us the proper understanding of how we would be expected to exit various types of aircraft and we practiced getting in, getting out, how we would be organized as a group of jumpers, called a "stick." Each time we piled into one of the mock-ups we saw and heard the nine jump commands demonstrated by hand and arm signals while they were being shouted out: Get ready! Outboard personnel stand up! Inboard personnel stand up! Hook up! Check static line! Check equipment! Sound off for equipment check! Stand in the door! GO!

Over and over these commands were shouted and executed as we jumped from inside the mock-up and hit the ground outside, executing a PLF (parachute landing fall), the only acceptable method of landing. By learning how to properly perform the PLF, injuries were greatly reduced.

When a jumper descends to tree-top level, he is taught to reach up, grab his parachute risers, and keep his eyes on the horizon and his head straight. In that position he will be unaware of exactly when he will hit the ground. At the first instant of contact with mother earth, each jumper should twist his body in one of four directions—right, left, to the front, or to the rear. The direction selected depends upon which way the wind is carrying the jumper. The sudden shock of impact is absorbed through the jumper's feet, the calves of his legs, his thighs, then his butt, and finally across his shoulders as he pivots his body to face the canopy. After completing several hundred PLFs and performing hundreds of push-ups as incentives to remember the proper sequence of jump commands, our performance of this routine improved.

With Ground Week also came other training, which included spending many hours hanging in parachute harnesses. After we had become familiar with that feeling, additional classes were taught that described how to prepare for difficult landings among rocks, in water, and in proximity to high-tension electrical lines. To help give each student a feel for being dragged over open ground by his parachute canopy, a wind machine was used to simulate the experience, and we were taught how to run into the canopy to collapse it. If that proved impossible, then the student was taught to release the parachute from its harness by disconnecting a release mechanism, known as a capewell, which would separate him from the chute.

The last and probably the most feared phase of Ground Week was having to face the thirty-four-foot tower for the first time. It was at this point that most students began to wash out. The jump from the training tower, while attached to a parachute harness, allowed each of us to experience the feeling of having to "stand in the door" and then undergo the gut-wrenching shock of canopy deployment.

I jumped out the way I had been taught in the mock-up door, then slid down the cables on a trolley to a sawdust mound where I was unhooked before double-timing back to the base of the tower to receive a grade from an instructor. Satisfactory completion of Ground Week moved each of us into the second phase of training, Tower Week.

Tower Week consisted of five days dedicated to learning about parachute construction, how main and reserve parachutes were packed, and how to handle a malfunction. Of course, as the name implies, Tower Week completion meant having graduated from first using the two-foot-high mockups, the thirty-four-foot tower, and the 250-foot-high training device known as the free tower.

A trip to the free tower meant that each student jumper was placed in a specially designed harness and parachute and was then hauled to the top of one of the tower's four arms. The Army's instructors on the ground beneath the tower were armed with bullhorns and would talk to individual students as we were being hauled skyward, coming to rest 247 feet above them. On a given command the control NCO released each jumper and we descended the way we would on a live jump. We were closely graded to see if we could put all of our previous instruction into a satisfactory descent, which included slipping away from the tower and performing a proper parachute landing fall. After the free tower, all that remained was Jump Week.

The final week of the course was used to teach us how our personal and combat equipment was to be properly packed and secured inside of an aircraft before we moved down to the airfield for the first of our five scheduled jumps. The first two jumps were conducted in one day without the use of excess equipment, and were called "tap-outs" because the jumpmaster physically tapped each student as we exited at 1,250 feet from Fairchild C-123 aircraft. Our third jump was a mass exit wearing a partial pack and the fourth jump was done with a dozen aircraft flying in close formation. This exercise was as much for the learning experiences of our jumpmasters and the pilots as it was for us students. Our fifth and final jump was a thirty-six-man mass-exit jump with full combat pack.

Graduation from the Basic Airborne Course was a big moment in the life of every Marine student. We felt that we had cheated death and had lived to tell about it. We also looked forward to getting away from the U.S. Army and returning to our parent commands, and to begin spending the additional $55 per month that was paid to each jump-qualified Marine. The three units of the Corps that actually rated jump pay were Recon, Air Naval Gunfire Liaison Company (ANGLICO), and the Air Delivery Platoon.

I returned to Camp Pendleton and resumed my duties as the pathfinder platoon sergeant. I was introduced to our new platoon commander, a squared-away captain named Davis, whose primary goal in life was his concern for improving our training. He wasted no time in letting it be known that he wanted the Marines of his pathfinder platoon trained in every aspect of long-range reconnaissance patrolling.

Although our company strength was small in numbers, it was apparent that there was a division in attitude between those assigned to the pathfinder platoon and those assigned to one of the reconnaissance platoons. The reason for this attitude was because of the difference in the missions given to the platoons. The Marines who made up the recon platoons were superb swimmers and highly trained as scuba divers, and the unspoken feeling within the company was that anyone joining the company who wasn't scuba-qualified should be assigned to the pathfinder platoon. The pathfinder platoon, on the other hand, had the reputation of being the home of the more-accomplished parachutists in the company. Captain Davis, Staff Sergeant Jerry Lundermo, and I wanted to put an end to this belief. We knew that it would take some doing, but we felt that if all of the platoons trained as one, this individuality crap would disappear. Intensified unit training became the common goal.

At the time, the pathfinder platoon consisted of only one officer, one staff noncommissioned officer, and four ten-man teams. Our company training program dictated that every team member be capable of participating in the many different types of training required of a reconnaissance Marine. This included parachute operations, free-fall training, scuba operations, submarine operations, pathfinder operations, rappelling operations, and initial terminal-guidance operations for helicopter landing zones. Those other functions associated with our intelligence gathering, such as detailed area studies, debriefing of patrols, the compiling of reconnaissance-patrol reports, and preparing information for radio transmission, were taught by the company intelligence officer, assisted by the platoon leaders and platoon sergeants.

Beginning in February and for the next several months, we participated in an intensive training program that began with a five-week training package at the Mountain Warfare Training Center at Bridgeport. It was designed to help prepare us for a future six-month deployment to some of the more remote areas of the Philippine Islands. Again leaving the lower altitude of southern California for training above the eight thousand-foot level at Bridgeport, we participated in classes taken from both the winter and summer courses.

We learned about rock climbing and mountaineering equipment, practiced mountain-warfare tactics, and how to cross rapidly flowing mountain streams properly. We also learned about the care and use of our special equipment under the extreme conditions of snow and ice, realizing that these same lessons would prove invaluable in any type of terrain. At the time, there were only two military training sites in the country that provided courses in mountaineering, rock climbing, and cold weather survival: an Army school in Alaska and the Marine Corps' site at Pickle Meadows. The time spent at Bridgeport was viewed as a welcome change from our training at Camp Pendleton.

Five weeks later, we returned to the lowlands of San Diego County, feeling physically fit and ready for another training challenge. We didn't have to wait very long.

We got the word that some of the jump-qualified Marines in the company were to be flown from Camp Pendleton to El Centro, California, to be used in a testing and evaluation program to determine why several modified military parachutes had ripped apart in mid-air during a recent jump exercise. Our stay at El Centro allowed us the opportunity to participate in dozens of static line and free-fall parachute jumps over the Imperial Valley. We soon discovered that the earlier parachute malfunctions had occurred because a twenty-eight-foot parachute pack was being used to hold a thirty-two-foot military canopy. When the too-large parachutes deployed without the use of protective sleeves, friction weakened the nylon fabric and the canopies ripped apart in midair. Fortunately, no one had been killed because of the resulting malfunctions, and the potentially deadly problem was corrected. We returned to Camp Pendleton, rejoined the pathfinder platoon, and completed final preparations for overseas deployment.

We flew from Travis Air Force Base to Clark Field, outside of Manila, then were taken by bus to Subic Bay. From the Navy base at Subic, we flew south by helicopter, to the island of Mindoro. Our six months of jungle training was made all the more enjoyable after we learned that we would be taught the finer points of jungle-survival skills by the true masters of the Philippine jungles—the Negritos, aboriginal natives who had found their way to the Philippine Islands by way of Asia more than twenty-five thousand years ago. Though not exceeding a height greater than four and a half feet, the Negritos were skillful hunters, trappers, and fishermen, allowing the jungle to provide for all their daily needs. Rumored to be head-hunters, savages, and cannibals, their reputation helped to keep the majority of the Filipino population at a distance. But those few Negritos who were persuaded to leave the jungle and work for the military as expert trackers, guides, and teachers earned the respect and admiration of every Marine student. And we learned from them.

First, the Negritos taught us that just the simple act of staying clean could make the difference between an effective fighting man and one who has to be taken out of action because he has come down with some jungle disease. We also learned how to make comfortable shelters from material found in the dense vegetation. Keeping warm and dry was an important part of learning how to live in this unfamiliar territory. Other classes taught us what could be eaten and what was injurious. The jungle was a vast storehouse if we knew what to look for. We learned that some of the edibles were not as good-tasting as mom's home cooking, but could keep us alive and healthy. Learning that some plants like bamboo naturally store water could mean the difference between surviving or dying of thirst in a rain forest. The Negritos said, "When in doubt, watch what the monkey will eat, and then eat the monkey."

Their survival lessons were never dull, and we watched in fascination as they showed us how to prepare a typical Negrito jungle meal by taking a short section of bamboo, filling it with dried rice, frogs, snails, and water, and then placing it beside the coals of a small campfire. After about one hour's time they would remove the bamboo from beside the fire, split the section in half, and present us with dinner for two!

Our time spent learning secrets from the Negritos paid off, and soon each of us had learned how to properly construct a good jungle hooch, complete with a one-man hammock. We also learned the safest way to rise after a good night's sleep: making certain that there were no unwelcome guests crawling around outside your bed before you put feet on the ground and searching the folds of your uniform before putting it on. One bite from a spider or from a poisonous scorpion, or the sting from a hidden yellow wasp, could put a man out of action for several days. If an insect bite went untreated and became infected, it could eventually kill a man.

Probably the most important class taught to us was the lengthy land-navigation course. There were two phases— one for day and one for night. We learned to move over mountainous terrain, across deep river gorges, and through the dense jungle. The most difficult portion of the course came at night: Learning to cope with unusually high temperatures, constant humidity, torrential downpours, and the constant buzzing and biting insects during periods of total darkness made us much more confident in our ability to traverse the jungle safely.

Only one training "incident" occurred during our deployment to the Philippines, which otherwise could be described as "safe." As a member of one of our reconnaissance platoons, twenty-one-year-old Lance Corporal Dennis Boyle, a native of Mitchell, South Dakota, was part of a six-man stick that was making a routine parachute jump over Subic Bay. Captain Miller, the commanding officer of the U.S.S. *Bennington*, a Navy carrier that was acting as the temporary home for the members of a reconnaissance platoon, had requested that the platoon members make a static-line jump so that his crew could photograph the 425th jump conducted by the company since its inception in 1957. The Marines wanted to have a "tight" stick so that the photograph would reveal how well they performed as jumpers, but in their haste to get everyone out of the TF-1 prop-driven aircraft, Lance Corporal Boyle accidentally stepped over the static line of the jumper positioned in front of him. The static line wrapped around Boyle's right leg and pulled him out of the airplane, flying at 120 knots.

Helplessly suspended upside down and eighteen feet beneath the aircraft, Boyle managed to keep his cool, and signaled the jumpmaster, 1st Lieutenant Phillips, that he was still conscious by placing his hands on top of his helmet. The pilot of the TF-1 immediately gained altitude, while Boyle hung beneath the plane for nearly four minutes and the jumpmaster tried to figure out which static line was the lance corporal's. Had the jumpmaster not cut the correct static line, Boyle's main parachute would have gone from being partially open to fully deployed, and would have have ripped him apart as it opened in the 120-knot slipstream. Fortunately for Boyle, he was able to remain conscious while he was suspended beneath the aircraft. Once cut free, he descended 1,300 feet, landing in a palm tree. He was taken to the base hospital for an examination and, after being treated for a sprained knee, was released to full duty. He was one very lucky Marine!

Our platoon returned from the Philippines in June 1962, and I was no sooner getting accustomed to life back at the company area at Camp Del Mar when I was presented with a new set of orders that directed me to attend pre-scuba school. This preparatory school lasted for two weeks. During this time I prepared myself both mentally and physically for the rigors of formal training to become a qualified scuba diver at the Navy's Underwater Swimmer's School (UWSS) located at Key West, Florida.

Our scuba-school class at Key West initially numbered fifty-five students, including thirteen Navy midshipmen, who had taken leave from their classes at the Naval Academy in Annapolis. Twenty-three Marines, including one major, two captains, and three lieutenants, who came from the two reconnaissance companies located on either coast, a U.S. Air Force staff sergeant, a U.S. Army sergeant, and a technical sergeant named Soo Yee Kim, from the Republic of Korea Marine Corps, also attended.

We began the four weeks of intensive underwater training the same way we had begun every other military class—with lots of early morning physical-fitness training as part of the conditioning program. Enlisted Marines over the age of thirty-one were not allowed to attend this school and all students had to be excellent swimmers and able to pass a demanding physical examination. Those men who could not handle the demands of scuba school were immediately dropped from the class and found themselves headed back to wherever they had come from.

What we would learn at Key West was designed to enable us to use the water as a vehicle and to move silently onto an enemy-held beach, map out the enemy defenses, accurately chart the hydrographics of a landing area, and return safely to friendly forces with the information. The emphasis of our basic training at UWSS was divided into four areas: physical conditioning, knowledge of our diving equipment, medical knowledge, and practical application.

Training in medical skills was heavily stressed because there was so little margin for error in scuba diving. Although these classes seemed to be boring, they were in fact the most important classes of all. Once we became more familiar with the demands that swimming and scuba diving could place on our bodies, we became more relaxed in our new liquid environment. We learned the causes of pressurization; the effects that water would have on us; and that the body contains fluids and tissues that are incompressible and automatically equalize with outside pressure. However, within the body, certain areas must be forcibly equalized— the lungs, ears, and sinuses—and because these areas could be quickly damaged by unequal pressure, we relied upon compressed gases in scuba tanks to equalize it.

Our physical conditioning had to be at a peak level whether we were on or below the surface of the water. Daily sessions of endurance runs, countless flutter kicks, and long hours spent in open water kept our fitness level on par. We were graded in three surface swims out to a thousand yards, and four scuba swims at five hundred, seven hundred and fifty, and a thousand yards during the day, and one at night. We also were graded in day and night compass dives that covered more than a thousand yards. Expert knowledge of our diving equipment was mandatory; a scuba diver can't trust his life to a piece of equipment that he doesn't thoroughly understand. To insure that we knew our equipment inside and out, we were taught how to disassemble and assemble the different types of regulators and valves that we would be using daily.

The practical application of diving was, by far, the most interesting portion of the course. To enable us to swim to greater depths, we were introduced to a series of diving bells that were suspended below the surface of the water in increments of twenty feet. The diving bells could accommodate groups of up to six divers, and after short periods of rest between the diving bells we would exit and swim down to the next, deeper, bell. As a safety precaution, sets of scuba tanks were suspended on anchor lines between the diving bells for student divers who might require an immediate resupply of compressed air. After we had demonstrated our abilities as swimmers and had begun to feel more at home wearing scuba gear, we began to practice infiltration techniques that enabled us to swim undetected and to place explosive charges and different types of mines on ships, submarines, or against other types of structures that would require destruction by explosive ordnance. To make sure that we could easily recognize a submarine, our kindly instructors arranged for us to spend the better part of one day chipping paint from the side of one.

On several occasions our class was divided in half, with one group of student divers placing explosives on a submerged structure, while the second half of the class was required to locate and defuse the hidden charges.

The use of the buddy system was the only means that allowed us to train in this manner, and our Navy instructors wanted us to experience as much hands-on time as possible.

As part of our final scuba dive, we were required to dive to sixty feet and, working as two-man teams, locate a large iron flange on the bottom of the Gulf and then bolt on twelve steel bolts that we carried with us. The next two-man team was then required to find the flange and remove the bolts. The process was repeated by all students. In this way we demonstrated our ability to work as a team under water.

On August 31, 1962, I graduated from the Underwater Swimmer's School, fifteenth out of thirty-nine graduating students. I would not have done that well if it had not been for the continuous help of my diving partner, a young midshipman named Gary R. Hosey, who spent hours tutoring me in the more difficult mathematical problems that we were supposed to master at the school. Midshipman Hosey was majoring in engineering at the Naval Academy, and his willingness to help me and his patience in teaching me were put to the test every day. Again, the use of the buddy system paid off for me in a very big dividend.

When we returned to Camp Pendleton, we found that the company had once again become a beehive of activity. New orders had arrived that directed the deployment of our pathfinder platoon to the island of Okinawa for one year, beginning in October. To be considered ready for the deployment, all members of the pathfinder platoon were required to complete a number of parachute jumps that would bring the platoon's parachuting proficiency up to speed prior to departure. Familiarization jumps, with and without equipment, were a standard part of our training schedule, and these numerous jumps made during the day and at night from various types of Navy and Marine aircraft added to our proficiency as a team.

To help get the platoon prepared for our lengthy deployment, I sought out the advice of some of the senior Marines within the company whom I knew I could depend upon for sound guidance, asking them to tell me as much as possible about their last deployment on Okinawa. I wanted to know if there was anything they could think of that might prove valuable to me and to my Marines. Gunnery Sergeant Julian "Spider" Parrish, our company operations chief (S-3), Gunnery Sergeant John Massaro, our company gunnery sergeant (later to become the Sergeant Major of the Marine Corps), Staff Sergeant Jerry Lundermo, and Sergeant Mike Ratliff topped my list of those professional Marines I could depend upon for any additional help. The junior Marines in our company also knew that these noncommissioned officers could be approached at any time for a straight answer. These noncommissioned officers were to become my mentors. They simply lead their lives by being good examples for the rest of us to follow.

Armed with what we felt was the best checklist of equipment, maps, tools, and hard-to-find items that we could put together for the deployment, pathfinder platoon continued to prepare themselves for departure. Finally, with the majority of the platoon's equipment packed up in "mount-out" boxes, our remaining days at Camp Del Mar were scheduled for parachute operations that would help qualify several Marines within the company as jumpmasters.

18

A Jump in the Wind

Within my twelve-man pathfinder team were seven jump-qualified Marines who were originally scheduled to go to Okinawa, along with the rest of the Marines in the platoon, but because these seven men did not have enough obligated service time in the Marine Corps for our one-year deployment, they had to either extend their periods of enlistment or reenlist for two more years of duty so that we could stay together as a team. Those seven Marines did reenlist just prior to their deployment date, best describing how truly dedicated and committed they were in their desire for us to remain together. Certain that our deployment to Okinawa would now be a very memorable event, a fresh feeling of confidence and anticipation swept over the pathfinder platoon.

On the night of September 20, 1962, our group of jumpers, consisting of Sergeant P. J. Orlett, corporals J. L. Rosas, J. D. Rich, A. A. Analla, B. Martin, C. Kirehoff, and lance corporals R. Saenz, D. McLean, C. D. Knight, R. L. Cross, C. E. Hemphill, J. Vandergaag, Jr., A. Jesperson, L. Mendoza, and Private First Class D. L. Trillo joined me as we boarded a Marine HR2S helicopter just after dusk and departed the airfield at Camp Pendleton to fly in a northeasterly direction to our designated drop zone. It was located less than four miles from the airfield and positioned next to the 1st Marine Division's tank park at Camp Los

Flores. Our drop zone was simply referred to as the "Tank Park DZ" and was familiar to all of us. We carried no extra equipment other than our standard gear—helmet, knife, and signaling flare. We used our main T-10 parachutes and reserve chutes.

This night jump was the next-to-last jump that we would make prior to our departure for Okinawa, and it would also help to qualify one of our new jumpmasters. On his signal we exited the helicopter and experienced no problems. All that remained for us to do was participate in the next day's jump, over this same drop zone, before we packed up our parachutes and departed California for deployment to Okinawa.

The following day's activity was considered by the Marines of the pathfinder platoon to be just a hot-dog jump, because static-line jumps, performed without the burden of extra equipment, were always fun, and left little room for injury. This would also be our last opportunity to jump as a platoon before we left Camp Pendleton.

On the morning of the 21st, a typical weather pattern for southern California greeted us. The cool ocean air had created a thick layer of low-level clouds covering the coastal plains, but by 1000 the warming sun had broken through the fog and patches of blue sky meant that our drop zone would be visible by 1100.

Our departure from the Camp Pendleton airfield was scheduled for 1030, with one Marine GV-1 aircraft assigned the mission of dropping us over the zone. As we stood by waiting for the arrival of the big airplane, we went through the elements of our jump brief for the last time.

Ten of us made up the first stick of jumpers, with myself positioned as the last jumper, so that I would have the honor of pushing the stick out of the plane. We knew we had arrived at the correct jump altitude when the crew chief came back to where we were seated and set the hydraulics in motion to open the huge cargo doors at the rear of the aircraft. Receiving the signal from our jumpmaster, ten of us stood up, hooked up our static lines, and moved in a penguinlike shuffle toward the rear of the plane. On the command "Go," I started pushing the Marine in front of me and the momentum carried the stick of jumpers forward. We cleared the plane in seconds.

After I exited the aircraft, I waited for the familiar tug of my deploying canopy, looking straight up when I felt the jolt to make sure I had a good canopy opening. I unhooked one side of my reserve parachute from my main harness so that it would drop away and permit me to take a good look around and then orient myself to the drop zone. At a height of about eight hundred feet, I noticed that I was drifting toward a series of high-tension lines than ran close to the drop zone. I tried to slip against the wind and get away from these by pulling down on my risers. My efforts began to pay off, but as soon as I stopped slipping away the wind began to blow me back toward the power lines, just as if there were a magnetic attraction between myself and them. At that point I tried to change my strategy and began slipping with the wind to pass over the lines. When I was less than fifty feet from the ground and preparing myself to land, I let up on my risers, but as soon as I did the wind changed again and blew my parachute upward and back toward the high-tension wires.

The cooler wind from the Pacific Ocean was meeting with the prevailing warmer desert air and the gusting winds hit off the hillsides near the drop zone, causing my canopy to become caught in the middle of this tug-of-war with nature. It finally ended with my chute becoming entangled in the 69,000-volt lines. Helplessly suspended beneath those big lines I swayed above a lower set of three 12,000-volt lines that ran parallel to the main lines. The momentum of being carried between the lines caused me to swing out; as I swung back I could feel myself drop a little. My left foot hit the middle 12,000-volt line and I drove it against the outside line. When those two lines made contact I was the only obstacle between the humming 12,000-volt and 69,000-volt lines.

I felt the electrical shock as it came up from beneath me.

Everything around me turned bright yellow and I could hear a loud "boom" ringing in my ears. To this day, I can still remember that moment: I looked out toward the west and noticed a large Navy ship moving through the water close to the shore. That ship and the Pacific Ocean appeared as black as coal, while the sky remained bright yellow.

The Marines in the drop zone could only stand and watch as a bluish-white flame shot up from the electrical lines and arced against my left foot. The spark traveled up and over my body, moved back down my left, followed by an orange flame that shot up from the lines, passed over me, and continued moving straight up my parachute risers, causing my nylon canopy to smoke. When the canopy melted, I dropped thirty feet to the ground from where I had been suspended. I remember falling, but it seemed more like I was floating down to earth rather than crashing to the ground. However, I'll take the word of those Marines who witnessed what happened. They said I fell like a ton of bricks.

I remember lying there on the ground and trying to move, but I couldn't. One of the electrical lines had snapped in two and fell to the ground still sparking, whipped around in the dry brush, and ignited grass fires everywhere it touched down. I watched as the fires began to spread out from the points of origin and tried helplessly to reach for my signaling flare, but I didn't have the strength to pull it away from my harness. Our training had been so repetitive that it was an instinctive reaction to try and get my signaling flare ignited and let someone know where I was and that I was still alive. I can remember trying to holler, but no sounds came out of my throat.

The next thing I recall was the arrival of the first Marine to reach me, Sergeant Ratliff. He had jumped before me and had watched as I had swung into the power line, caught on fire, and then had fallen to the ground. He reached for my harness so that he could open the capewells, but he jerked back his hands after getting burned from touching the hot metal clips. He was joined shortly by another Marine, by which time the metal had cooled enough to enable them to pop the capewells and pull me out of the smoking harness and away from the approaching brush fire.

One of our company corpsmen, a guy we always referred to as "Pappy," was the next person to join us. (Pappy's real name was O. D. Fikes. As luck would have it, he was about to retire from the Navy after twenty years of service, and after being discharged from Camp Pendleton a few days after my accident, he was killed in an automobile accident in route to his retirement home in Texas.) Pappy grabbed a pair of dressing scissors from his medical bag, cut open the legs of my trousers to expose the burns, and then used his scissors to cut the laces from my jump boots. Because my left jump boot was still smoking and literally too hot to handle, a field jacket was wrapped around the boot so that it could be carefully slid off my foot.

Pappy placed the boot beside me on the ground, and I noticed that the three brass cobbler's nails in the toe of my Corcoran jump boot had actually melted and now hung beneath the boot's tip like three drops of brass-colored water. Until that moment I had not experienced any pain, but when my boot was slid away from my foot, my green wool sock slid away with it and I remember seeing that my big toe was gone. In fact, my toe was inside of my sock and the stench of my own burned flesh filled the air around us.

I grabbed for Pappy's arm and asked, "How bad is it, Pappy?" The thoughts of suddenly not being able to take my pathfinder team overseas after all that they had done to try and stay together began to upset me. Then, selfishly, I thought about myself and wondered if I would be able to jump again, even though I was missing a toe. It still hadn't occurred to me that I was not able to move.

Pappy patted me on the shoulder and spoke softly. "Ham, I wish I had some morphine to give to ya', but it got crushed the other day while we were in the field. We've got a rescue chopper headed in here, right now, and we'll have you over to the base hospital in just a couple of minutes.

Just try and stay cool, and you'll be fine. Just don't try to move. We'll put you on a stretcher and load you into that rescue bird as soon as it gets here."

When the little Kaman HOK-1 Husky rescue helicopter landed in the center of the drop zone, I was placed on a stretcher and carried to the rear of the waiting bird. My stretcher was then placed along a metal railing and I was shoved, head first, into a slot and strapped into position between the pilot and copilot. They both looked down at me, and gave me a "thumbs-up" before we took off, without a word ever being spoken. Less than five minutes had passed from the time that Pappy told me about the inbound rescue helicopter until I was picked up and carried into the emergency room of the naval hospital at Camp Pendleton.

My arrival at the naval hospital came at the worst time possible—lunch time. The duty corpsman who had met the rescue chopper had been told only that the hospital was receiving a burn victim, and had no idea as to the extent of my injuries. Most of the hospital's staff were enjoying their noon meal and, when the word was passed that an emergency medevac patient suffering third-degree electrical burns had just been brought into the emergency room, they thought that the news was either a joke or some sort of drill. It was neither, and I was starting to feel considerable pain.

The first Navy doctor who appeared in the emergency room, a young lieutenant commander named Lamont, politely introduced himself and then quickly ordered one of his attending corpsmen to cut away the rest of my utility uniform as I lay there on the stretcher. After carefully examining my left foot, he looked up at me, and with all seriousness asked, "Just how many days has your foot looked like this?"

Surprised at his question, I told him exactly what had happened. He stood there motionless, apparently in disbelief that I was not only able to tell him the details of what had just happened, but that I had survived the electrocution as well.

I was given a spinal and all sensation of pain left me. It was noted on my admission form that I had been burned on my right side, just below my hip. Luckily the .45 pistol I had been carrying had not been loaded, because the 69,000 volts of electricity that had passed over me found every piece of metal that was attached to my body. My Colt automatic had been heated up and had burned through its leather holster, causing the third degree burns below my right hip. In fact, wherever metal had been close to my skin, I was burned.

I was moved from the emergency room to the intensive-care section of the hospital and tried to sleep during the next several hours. The pain medication was doing its job, but so was the hospital's staff. I was X-rayed from head to toe, examined by other doctors and nurses, photographed by a surgical team, and had numerous samples of blood taken while I tried to make some sense out of what had happened and to learn whether or not I would be able to heal fast enough to join my platoon while it was on Okinawa.

Late in the afternoon I was awakened by my first visitor, my company commander, Major Jim McCallister. He had left the company office at Camp Del Mar as soon as he had learned about the accident and had remained at the hospital all afternoon, waiting for permission to get to see me. He had not come alone, but was accompanied by several other company officers. The doctors had asked them all to wait until I was a little more prepared for visitors, but had made an exception for Major McCallister.

His visit was short, but he told me how very sorry he was to see that I had been injured and offered to help me in any way possible. Smiling, he told me that he had to stop a mass exodus of Marines from leaving the company area at Del Mar when they had heard about my injury. With a reassuring handshake he told me that he would see to it that I would get the very best care possible, and promised to return every day to check on my condition. I have never forgotten that man's kindness.

That evening, Lieutenant Zeweber, one of the Navy nurses who was assigned to the intensive-care ward, told me that a Navy captain, a gentleman named McCullum, was going to examine me in the morning. As she worked at changing my bandages, she told me that it was considered nothing short of a miracle that I had survived the electrocution.* She also said that Captain McCullum was the one man who would have the answers to all of my questions. Thinking that there was a good chance that my foot might heal up, I spent a restless and painful night drifting in and out of sleep, waiting for the arrival of Captain McCullum, United States Navy.

*A number of newspaper and local and national magazine articles were written about what happened to me at Camp Pendleton on that morning of September 21, 1962. Though there was a fair degree of accuracy in many of those articles, a good deal of inaccurate information was also given. These inaccuracies were the result of a combination of misinformation, pure speculation, and "second-hand" eyewitness accounts that caused more than a little embarrassment to me.

Magazine articles stating that I had been awarded numerous medals for heroism during the Korean War, along with newspaper articles stating that I had been left for dead for several hours, lying on a stretcher waiting for help, served no useful informational purpose. Other stories that were published were simply untrue, or written only to sensationalize the incident. With this opportunity to tell the story about my years of service in the Marine Corps, I believe that it is necessary to set the record straight once and for all about what really occurred on that windy September morning.

19

Fun in the Hospital

As I lay in my hospital bed watching the morning light move through the venetian blinds, my attention was drawn by the movement of white shapes approaching the room. These forms came into focus as a gaggle of starched white doctors and nurses who had begun the morning ritual, making rounds through the intensive-care ward of the hospital. It had been less than twenty-four hours since I had parachuted into the electrical lines, but during that short period of time I had been thoroughly examined, X-rayed, photographed, medicated, and bandaged and I had quickly learned to endure having multiple samples of my blood drawn into color-coded test tubes hourly. Two large areas of my right side and my right leg had been badly burned, and my left leg throbbed. It was wrapped in layers of white cotton gauze, but I was beginning to get impatient for someone—anyone—to come in and tell me just how badly I had been injured. The sight of the Navy doctors making their rounds gave me hope of getting some answers to my questions.

Captain McCullum, the naval hospital's chief of surgery, led the group of staff officers. As they came to a halt in front of my room the captain spoke quietly to them and they departed, leaving the good doctor and me alone. He approached my bed, stopped, and bent down to remove the medical chart from its frame at the foot of my bed. I watched his eyes as they moved slowly across the pages containing my medical history and describing the previous day's emergency-room treatment. The results of the laboratory tests had been stapled to the pages on the left side of the chart. When he had finished reading, he placed it back in its frame and turned his eyes on me.

"Good morning, Staff Sergeant Hamblen, my name is Doctor McCullum. I'm the head surgeon here at the hospital. I don't know what you've been told since you've arrived, but I want you to know several things right from the start. First of all, I have to say that you must be one lucky son of a bitch. To have fallen more than thirty feet without breaking any bones is a miracle, but to have survived an electrical shock of that magnitude can only mean that you must live a very charmed life. Your good physical condition has played an important role in your being alive today, but there're some things that I'm going to tell you that will require a great amount of strength on your part—inner strength."

The captain pulled a chair up next to my bed and told me what he had read in my medical chart. He explained the reason why so many samples of my blood had been taken during the past twenty-four hours—that because my left foot had been so badly burned, he feared that a gangrenous infection had already set in and that the only way to determine if that was so was through the numerous blood tests. He added that because of the unknown damage to the circulation system in my leg it would take several days before he could make a complete diagnosis.

Because the captain was so straightforward and took care not to give me reason for false hopes, I believed what he said and felt comfortable in trusting him.

Three days later, I guessed that Captain McCullum must have been the doctor who had drawn the shortest straw: He came into my room and told me that most of the flesh on my left foot had been completely destroyed. As he had feared, gangrene had set in. He told me that I would live, but that he would have to amputate my lower left leg in order to save my life.

His words sent a cold shiver up the back of my neck. The first question I asked him was, "When will the operation take place?"

"We'll pack your leg in ice tonight. I'll perform the surgery first thing in the morning."

"How far up are you going to take it?"

"What the hell difference does it make?" he shot back. "You'll still have your knee, and that'll allow you to walk normally. The good news is that you won't look and feel like someone who has lost his leg. You're a strong man and you've got a lot to live for."

From that moment on, Dr. McCullum and I became good friends. He had tried in every way possible to save my leg, but it was burned beyond repair. He had not wanted to be the one to have to tell me that I was going to lose my leg, but because the commanding officer of the naval hospital didn't have the guts to tell me himself, he had ordered Captain McCullum to do the unpleasant job for him. Dr. McCullum hadn't been angry with me; only in having to be the one who had to tell me about it.

That night a makeshift pan was brought into my room and my lower left leg was packed in ice, making any chance of getting some sleep impossible. I dozed off and on that night, thinking about my future.

Early the next morning several hospital corpsmen came into my room and with their help I was placed on a gurney, then taken by elevator down to the operating room. While parked outside of the OR, I was given an injection of Demerol that was supposed to make me sleepy, but I was very much awake when they wheeled me in. The last thing I remember was the beelike sting from the spinal.

It was sometime late in the afternoon when I finally awoke. I couldn't feel that part of my left leg was gone, but when I focused my eyes and glanced down at the foot of the bed, the empty space below my left knee—that place beneath the pale blue sheets where my leg and foot should have been—was flat and empty. It was that empty space that constantly reminded me that my lower leg was gone forever, and I spent the rest of that afternoon looking down at it, wondering what life was now going to be like for an infantry Marine with only one leg.

When Dr. McCullum came in to visit with me later that evening, he told me that he had rounded off the end of my tibular and fibular bones, and that he had left the skin below my knee looking "dog-eared" so it would properly drain. He was pleased with the way the operation had gone and he thought that I would have an excellent chance of being able to walk normally. He also said that the electrical burn on my right thigh was much deeper than they had originally thought, but there appeared to have been no damage done to the bone. He added that the burn area under my right arm would heal after several skin grafts, which would be performed at a later time.

"There's still a lot of work to be done, Hamblen. You'll have to remain here on the intensive-care ward until we're absolutely sure that there is no sign of staph infection, and we'll watch that left leg closely to make certain that we don't have to take any more off it. After you're out of intensive care and we've completed those skin grafts, you can begin the process of physical rehabilitation, which will prepare you for transfer up to the Oak Knoll Naval Hospital, in Oakland. It's the best military hospital on the West Coast and active-duty military patients who are candidates for a prosthesis are sent there. They do really good work."

Dr. McCullum had done his job, but I knew that it was up to me to get into shape and become fit for duty. The only thing that stood in my way was the time required for my burns to heal and the slight inconvenience of having to learn, once again, how to walk. I had been in the Marine Corps for twelve years and, not counting the ten days I had spent in a battalion aid station after being wounded in Korea, I had never been hospitalized. I thought that with a little help from the Navy, I would soon be as good as new. Little did I realize what lay ahead.

My road to recovery started, the very first Sunday morning after I had lost my leg, with the unauthorized visit to the intensive care ward of two "family" members— Sergeant Paul Moyer and Sergeant "Nelly" Nelson. Both of these Marines were members of 1st Force Recon Company, but Sergeant Moyer happened to be a patient in the naval hospital because he had managed to survive falling off Demonstration Rock at the Mountain Training Center at Bridgeport. As a result of his nearly fatal fall, he was wearing a body cast and was pushed along in his wheelchair by Sergeant Nelson, who ran the recon company's scuba locker. These two Marines were inseparable friends, and when Sergeant Nelson had come to visit Moyer with the news that I, too, had been hospitalized, the two of them decided it was proper and fitting to pay me a visit bringing with them a Sunday newspaper and a half-empty bottle of scotch they had "tested" prior to coming to my ward. Breathing scotch fumes all over the duty corpsman, the two said they were related to me, and demanded to know what room I was in. When they left to find me, the duty corpsman ran off to find the ward nurse. Later, though found innocent of having invited my two "brothers" to join me for a drink on the intensive-care ward, I was cautioned by the nursing staff not to expect any more lenient treatment for other "family" members who didn't understand the visiting rules of the naval hospital.

With the permission of the base hospital's chief of surgery, our company commander, Major McCallister, arranged for a vehicle, a weapons carrier, to be made available to the Marines in the company who wanted to travel the ten miles from Camp Del Mar to the naval hospital and visit me. Both officers thought this would be good for my morale. They were right.

Just two days prior to the pathfinder platoon's leaving for its one-year deployment to Okinawa, I was surprised to see the entire platoon, less two Marines who had duty, come into the intensive-care ward wearing their Class-A uniforms and surround my bed to have a farewell picture taken. Their thoughtfulness was better for my spirits than any medical treatment I had received since arriving at the hospital. Though I was saddened that they would be leaving California for a year, their departing gift gave me encouragement to work even harder at getting discharged from the ward and move on to the physical therapy that would possibly help me back to full duty.

Only a few days after the Marines of the pathfinder platoon had left for Okinawa, I was surprised by a personal visit from the commanding general of the 1st Marine Division, Major General Herman Nickerson, Jr. As his aide kept watch, the general came into my room and stood beside my bed.

"Staff Sergeant Hamblen, I had my aide check to see if I could get in here to the hospital without raising some kind of official fuss. I know that you don't need any unwanted visitors, but I just wanted to have a few minutes to visit with you. I've spoken with Captain McCullum, and he's kept me informed as to your daily progress. He seems to be pretty impressed with you, and so am I. Major McCallister tells me that there's a parachute jump scheduled for next week, and I plan to come over here and get you, so that the two of us can go to the drop zone and watch it. I'll be back for you next week. In the meantime, Marine, if there is anything that I can do for you, just pick up the telephone and call me personally. And I mean that."

Exactly one week later I was wheeled out of the hospital and brought to the waiting general's jeep for a three-mile ride over to the selected drop zone, located near Camp Margarita, the home of the 5th Marine Regiment. From the relative comfort afforded by the jeep's seat cushion, Major General Nickerson, his driver, and I watched through binoculars as several sticks of 1st Force Recon Company Marines exited a GV-1 and slowly floated down to the drop zone. Satisfied when everyone had safely landed, the general delivered me back to the waiting hospital staff. As I was being helped out of his jeep, the general thanked me for riding along with him and for answering some questions he had asked about military parachuting. He surprised me when he told me that the two of us had more in common than me being one of the Marines in his division. He reminded me that while I had been a young squad leader in Korea, he had been on my right flank as the regimental commander of the 7th Marines. Before he left, we shook hands and he repeated his generous offer of personal assistance, "anytime, anywhere." There was no doubt in my mind that his concern for my welfare was personal and heartfelt. He cared greatly for his Marines.

I spent the following weeks in the naval hospital working hard on improving the strength in my left leg. I had been fitted with a plaster cast that covered my stump, and attached to the lower end of the cast was a steel O-ring. A section of rope was run over one of the "monkey bars" above my bed frame and attached to the O-ring. By pulling up and down on the rope, I could raise and lower my leg, thereby beginning to increase the strength in my arms and in my left leg. I had also asked the hospital's physical therapists to construct a "stump block." This device was really nothing more than a ten-inch-high wooden block, covered by padded carpeting. As part of my daily exercise program, I would lie down on the floor with the padded block positioned beneath my left knee and do leg lifts to strengthen my injured leg. I was told that by doing these types of exercises I could greatly reduce the possibility of later having to walk with a limp. A steady increase in the number of push-ups that I did every time I got down on the floor helped me to maintain the strength in my arms.

I wanted to show my progress to the Navy doctors who had been there when I was first admitted to the hospital but, ironically, what was later to become known as the Cuban Missile Crisis had begun, and the majority of the Navy doctors assigned to the hospital at Camp Pendleton were flown east to Norfolk, Virginia, to be on hand in the event that war broke out between the United States and Cuba. With many of the doctors unavailable to notice the changes in my progress and recommend my transfer to Oak Knoll,

I had to remain at the base hospital and work on getting stronger while I waited for their return.

Because my parachuting accident had been the subject of several stories in the base and local newspapers, I began to get a great deal of cards and letters from people who wished me well. Marines, Army paratroopers, and civilians took the time to write me words of encouragement, which meant a great deal to me. I tried to set aside a period of time each day to reply to those people who had sent me a get-well card or note. It was during one of these letter-writing sessions that I was visited by our company 1st sergeant, "Top" Echols, accompanied by our administrative chief, Staff Sergeant Riedl. The 1st sergeant told me that he had specifically come to the hospital to hand-deliver one letter. Upon opening the letter I was dumbfounded to find a bill from the San Diego Gas and Electric Company, addressed specifically to me, demanding that I pay SDG&E the hefty sum of $179.32 for damages and for having interrupted the electrical power on the morning of September 21, 1962. At first I thought the bill was some sort of poor joke, but it wasn't. The 1st sergeant had brought along Staff Sergeant Riedl, who handed me an allotment form that would remove a specified amount of money from my monthly paycheck to be given to SDG&E until my "electric bill" was paid off. He, of course, was kidding, but had it not been for the Marine Corps getting directly involved in the settling of this bill, I would have been held responsible.

As the days of October became the weeks of November, my resolve to get discharged from the ward became stronger. I had forced myself to get up and move from my bed to the chair beside my bed only two days after my leg had been removed, and learned then that I no longer had a sense of balance. However, within a week I had become accustomed to looking at my stump, and I was able to change my own dressings, realizing that this was the only way that I could begin to accept what had happened and, more important, to feel like there actually was something I could do about my condition.

In early November I was transferred from the intensive-care ward to the hospital's orthopedic ward to master the use of the wheelchair and crutches. As a staff sergeant, I rated a semiprivate room and upon my transfer I was introduced to my new roommate, a crusty old gunnery sergeant named Bill Grammy. Gunny Grammy was an explosive ordnance disposal expert (EOD) who had miraculously survived the sympathetic explosion of three "inert" rifle grenades he had been carrying in his right hand. The surprise detonation of the rifle grenades had sent fragmented chunks of steel ripping through his right side and into his legs. He'd lost some of his right hand and his right eye, but what he had not lost was his sense of humor. Having been hospitalized for several months prior to my arrival, he knew his way around the hospital, and because of his attitude toward getting better he became one of my mentors.

It became part of Gunny Grammy's physical-therapy program to push me around the floors of the hospital while I sat in my new wheelchair. Having himself graduated from a wheelchair to crutches, he was able to walk without much assistance, and the handles on the back of my wheelchair provided him with an intermediate aid in balance before he relearned the skill to walk unassisted. In a strange way, we were partners: helping each other and showing the patients on our ward what could be done with just a little teamwork. The gunny was always fun to be with and his stories about his life in the Corps were fascinating, but having quickly become bored with the daily routine, he decided one morning that we should do something to liven things up at the hospital. As we made our way around the wards that morning, we stopped to visit with one of the orthopedic specialists. Finding that his office was open but empty, we began to study a full-size human skeleton that hung from a metal stand in the corner of the office. The skeleton was used as a teaching aid for staff members and patients, but we decided to use it for fun. The gunny unbolted the skeleton's left leg and handed it to me, and I placed it in my empty pajama leg before we resumed our tour. As we moved onto one of the adjoining wards, a small boy was standing next to his mother when he noticed the gunny and me approaching. He grabbed at his mother's coat and screamed, "Look, Ma, look. That man has a dead leg." The poor woman, horrified at what she saw, slapped her hands over her son's eyes and headed for the door. We thought it was comical, but unfortunately our sense of humor was not shared by the hospital staff. Such was life on the wards.

Only a few days after Gunny Grammy and I became a mutual support team, an aircraft loaded with civilian sport parachutists from the town of Santee was flying to Oceanside, when it ran afoul of bad weather and crashed into the waters of Lake Henshaw, California. This terrible accident became a very big news story, and the gunny decided to capitalize on it. As we moved along the wards on our daily stroll, new patients often asked us how we became hospitalized. That was when the gunny began to tell them that he was the pilot of the doomed airplane, and that I was one of the jumpers who had his leg ripped off while trying to escape from the descending aircraft. We did look the part, but when the story of "the two Marines who had survived the crash" got back to the nurses on our orthopedic ward, we were told to stop telling the story to the new patients. It was fun while it lasted.

With the encouragement of Gunny Grammy, I was soon able to walk around the naval hospital using only my crutches. I also learned from listening to him that using the wheelchair would put me on the road to becoming complacent. I didn't want or need that luxury. What I needed was a change.

For a stabilized, long-term bedridden patient, the daily routine of hospital life is usually very boring because it is so damned orderly: wake up, wash up, change your pajamas, make your bed, eat, wait for the doctors and nurses to make their rounds, find something to do until noon, eat, take a nap, find something to do until the evening meal, eat, find something to do until it's time for lights out, and then go to sleep, only to repeat the process the very next day. Fortunately, in mid-November I was given the rare opportunity to break away from this terrible routine, thanks again to my company commander, Major McCallister.

A group of twelve Marines from one of the company's reconnaissance platoons was scheduled for a static-line jump from a Douglas R4D aircraft, and Major McCallister had asked my doctors if there would be any objections to letting me go along for the ride. There were none. I was thrilled at this invitation, but I don't think that my degree of enthusiasm was shared by all of the Marines scheduled to jump that day. When the major came to pick me up, I greeted him standing on my crutches with my right arm sticking out from my body because of a wooden brace that had been attached to my arm cast. A skin graft had been attempted only a few days before, and this cast and brace were designed to immobilize my right arm, keeping it up and away from the grafted area.

I had boarded the R4D before the jumpers arrived and upon seeing me seated across from the plane's exit door, their facial expressions changed from amazement and surprise to shock, thinking, no doubt, that what had only recently happened to me could happen to any one of them. Still, we joked and kidded as we took off and gained altitude, and the jump went off without any problems. Nevertheless, after landing I told Major McCallister that the next time I took to the sky, I would really like to be a part of the group doing the jumping, not just a reminder of the more dangerous aspects of what could happen. He readily agreed.

The mood of the hospital shifted with the coming of the holiday season, and by December I had come to know all of the nurses and corpsmen who worked on the orthopedic ward. It was probably because I had developed a rapport with them that I was approached by one of the ward's senior nurses, a lieutenant commander, who was concerned by what she believed was a "downward trend" in the attitude and performance of one of her corpsmen. She asked me if I had noticed any changes in the man's behavior, or if I had smelled alcohol on his breath. I said that I hadn't seen any changes in him, nor had I ever smelled any alcohol, but I promised her that I would watch and see if her observations were correct.

The young corpsman who was the subject of her concern had always presented himself as a hardworking individual who seemed to get along well with all of the patients on the ward. He enjoyed talking with Marines, and when the opportunity for me to talk to him presented itself, I asked him how things were going and if there was anything wrong. He told me that the holiday season had made him homesick, and that to cope with the problem he had been drinking more than usual. I warned him that he should be careful and explained the dangers of getting caught working under the influence, but I guess that my advice didn't do much good.

In her efforts to make the ward feel more like home, the lieutenant commander had brought in a Christmas tree, making a little ceremony out of decorating it with lights, tinsel, and ornaments. She also brought to our ward a hand-painted clay manger scene complete with straw, and had set it up on a large wooden table near her desk. It did add something of a holiday touch to our ward, but in her attempt at making the patients happy, she only depressed the unhappy corpsman more. I noticed that he was spending a great deal of time stopping by the manger scene, and wondered why. Then I discovered that he was using the hay in the manger as camouflage. He had hidden a pint bottle of whiskey under one of the sheep and as he passed by the manger on his rounds he would stop in for a quick nip if he thought that no one was watching him. His downfall came one night just before Christmas when I had asked him if I could get a shot that would help me to sleep after I had put myself through a lengthy and painful session of physical therapy. When the corpsman returned to my bedside he showed me the syringe before injecting the sedative into my arm. He wiped a spot on my arm with an alcohol swab and then fell forward as he plunged the needle into me, but I felt nothing. I was about to congratulate him on his ability to give a painless injection when I realized that he had driven the syringe into my pillow. He had done this in full view of the lieutenant commander who was watching from the shadows. That was his last night on the ward.

By late January 1963, my condition had improved, and my doctors felt that I was ready to be transferred to Oak Knoll Naval Hospital in Oakland, California. I had progressed well during my stay and I was able to get around on my crutches. I had also demonstrated that not only was I able to get in and out of my car, but that I could drive it without any mechanical modification being required. A special driving course had been designed for handicapped servicemen to complete before they were allowed to get behind the wheel of an automobile, and I had managed to pass this course with flying colors before I was discharged from the Camp Pendleton naval hospital.

On January 30, I loaded the few belongings I had into the trunk of my car, and went to thank Captain McCullum and the nurses and corpsmen who had worked on the intensive-care and orthopedic wards for all of their help. Then I made one stop at the 1st Force Reconnaissance Company area and after thanking Major McCallister and the Marines in the company for their help and support, I headed north to Oak Knoll.

I arrived there on a Sunday afternoon, wearing my Class-A uniform, and after checking in with the hospital's Marine Corps liaison officer, Chief Warrant Officer M. A. Zimmerman, I followed his directions to the ward that was to be my home for the next two months. However, my arrival was not without incident.

A portly Navy lieutenant commander, who wanted to establish her position of authority before I had even been assigned to a bed, met me at the entrance to the ward. She held out her hand, anticipating the immediate surrender of my travel orders and medical records, and then gave me the once-over before she spoke. "Honey, before you take another step, let me tell you something about the rules on my ward. On my ward you don't have any rank. You hang up your rank before you come into my ward, and you can pin it back on after you leave here. Is that clear?"

"Lady, I don't know just who the hell you think you are, but I'm a staff sergeant in the United States Marine Corps. My name is not Honey, it is Staff Sergeant Hamblen, and I will wear my rank exactly where I've always worn it: right here, on my goddamned shoulder. And, I will wear it on and off of your ward as long as this is still a military hospital. Is that clear?"

Understandably, our relationship went downhill from there.

Oak Knoll was very different from Camp Pendleton, and it didn't take very long for me to find out why. There were only two types of patients at Oak Knoll—those who wanted to get on with their lives, and those who had given up living.

I was to learn much more about myself and about other people who had lost their arms or legs, and this education began with a weekly event known as the "Freak Show." The Freak Show began exactly at 0800 every Monday morning with all of the patients assembled in one large room for an inspection by the hospital staff. The dress code for the Freak Show was always the same—we wore only our bathing suits. This enabled the doctors to get an unobstructed view of their patients and to take notes on those who would benefit from a prosthesis. The Freak Show was a humiliating affair the first time around; however, the doctors' observations meant that some of our lives could return to a state of near normalcy. Within a few days I had been measured and fitted for my first prosthesis. It was designed to match my right leg and built strong enough to support the life-style of a thirty-year-old Marine.

I was anxious to walk again, but in 1963 "state-of-the-art" artificial legs had problems with artificial joints. On more than one occasion, I was asked to test newly designed ankle joints that were built into my prosthesis. I would climb several flights of stairs and jump up and down, but the stress that I applied to the ankle joint caused the seals to rupture, leaving a trail of yellow hydraulic fluid dripping from my ankle. By mid-February I had grown accustomed to strapping on my new leg and walking around the hospital grounds as I continued physical therapy to make my legs stronger.

The Navy and the Marine Corps were very interested in my prognosis, but each for a different reason. The Navy wanted to know my physical status to determine that I could not return to duty, while the Marine Corps wanted to know when I would be returned to either a limited or a full-duty status. There was no question in my mind that return to full duty was my only objective. I had already made this decision when I was at the naval hospital at Camp Pendleton, waiting to be found qualified for transfer to Oak Knoll. The decision was reinforced on the day I had my only negative experience there—with an official from the Veterans Administration who came to visit me.

This individual, a former Navy chief, came into my room on the ward and told me that he had heard about my accident. He said that, in his opinion, I was making a very big mistake by trying to go through with rehabilitation and with the fitting of a prosthesis in the hope of being retained on active duty. He said that what I should do was consider taking a disability retirement from the Marine Corps and go into business.

"What kind of business are you talking about?" I asked him.

"Plaques, Hamblen. Plaques. The way I've got it figured is that you're no good to the Marine Corps anymore, so I'll set you up in a new business that will make us both a lot of money. That business is selling plaques. When a guy leaves his ship, or transfers from his old unit or base, we can have a plaque made up with his picture on it and it can be engraved. You can sit in your wheelchair out in front of the Navy or Marine Corps Exchange, and once those people see that you haven't got a leg, they'll feel sorry for you and will buy a plaque. What do you think about that, Hamblen?"

"I think that if you don't get the hell out of this room, pal, you're the one who's going to need this goddamned bed. If you ever come near me again, I'll make you wish to God that you were never born. Now, beat it!"

I never saw that clown again, but his message was loud and clear. My resolve not to leave the Marine Corps to "sell plaques" was what really had driven me to Oak Knoll.

Not long after I had settled into life on the ward at Oak Knoll, I was told that I would be assigned to a semiprivate room and that my roommate was a new arrival, a Navy chief named Fred Williams. The chief had been assigned to duty aboard the aircraft carrier U.S.S. *Constellation*, and happened to be walking across the ship's flight deck one day when one of the aircraft arresting cables snapped. The heavy steel cable whipped across the flight deck like a bullwhip and struck the chief just below his knees, amputating both of his legs in the blink of an eye.

Any thoughts of self-pity that I had previously entertained over the loss of my leg vanished when Chief Williams became my roommate. Like Gunny Grammy, the chief and I became a team, and as part of our physical therapy, I was given the job of pushing Chief Williams around the hospital corridors while he became accustomed to his wheelchair.

Because he'd lost both legs, the chief had also lost his center of gravity and tended to slump forward in his wheelchair. His "head-down" position caused him to suffer greatly from headaches, which were relieved by the doctors allowing him to drink one glass of wine each night. Whether or not the glasses of wine were a cure for his headaches is debatable, but I know that the chief enjoyed a drink and complained of having headaches as long as he remained in the hospital.

The more active I became at Oak Knoll, the more responsibilities I was given, and within a time span of just a few weeks I was placed in charge of two wards, responsible for insuring that patients cleaned around their beds and windows, and making certain that their living areas were maintained in as military a manner as was possible. The majority of patients helped out as best they could, but one individual stands out as the only problem child I encountered while I was hospitalized at Oak Knoll. My solution to solving his problem nearly cost me my career.

Marine Private Simpson (not his real name), had been assigned to a supply battalion at Camp Pendleton and one day was working off-loading a truck on one of the supply docks. The truck driver had failed to notice Simpson standing behind his vehicle and when he mistakenly put the truck in reverse he pinned Simpson against the loading dock, crushing his right leg against the truck's steel bumper and the concrete locking dock. Private Simpson was admitted to the Camp Pendleton naval hospital about the same time that I was there, but unlike me, he did not have to have additional surgery and was quickly transferred to Oak Knoll as a potential candidate for a prosthesis. Simpson was still at Oak Knoll when I arrived, four months after his accident. The problem with Simpson was that there was always an excuse why he could not be correctly fitted for a new leg.

His mother had flown from Texas to California to be closer to her injured son. She had rented a hotel room nearby, and every day Mrs. Simpson came to the hospital to sit beside her young Marine son. Every weekend mother and son left the hospital so that they could be together while he was on liberty, but when Simpson returned to the hospital each Monday morning at 0700, he was always too sick, too weak, or too tired to participate in any of the physical-therapy sessions that began after the Freak Show, which might have helped him get onto his feet and out of the hospital. In hoping to get Simpson up and out of his rack, I had tried on many occasions to encourage him, but he wanted no part of me or my suggestions.

One Friday morning, there was Private Simpson, dressed in his Class-A uniform and sitting on his rack, waiting for

Mommy to come and get him. The area around his rack was a mess and the windows next to his rack still had not been cleaned, but Simpson couldn't do any of that. He could only get dressed and sit, waiting for his Mommy. I had had enough of Simpson and walked over to where he sat. "Simpson, where the hell do you think you're going? Again, you haven't done what you were told to do. But you look like you're all ready to head out of here on liberty. Answer me, Simpson: Where do you think you're going?"

"I'm going on liberty with my mother, Staff Sergeant Hamblen. The doctors said that I could go."

His pathetic little whine made my guts tighten and I tasted my own bile. "Well, Simpson, if you're going out on liberty, you little shit, then you won't be needing these anymore."

I grabbed his unused aluminum crutches, lying next to his bed, and smashed them over the rim of a nearby trash can, bending them into unusable right angles. My yelling at Simpson and the sound of metal smashing against metal drew the immediate attention of my friend, the fat little Navy lieutenant commander, and within an hour I found myself standing at attention in the office of the hospital's commanding officer.

"Staff Sergeant Hamblen, you must understand that you simply cannot treat our patients like they were your Marines down at Camp Pendleton. Have you got anything to say for yourself over the way that you treated Simpson?"

"Yes, sir, I do. I wasn't treating Simpson like he was a Marine of mine at Camp Pendleton. I don't treat my Marines that way. I respect my Marines, sir. But when Private Simpson plays sick all week long and then is the first one ready to go out the door on liberty call and is the last one to return, I lose any respect I might have for him. Why is he allowed the same privileges as those men who do what they're asked and work hard at getting out of here? Captain, I'm not sorry about what I did. I'm only sorry that I wasted the way I feel on Simpson. If he isn't made to get out of bed and made to try and walk on a new leg, then he'll never do it. Not here. or anywhere else."

I was relieved of my duties on the two wards, and the captain cautioned me not to let my emotions stand in the way of good judgment, but my feelings remained the same. I thought that if my chances for being retained on active duty had been damaged because of this one incident, and that I was going to get a medical discharge, then the hell with it. I'd still try and make a difference if I could. Now, with less responsibility and more time to work on mastering the use of my new leg, I worked at improving my balance and coordination.

Oak Knoll's policy was to get its patients properly fitted with their prostheses and return them to society as quickly as possible, feeling confident, accepted, and productive. In watching how other patients dealt with their particular situations, I learned how to better my own. I knew that the key to a rapid recovery was more of a mental effort than a physical one, and I wanted to be able to show those men and women who would evaluate my condition that I could do more than sit in a wheelchair and sew a pair of leather moccasins together. I needed to be able to stand, walk, and run if I was to be taken seriously in my request to stay in the Marine Corps.

One day in late March, Chief Warrant Officer Zimmerman, the hospital's Marine liaison officer, came by to visit me and told me that I was about to be discharged from Oak Knoll. I had demonstrated to the satisfaction of my doctors that I could walk, hop, run, fall down, and recover without fear of injuring myself. I had been something of a human guinea pig for the doctors at Oak Knoll in testing the strength and construction of newly designed ankle joints. In thanking me for helping them, they provided me with two extra legs. I was satisfied and so were they, but it was Gunner Zimmerman who really helped me out more than anyone else. He knew that if I had stayed at Oak Knoll for more than sixty consecutive days, the Navy would be required by law to send me before a medical evaluation board, where I could face the possibility of a medical discharge. By his discharging me from Oak Knoll before the sixty-day limit, I was able to receive a set of orders and return to my original command, 1st Force Reconnaissance Company at Camp Pendleton, in a "limited duty" status.

On the evening of March 28, 1963, fifty-eight days after I had been admitted to Oak Knoll Naval Hospital, several of the nurses assigned to duty on my ward helped me load my seabag and two extra left legs into my Chevrolet. After saying my good-byes to Chief Williams, Mister Zimmerman, and to Private Simpson, I headed south to rejoin 1st Force Reconnaissance Company at Camp Del Mar.

Back to Full Duty

With the company's pathfinder platoon only halfway through its year-long deployment to Okinawa, I returned to 1st Force Reconnaissance Company and was reassigned to my primary duty as the company's assistant operations and training chief. Because the Marine Corps' regulations on parachuting were explicit, my "limited duty" status prevented me from participating in jumps, but I was allowed to be the jumpmaster. I was also permitted to participate in the company's scuba diving operations and took every opportunity to suit up and get into the water. Participation in both scuba diving and open-sea swimming not only showed me my new physical limitations, but provided me with a way to overcome them. I knew that if I was to have any chance at all of reclaiming my "fit for full duty" status, I would be required to demonstrate that I was as physically fit as any Marine in our company. That became my goal.

As a scuba diver I would require a great deal of flexibility in my ankles. To get this flexibility I took one of my extra legs to a prosthesis shop in San Diego owned by Mr. H. Wayne Wilkerson and explained my situation to him, and he agreed to help build a "swim leg" that would meet my needs. My new leg had an ankle joint made of aluminum and was designed with a multiple-position setting system so that I could select a particular angle for the foot based on the type of swimming I was to do, and lock the ankle joint in place using an Allen wrench. In the shop my new leg looked great, but in the water it didn't function as we had planned. The stress and strain that my swim fin placed on the aluminum joint ruined the leg within a short period of time, and within a day it was back to the drawing board to come up with a better design. What finally proved to be the best swim leg was a standard wooden "peg leg" that had a groove cut into the wood, just below the knee. By placing the strap of the swim fin into this groove, I had a nonflexible swim leg that worked perfectly.

During the seven months that I had spent away from the company, changes in personnel had occurred both within the unit and at the division level that would affect my chances of being placed on a full-duty status. I had returned to find that Major Jim McCallister had relinquished command of the company to Major Tom Gibson, and that Major General Nickerson had received orders that directed him to leave the 1st Marine Division with Brigadier General Fairborn in command. Concerned that those Marine officers who knew of my request to be considered for full-duty status were leaving, I met with our company executive officer, Captain Patrick J. Ryan, and asked that I be given the opportunity to speak with General Nickerson before he departed Camp Pendleton. Captain Ryan agreed that it was a good idea and arranged for the meeting.

As I entered the division commander's office, General Nickerson came from behind his desk to take a better look at how well I had recovered since the last time he'd seen me and offered his huge hand. He invited us to sit down and then asked Captain Ryan to tell him about the urgency of our visit.

"General, I asked the chief of staff if we could please have a few minutes of your time to explain Staff Sergeant Hamblen's current medical status. He has officially requested that he be granted full-duty status and, as you know, that's up to the Navy, based on his medical status and the recommendations of the Marine Corps. Staff Sergeant Hamblen is a qualified jumpmaster with more than two hundred jumps, and he feels that he is physically capable of performing all of his duties. After seeing him do PT, scuba-dive, run, and instruct classes, sir, I completely agree with him. Sir, the question is, what must he do to be allowed to regain his full-duty status?"

The general wasted no time in explaining. "Captain Ryan, before I agree to Staff Sergeant Hamblen's request to be considered fit for full duty, he must take and pass the Physical Readiness Test. I know Staff Sergeant Hamblen, Captain Ryan, and I know how much he is desirous of remaining on full duty, but I can not, and will not, lower our standards for any one Marine."

Captain Ryan then asked the general if he would allow me to take the same test that the U.S. Army used to determine if their prospective Airborne Course candidates were physically qualified. That was not a good move.

General Nickerson's eyes narrowed and he said, "Captain, I know that the U.S. Army only requires their soldiers to run one mile, but this is not the Army. We require our Marines to run three miles, Captain Ryan, for a good reason, and I will not lower our standards. If Staff Sergeant Hamblen can pass the Physical Readiness Test, and pass those individual training events required of a Marine platoon sergeant, then I will agree to recommend him as fit for full duty. Now, is there anything else that I may help you two gentlemen with today?"

Captain Ryan and I took the general's not-so-subtle hint not to press our luck and, thanking him for his time, we departed the 1st Marine Division command post and retreated to the safety of Camp Del Mar. I had been given the chance I needed.

During the next several weeks I worked at improving my strength and endurance for the Physical Readiness Test with a vigorous early-morning and evening routine that included a two-mile run wearing a field-marching pack, a weight-lifting program, and a one-mile open-ocean swim. When the day of the scheduled test came, I felt that I was ready and able to pass all of the events, and I received additional encouragement when a number of Marines from the company came out to watch my progress and to cheer me on.

My first test was a timed event commonly known as the fire-man's carry. Dressed in my utility uniform, I was required to run the full length of a football field, pick up a 170-pound Marine volunteer lying flat on the ground and wearing a 40-pound field-transport pack, lift him up and onto my shoulders, and run back with him to the starting point. I knew that I had the physical strength to perform this feat and hoped that my artificial ankle would not fail me. It didn't, and I completed the event without any problem. Next came the rope climb, and because this event did not involve too much use of my legs, it too was not difficult. I was then required to run and jump across an open, eight-foot-wide ditch. This was one event that gave me problems, but they were self-inflicted. The first time I ran at full speed toward the ditch, but forgot about my leg and attempted the jump stepping off on my left leg. Without the help of muscle to get me up and over the obstacle I fell short of the far side of the ditch. I was given a chance to repeat the event and this time, using my right leg to get the required amount of lift, I cleared the ditch. I knew that the final event, the three-mile run, would be the most demanding of the events, but having practiced running for several weeks, I knew that I had the endurance to complete the run in the required time. Strapping on my field-marching pack, I went to the starting line and waited for the signal to begin the run. Once the command of "Go" was sounded I set off to the cheers and whistles of those Marines who had come to watch this one-legged Marine run for his life.

Thirty-six minutes was the maximum time allowed for a three-mile run, wearing combat boots and carrying a field-marching pack. With a lot of encouragement from the Marines of 1st Force Recon Company, I managed to finish the run with two minutes to spare.

When Captain Ryan came to where I was standing and congratulated me on my performance, I thanked him for having confidence in me. After he and the Marines who had witnessed the test had walked away, I sat down to remove my artificial leg and poured out a half-cup of blood that had collected in the leg's cavity, as a result of scar tissue splitting open during the run. Satisfied that I was now considered physically fit in the eyes of the Marine Corps, I returned to the S-3 office, happy that I had finally accomplished what I had set out to do.

To help and expedite the Marine Corps' administrative processing of my request to be found fit for full duty, I requested "Mast," that is, I asked to speak to the visiting Marine Corps inspector general, who as the senior officer of a mobile inspecting team had been sent by the Commandant to report on Marine Corps readiness. The process of speaking to the senior member of the inspecting team allows for any Marine to present a problem to a higher authority for fast resolution. My request was granted and I told the inspector general that I had fulfilled my obligation of meeting Major General Nickerson's standards, and asked the IG to insure that Headquarters Marine Corps would recognize my improved physical condition and pass their recommendations on to the U.S. Navy. Less than one week passed from the time that I had met with the IG before I was called into Captain Ryan's office. Not knowing what to expect, I prepared myself for the worst.

"Staff Sergeant Hamblen reporting as ordered, sir."

"Please come in and sit down, Staff Sergeant Hamblen. I have a letter here, from the office of the Marine Corps' inspector general back in Washington, D.C., and I think that you should listen to what he has to say to you."

In part, the IG's letter read:

Staff Sergeant Hamblen, I have personally spoken with our Commandant and I did not have to pursue him in any manner for him to agree to assist you in your hard-fought efforts to be found qualified as fit for full duty. A personal message from General Shoup will be forthcoming which will direct that you be found fit for full duty. You must then decide if you want to accept this medical status. This decision is not to be taken lightly, and I direct that you seek the guidance of a senior Marine officer and discuss your decision in a serious and thoughtful manner.

If, however, you decide that the physical demands associated with life in the Marine Corps are too great, and should you decide to accept a medical discharge due to your physical condition, you must do so. The current amount of medical disability allowed to you would be in the amount of $260.00 per month.

If you care to pursue civilian employment aboard the base at Camp Pendleton, this office is prepared to assist you in every way possible. If you are found not qualified for a particular position due to educational requirements, the Marine Corps will assist you in attaining the level of education required to perform that particular job.

If it is your intent to remain on full active duty then you must respond in writing within fourteen days from receipt of this letter. Please inform Major General Nickerson of your decision in person.

Captain Ryan handed the letter to me and said, "Staff Sergeant Hamblen, I think that we had better get you over to see Major General Nickerson with your decision before he leaves here. His change-of-command ceremony is only a few days away."

Our visit to the commanding general's office was even shorter than our previous one. Major General Nickerson had read a copy of the letter from the inspector general long before Captain Ryan had seen it, and knew that it would only be a matter of time before I would ask to speak with him.

"Staff Sergeant Hamblen, all I need to know is what you have decided to do. Are you in or are you out?"

"Sir, I want to stay in the Marine Corps, and that's all I've wanted to do since the day I joined."

"I was afraid that you'd say that, Hamblen. I've told Brigadier General Fairborn about your case, and he is in complete agreement with me. Consider yourself on full active duty. And welcome back, Marine."

I left Major General Nickerson's office walking ten feet high off the deck.

The 1st Marine Division's regulations on parachute operations required that anyone who had been injured in a jump to the extent of having suffered any broken bones could only resume jumping by first making a jump that had a body of water designated as the drop zone. To those who have not tried it, a water jump sounds easy, the false impression being that in the event of a parachute malfunction the water below will allow for a soft, comfortable landing. In reality a water jump can be much more dangerous than a normal landing. If a parachutist lands in deep water and fails to remove himself quickly from his harness, he can be entangled in the nylon canopy and shroud lines and easily drown. However, on the eleventh day of September 1963, with Captain Pat Ryan designated as the jumpmaster and myself as the assistant jumpmaster, we and ten other Marines from 1st Force Reconnaissance Company, along with two Navy lieutenant commanders, took off from Camp Del Mar's Landing Pad 21 in a CH-37 helicopter and prepared to make a static-line jump into Lake O'Neil from an altitude of 1,400 feet.

After the first five sticks of jumpers had safely exited the helicopter, we waited for our pilot to gain altitude and realign his bird for our jump before Captain Ryan made his way to the exit door and gave me the familiar thumbs-up gesture. I moved to the door and after I had determined when I was in the best possible position to jump, I exited the helicopter with the captain right behind me.

The news that the jump-qualified Marines from 1st Force Recon Company were making a parachute jump into Lake O'Neil, with me making my first jump since my accident, had attracted the interest of the press. As I looked down at the drop zone from my comfortable position nearly eight hundred feet above the lake, I could see that many people had come to the shoreline to watch the action. I wasn't as interested in seeing them as I was in trying to locate the position of two pickup boats that we had put into the lake. Once I had spotted them I turned into the wind to slow my descent and position myself for a landing close to one of them.

As I had done many times before, I unbuckled my reserve parachute from where it was connected on my right side and then hit my quick release button located in the center of my chest to disconnect the buckles of my parachute harness, allowing me to slip out of the nylon harness and away from the canopy seconds before I landed in the lake. With only those few seconds remaining before I hit the water, I looked over at the nearby naval hospital and thought about the many people there who had helped to make the jump possible, but the sudden shock of plunging into the warm water brought me to my senses. Within seconds of landing I surfaced to find the recovery boat beside me and felt anxious hands pulling me aboard.

A little less than a year had passed since I had last exited an aircraft, but with the help of a great many people, some of whom I never knew but who gave me words of encouragement, I was able to do what some people thought either foolhardy or impossible. To me it was neither. I knew that I had only lost a part of my body, but I had also learned enough during my thirteen years in the Marine Corps to know that no goal is impossible to reach if you put your mind to it. By making that parachute jump into Lake O'Neil, I thought that I could clear the field of those narrowminded skeptics who believed that handicapped people are something less than whole.

As the recovery boat drew alongside the dock, I could see that so many people had managed to get onto the dock that their weight had caused several inches of water to cover its wooden surface. The newspaper and radio reporters ran toward me, and before I could get out of the little boat several microphones, attached to outstretched waving arms, were shoved in my face.

"What was it like, Hamblen? Did you think you were going to die? Were you afraid? How does it feel to be missing your leg? Do you think that you'll do this again?"

I was surprised at the insensitivity of the questions and jokingly tried to pass them off while attempting to get to one of the jeeps that would take us back to Camp Del Mar. But my path to the waiting jeep remained blocked by several members of the press until I agreed to answer their questions. The fact that so many of these professionals acted with such callousness surprised me until I learned that their motivation was based solely on their ability to sell a story. And, with only a single telephone booth located near the boathouse at Lake O'Neil, it was not difficult to believe the story that one reporter had physically jammed himself inside the booth and denied the use of the telephone to all but the highest bidder.

With this final hurdle out of the way, I was placed on jump-qualified status and resumed my place as one of the company's parachutists.

In early October, teams from 1st Force Reconnaissance Company were assigned as the aggressor force during a joint Army-Navy operation conducted inside the coastal area of the state of Washington and within the boundaries of Washington's Olympic National Forest. Assigned as the reconnaissance liaison officer, I was sent to the U.S. Coast Guard station located on the Strait of Juan de Fuca, near Port Angeles, to monitor our recon teams' radio transmissions and to help direct their movements. Before leaving southern California, our teams were given a detailed situation brief by our company's intelligence chief, Staff Sergeant "Big" Ron C. Kunsaitas. It was his professional opinion, based on studying the seasonal weather reports from the past three years, that there was absolutely no chance of any of us experiencing extreme weather conditions, with the possible exception of some measurable rain. Thus, we dressed accordingly.

Our part in the tactical problem was to use Navy seaplanes to insert four-man recon teams along the coast near the towns of Dungeness and Sequim and to parachute additional four-man teams into areas within the Olympic National Forest. Confronting our aggressor teams was supposed to be the primary objective of infantry patrols conducted by U.S. Army infantrymen from nearby Fort Lewis and we thought that we could easily outmaneuver them. However, two things that we had not taken into consideration were the local population's involvement in the operation and the unpredictable weather of northwest Washington.

The day that the operation began the sun was shining brightly and the temperature was a mild sixty degrees. But by late in the afternoon, an unexpected storm front had moved down the Strait of Juan de Fuca, and by midnight five inches of heavy, wet snow blanketed the Olympic National Forest. At this point our radio-message traffic began to indicate that there were going to be some problems.

With the presence of the large U.S. Navy bases in nearby Puget Sound, home to several naval air squadrons at Whidbey Island and submarines home-ported at Bremerton, infiltration by Soviet small-unit forces had been considered as a real possibility from the early days of the Cold War. Moreover, because of the size and the remoteness of this vast northwest area, the locals knew that they might someday be called upon to help guard against this real enemy threat and decided to use this particular joint operation to exercise their own defense plans.

Assisted by the area's Civil Defense authorities, the local newspapers and radio stations had alerted the townspeople that U.S. Marines, acting as aggressors, would soon try to infiltrate the Olympic National Forest, coming in from the sea and using parachute insertion. They also urged the locals to help the U.S. Army locate the small bands of aggressors, and went so far as to offer free tickets to local movie theaters and complimentary dinners as incentives to those who helped in the capture of our teams. After we learned of these "defensive plans," our recon teams were alerted to the situation by high-frequency radio messages.

By early morning we knew from their radio transmissions that the teams that had been dropped off of the Washington coast by seaplane had done very well at avoiding possible observation while swimming to shore and side-stepping the homemade "rattle-can" detection devices set up along the beaches. The recon teams that had been assigned to parachute into the national forest had not fared quite as well. Making their scheduled jumps early in the evening, most of the teams had managed to land safely within their preplanned drop zones, with only one team experiencing a temporary problem—one of its Marines landed in the top of a large pine tree. A lumberjack who lived close by witnessed the tree-top landing, strapped on a pair of climbing spurs, and, using a chain saw, topped the tree, sending it and parachutist crashing to the ground.

The unexpected snow made for a much more difficult situation for the recon teams operating in the higher elevations of the national forest. Without the use of cold-weather gear, the teams were forced to seek shelter wherever they could find it. Since safety was always our first consideration, there was no objection voiced to their breaking into line shacks they happened to discover. After we had noted the parachuting teams' positions on our situation map, we directed them to move down to the safety of the lower elevations and to stand by for their extraction by Coast Guard helicopters. The danger of possible frostbite and hypothermia added to the urgency of their extraction. While I rode along in the rescue helicopter to the various pickup points, the remaining teams began to move toward Port Angeles.

It took several days to gather up all of our teams, and during that time several unusual incidents made their way into the Port Angeles newspaper. One woman reported the disappearance of her husband's clothing from her clothesline. Ironically, another article told the story of a school bus that had been commandeered by a group of four suspicious-looking men, dressed in ill-fitting clothing and carrying M-3 "grease-guns" who had ordered the bus driver to drop them off at a remote intersection. Their last-known location was printed in the article and readers were even encouraged to search for them. After the joint operation ended in November, we returned to Camp Pendleton much wiser than when we had left. Not holding any grudges against our S-2 chief, we nevertheless now knew better than to rely on old information as a basis for future planning. We also learned how much influence the local population could have on a military operation. Unknown to most of us, this particular lesson would be repeated over and over again in the years to come in Southeast Asia.

Not long after the holiday season had ended, several teams from 1st Force Recon Company were sent aboard a Navy helicopter assault ship, the U.S.S. *Okinawa*, while it was stationed at Long Beach, California. It was during our stay aboard the *Okinawa* that I witnessed one lesson concerning pride of citizenship that has remained with me all these years.

A young sergeant who was one of the reconnaissance team leaders and a former citizen of Germany, Johann Haferkamp had received word from the ship's message center that his request to become a citizen of the United States had finally been approved. Words could not describe how thrilled Sergeant Haferkamp was when he learned of his long-awaited change in status, but his actions certainly did.

Finding this to be a very good reason to celebrate, several Marines invited Sergeant Haferkamp ashore, and as we sat in one of Long Beach's better gin mills dressed in our Class-A uniforms, we listened as Haferkamp spoke in his thick German accent and regaled us with stories of what life had been like for his family and him during World War II. While he spoke and told us how thankful he was now that he was an American, we continued to raise our glasses and toast our newest citizen many times before heading back to the ship.

We flagged down a cab to make our return trip just a little easier. At an intersection, as we sat in the cab waiting for a traffic light to change, Sergeant Haferkamp noticed that an unpardonable sin was being committed. The driver of the automobile in front of us had taken out his last cigarette, and as he reached for his lighter he crumpled up the empty cigarette package and tossed it out the window onto the street. Within seconds Haferkamp was out of the cab, had opened the door of the gentleman's car, and had yanked the petrified driver out into the street.

He jammed his finger into the man's chest and in the thickest of German accents, he shouted, "Gott damn it. I am now an American citizen and you will not throw your shit on my streets. Now pick up your trash!"

The terrified motorist, surrounded by four drunken Marines, grabbed for his crumpled cigarette package and apologized to Sergeant Haferkamp, telling him that he would never have littered the street had he known that United States Marines were patrolling Long Beach looking for litterbugs. He finally jumped back into his car and sped away.

Proud of having performed his first act of civic duty, Sergeant Johann Haferkamp, American citizen, climbed back into our cab and announced, "This is now my country and my home. I want everybody should keep it clean. Now let's go home."

Of course our cab driver, thinking that there was about to be one hell of a fight, had called on his radio for the Long Beach police. Luckily for us the cabby was able to radio back to his company and have his call for help canceled before the police had time to respond.

During the months of February and March of 1964, the Marines of the company's reconnaissance platoons flew from California to the Philippines, and participated in a short SEATO amphibious exercise known as Operation Tulunga. As the operations chief, I was assigned to the U.S.S. *Blue Ridge*, one of the Navy's command and control ships that operated between the Philippine Islands and the island of Taiwan. Along with a number of Marines from the division's 7th Communications Battalion, I became skilled in the use of high-frequency, long-range radios. While we were off the coast of Taiwan our radio-message traffic began to show a marked increase in communications concerning our military advisers in the Republic of Vietnam. Even in early 1964, most reconnaissance Marines knew little about that small Asian country. However, it had become readily apparent to those of us who were assigned to radio watches in the *Blue Ridge*'s command and control center that American military involvement was growing in Southeast Asia and that it would be only a matter of time before our reconnaissance teams would be operating inside of the Republic of Vietnam.

Our reconnaissance platoons returned to Camp Pendleton by early April, and as part of the company's continuous parachute training, I arranged for those Marines who had not completed their annual water-requalification jump to fly east in a Marine R4D to our designated drop zone—California's Salton Sea. As the jumpmaster scheduled to lead the group of fourteen Marines, I wrote the request for the aircraft support that would take us over the drop zone. As soon as the approved request came back from the Marine Corps Air Station at El Toro, the wheels were set in motion to complete the water jump.

We had been waiting only a short time at Camp Pendleton's airfield when our silver R4D landed and made its way to the runway apron for loading. The rear door of the aircraft opened and the pilot came out. He looked a little surprised to see that we were dressed only in T-shirts, brownies, and tennis shoes. To most of us, the jump was just a routine free fall, and we wanted to be as comfortable as possible as we headed for the heat of the Salton Sea area.

We had arranged for our drop-zone control team to be in position near the shoreline of the Salton Sea a day ahead of schedule. With our jump brief completed, we boarded the aircraft and took off for the drop zone, a little less than one hour's flying time from Camp Pendleton.

A short distance before our drop zone the pilot's voice came over the plane's intercom system.

"Jumpmaster, this is the pilot speaking."

"Yes, sir, go ahead."

"We've got a little problem with our port engine, Hamblen. My idiot lights tell me that we've got an engine on fire. I think that we can get it out, but I sure would like you and your Marines out of this aircraft. Do you read me?"

"Yes, sir. I'll get my people ready now."

All eyes were riveted on the open exit door. The men knew that we had been flying long enough to be close to the drop zone, but they had not received any word from me to prepare to jump. That changed very quickly. When I shouted the first command of "Get ready," they knew that something out of the ordinary was happening. On the command "Go," we cleared the now-smoking aircraft within six seconds.

Our pilot had radioed our exact exit location to the drop-zone control team when we exited the R4D, and without experiencing any injuries we landed close together in the Salton Sea. It took several minutes before we were picked up by the U.S. Navy recovery boats stationed there, and our pilot, Major C. E. Hill, managed to safely land his crippled aircraft. When we returned to Camp Pendleton, I learned that I was to report to Major R. R. Dickey III, our commanding officer, and pick up a set of travel orders that would take me and one T-10 parachute across the country to the city of Washington.

21

My Trip to Washington, D.C.

My surprise cross-country trip to the nation's capital did not start out very well. Prior to leaving Camp Del Mar that Sunday morning, I was told by Major Dickey that in recognition of my accomplishment in overcoming the loss of my leg and being found fit for full duty, my name had been submitted as a nominee to attend the ceremonies for the National Employ the Physically Handicapped Week as part of the Annual Meeting of the President's Committee on Employment of the Handicapped (E.O.H.).

Although I protested that I did not want to leave California to attend the week-long observance, I was told in no uncertain terms that I should enjoy this "once-in-a-lifetime" opportunity. Not only would I be representing the United States Marine Corps, but also all of those handicapped servicemen who were not physically capable of being there themselves. I tried, unsuccessfully, to explain how the Freak Show, the Monday-morning observation of patients at Oak Knoll Hospital, had been enough stardom for me, but my protestations fell on deaf ears. The Marine Corps had spoken. I had my orders.

To make matters worse, after the jeep driver left me at the San Diego airport I discovered that my military travel orders had not taken into account the excess weight of the T-10 and reserve parachutes that I had been requested to take along to the dog-and-pony show. Only after paying the additional baggage charges out of my own pocket was I allowed to board the commercial jet for the day-long flight to Washington's National Airport.

When I landed, I called the telephone number I had been given for the Washington Marine Barracks and asked the duty NCO if he would send his driver over to the airport to collect my baggage and me. The NCO on duty said that he was aware I was to be a guest at the barracks, but because he'd thought that I was not due to arrive for several days his driver had been dispatched elsewhere. He assured me that as soon as the duty driver returned, he would immediately instruct him to get me. The duty driver finally appeared three hours later, and though I didn't hold him personally responsible for the delay, I know that I wasn't very good company during our short trip to the southeast side of Washington.

The Marine Barracks at "Eighth and Eye" are truly a showplace with an impressive history. Since 1801, the barracks have occupied only two city blocks, bounded on the north and south by G and I, and on the west and east by 8th and 9th Streets. Though they served as the Headquarters for the Marine Corps from 1801 to 1901, they still remain the official residence of the Commandant of the Marine Corps and are home to the several hundred Marines who make up the Marine Band, the Marine Corps Institute, and the members of the Ceremonial Guard.

After I checked in, I was taken to my room at the staff NCO barracks. Since there were a number of Marines stationed at the barracks with whom I had served in years past, I looked them up in the directory and arranged to meet with them in the SNCO Club. I learned from several Marines who were assigned to the public affairs section that my time in Washington would not be my own. I would be shuttled around from one place to another during the week, wearing my Dress Blues. The schedule included a trip to a handicapped children's hospital, a meeting with Maine's senators Margaret Chase Smith and Edmund S. Muskie, a visit to the office of the Commandant, General Wallace M.

Greene, and a meeting with the President of the United States, Lyndon Baines Johnson. In addition, I was also scheduled to attend a number of formal luncheons, formal dinners, and to appear as a guest on Steve Allison's radio show. To make certain that I would be able to meet the demands of this busy schedule, I would be escorted by a hostess, a lady who knew Washington and would help direct me from one place to the next. My introduction to my escort and our busy schedule was to commence the next morning following breakfast.

Mrs. Earhart Twombley, a matronly D.C. socialite, looked exactly the way her name sounded. After being introduced to her and to several other volunteers, our tour began with a stop at a local children's hospital that specialized in amputee rehabilitation. Mrs. Twombley, stating that she "couldn't bear to see the sad little faces of those crippled children," opted to remain in the air-conditioned sedan while the rest of us went into the hospital for the tour. I was introduced to several of the children who had been selected to reflect the hospital's great work in rehabilitation. They had lost either their arms or legs to cancer, but it was obvious that they had not lost their hopes in overcoming their disabilities.

We had a commonality, and while we walked, talked, and even joked about life in the hospital, we knew that those of us who had metal joints had all been through the same hell. The brief time spent with those children was the most rewarding portion of my visit. While Mrs. Twombley still sat preening herself in the car's rear-view mirror, I left that children's hospital a much stronger person than when I had gone in.

Our next stop, and the reason for Mrs. Twombley's nervous concern for her personal appearance, was at the Capitol to visit Maine's two senators.

Senator Edmund Muskie presented himself as a very polite and uncomplicated gentleman who was quite interested in learning about me and the Marine Corps. He said that he was pleased to have the company of another native son from Maine and, following our formal introductions, he asked me to sit down and then proceeded to comment about the difficulties of getting good birch wood sent down from Maine for use in his small office fireplace. We had only been chatting for a few minutes when we were joined by the country's first elected woman senator, Margaret Chase Smith. She was a very gracious and charming lady, and I'm sure that I surprised her when I said that this was not the first time that the two of us had met. I could tell by the quizzical look on her face that she was preoccupied in trying to remember when she had last been in the company of a one-legged Marine staff sergeant, so I gently let her off the hook, reminding her that her niece, Miss Ann Saint-Ledger, and I had attended elementary school together in Winthrop, and that Ann's father, a Maine state policeman, was well known in our little town.

While I sat and answered the senators' questions, Mrs. Twombley was busy working behind the scenes, arranging for photographs, and making her own presence felt. But seeing that she was not to be included in our private conversation, she reminded everyone that our schedule was fixed and that we had to be moving on. We left the Capitol and headed off to attend a ladies' luncheon.

Having cracked the code on Mrs. Twombley, it didn't take very long for me to figure out that she considered me akin to some type of arm decoration and not much more. I had only seen a few women like her before, attending church services—the last ones to enter the church, always when wearing a new hat or coat, and always taking a place in the very front pew for all to see. It was also the habit of Mrs. Twombley to be "fashionably late" to every scheduled event, and she made her intentions known just before the luncheon.

"Staff Sergeant Hamblen, today's luncheon will be given by members of the President's Committee on E.O.H., and I want all of these ladies to know just how special you are to all of us. So, rather than rush in, I suggest that we wait for ten minutes before entering the banquet room to be seated. Of course, I want you to know that we will be seated at the head table, and after you escort me there, you may leave me and enjoy your lunch with your Marine Corps friends. I simply know that you'll understand."

She was quite right. I understood perfectly and decided at that moment that I had enjoyed about enough of Mrs. Twombley to last a lifetime. I began to prepare a plan for ridding myself of my overbearing hostess once and for all.

The next day was a wonderful reprieve from Mrs. Twombley. I had spent the previous night at the barracks, listening to sea stories retold by my old friends Gunnery Sergeant Person, Staff Sergeant Robbie Roberts, and Sergeant David Gonsowski. After a good night's sleep and a fine breakfast, I was taken from the barracks to meet General Wallace M. Greene, the twenty-third Commandant of the Marine Corps. The Commandant's office was located on the second floor of Headquarters Marine Corps, situated on a hilltop adjacent to the National Cemetery in Arlington, Virginia.

I was taken down a long corridor to the office of Sergeant Major of the Marine Corps Thomas McHugh. After meeting with him and listening to some interesting facts about the general, he escorted me to the Commandant's outer office. There, I was introduced to a colonel, the Commandant's senior aide, and he, in turn, took me in to meet the Commandant.

General Greene was a rather short, athletic-looking gentleman of fifty-seven years, with large dark eyes and dark-brown hair, which was starting to turn gray. A native of Vermont, the general had been born in the town of Waterbury. The son of a village storekeeper, he graduated from the Naval Academy in 1931. As Commandant, he had a reputation as being an innovative thinker and doer. His emphasis on physical fitness was well known and was the center of his conversation with me.

The Commandant told me that he was pleased to finally meet me and that he had reviewed my service record book before I had arrived. He noted that we had similar backgrounds—he, too, had grown up in the woods of New England, learning to hunt and fish along the shores of Lake Champlain.

He proceeded to tell me about his conversations with General Nickerson concerning my recovery progress and subsequent request to stay on active duty. He said that he was concerned about the ability of Marines maintaining themselves in top physical condition and wanted to know if I felt that I had done some good for myself and for the Marine Corps by requesting to be found fit for full duty.

I told the Commandant that while return to full duty might not be the best solution for every injured Marine, there were, in my opinion, career Marines who probably had a great deal to offer the Corps after injury. The General listened as I explained myself. When I was finished speaking he told me that he appreciated my candor and determination. He said that he believed our training to be the best in the world, but it all began at boot camp, where demanding physical conditioning set the standards for a Marine's career. He wished me well and said that he hoped we would meet again, adding that if there was anything he could do to make my visit more pleasant, all I need do was contact his office.

The following day, at a formal dinner to honor the national winners of the President's 1964 "Ability Counts" Contest, I was to meet retired Marine Corps Major General Graves B. Erskine, who had spent the years immediately following World War II as the chief administrator of the Retraining and Reemployment Administration, and was an early pioneer for the observance of National Employ the Physically Handicapped Week. General Erskine, who had gone to the Mexican Border in 1916 as a boy bugler, had ended up commanding the 3rd Marine Division during the battle of Iwo Jima. During World War I, he had fought at Soissons along with former Marine Corps Commandant Clifton Cates and had been hospitalized for nine months with blast concussion. General Erskine had spent two years as General "Howling Mad" Smith's chief of staff and, at the age of forty-seven, was well known as being one of the youngest and toughest generals in the history of the Marine Corps. This was one fine combat Marine whom I had read a great deal about. I was honored to meet him. He shook my hand and asked me if I would join him for a drink.

"Staff Sergeant Hamblen, I'm very honored to finally get this chance to meet you. I've heard a lot about you, and since I'm the guy who's giving today's keynote address, I thought that you'd be interested in knowing that you're one of the subjects of my speech. So, when I get up on that stage and start talking, you'll know that someone here in Washington is looking out for guys like you. I'll tell you one thing, Staff Sergeant Hamblen. I'd rather be facing a battalion of goddamned Japs than stand up and address some of these thoughtless bastards in D.C."

I was taken by surprise at General Erskine's comment, but he was known to be a fighter. When he marched up and took his place behind the podium, all eyes and ears were on him. In part, he said the following in his speech:

Ladies and Gentlemen, I am pleased to be aboard today not only to take part in the In Memoriam ceremonies for Mr. Mel Maas, but to look backward at where we have been these last two decades.

As I look back to 1946, and the real promotional efforts of NEPH Week, I am surprised at how much interest we stimulated, mainly with enthusiasm and hard work. There wasn't much money, and we were busy doing a dozen other things at the same time. But, we did establish the framework of cooperation between government and the private sector which has mushroomed into probably the least troubled area of labor-management/government-volunteer coordination in the public interest.

As the various states stood up to be recognized I am sure you were impressed by the large delegations from faraway states. Some of this was due to cooperation between the Pentagon and State Air National Guard Bureaus, but most of today's guests came on their own via scheduled transportation. That's real progress.

Way back in late 1946 or early 1947, I went over to the Pentagon for a swearing-in ceremony in the Army adjutant general's office. Retraining and Reemployment Order No. Nine had called for a maximum use of civilian injured and military wounded personnel. The Army was cooperating by reenlisting its very first amputee sergeant, not because he was an amputee, but because he was a damned good sergeant. We have another damned good sergeant with us today: Staff Sergeant Don Hamblen, Marine paratrooper and a member of the 1st Force Reconnaissance Company, an amputee who refuses to admit he is handicapped on the job.

As many of you know, the present Commandant of the Marine Corps, General Greene, is personally quite interested in the Corps' physical fitness program. He has kept the President's Committee advised of special devices the Corps is testing which increase and maintain muscular ability among Marines. The Committee is hopeful that the same program will be helpful in rehabilitation, both of the physically handicapped and also some of the retarded.

Jerry Walsh and previous winners of the President's Trophy have proven that the civilian handicapped can and will triumph over disability when provided with an opportunity. Staff Sergeant Hamblen, like the Navy's young double-amputee pilot, Lieutenant Frank Ellis, is proof that the armed services have both the courage and the sense to modify regulations in exceptional cases. Rules and regulations are necessary. We all agree to that. But, it is also necessary for decision makers to be sufficiently flexible to modify or to change rules and regulations in the face of unusual circumstances.

We have a phrase in the military which we call "for the good of the service." It was for the good of the service that Admiral John Hoskins, with one foot, went back to command the second *Princeton*. It was and is for the good of the service that Staff Sergeant Don Hamblen and Lieutenant Frank Ellis are on duty today. It was for the good of the service that Mel Maas was kept on active duty long after blindness overtook him. And, it is for the good of the service of our nation that employers today are more and more emphasizing the importance of what people can do and worrying less and less about the things they can't do.

When Mel Maas retired a dozen years ago he paraphrased General MacArthur's famous remark about soldiers. Mel said, "Old Marines never die, they just take one step to the rear and keep pushing the young ones forward." Well, Mel's work in the "rear rank" is done, but it remains our duty, yes, our privilege, to continue pushing the young ones forward, the Jerry Walshes, the Frank Ellises, and the Don Hamblens.

I am proud to join you in your rededication to that continuing effort, an effort which can only bring lasting benefit to our beloved country and God's richest blessing on those who carry on this noble work.

The General stepped away from the podium and as he walked back to our table the applause continued until he waved his thanks and sat down.

"Well, what do you think? That wasn't too bad for an old general. While you sit here and think that one over, Staff Sergeant Hamblen, I'm going to the bar and get us a couple more drinks."

A short time later, while General Erskine was in the middle of telling me about an episode on Iwo Jima, Mrs. Twombley made the conscious decision to join in our conversation.

"Staff Sergeant Hamblen, I've been thinking that it would be absolutely wonderful if we could arrange for you to take a morning walk with President Truman. Our former President takes a short walk every day and I just know that I have some very influential friends who can arrange for a meeting between the two of you. What would you say to that, young man?"

General Erskine must have known what I was thinking, for he turned his eyes away from Mrs. Twombley and waited for me to reply.

"Mrs. Twombley, President Truman is not one of my favorite people."

"I beg your pardon, Staff Sergeant Hamblen. What did you just say?"

"I said, former President Truman is not one of my favorite people. He hit a lot of Marines in a very sore spot when he referred to us as 'just a police force' during the Korean War. Even though he made a public apology later, the damage was done. I do not think that my meeting President Truman is a very good idea for another reason: My Purple Heart Ribbon and about a dozen other decorations, including several Silver and Bronze Star Medals awarded to Marines in our company, were sent back to President Truman in a Kotex box, along with a very short note that was signed, 'From the Marines of Dog Company, 2/5.' "

The words had no sooner left my mouth when I looked at Mrs. Twombley and thought that she was suddenly about to faint.

"Staff Sergeant Hamblen, I am afraid that I must leave now."

After she made her shaky but unescorted departure from our table General Erskine began to laugh. "Dammit, Hamblen, that's about the best one I've ever heard. Tellin' ol' Harry Truman where to go, on a note stuffed in a Kotex box full of medals!"

Nothing more was ever mentioned about my proposed walk with President Truman, but from that moment on I saw far less of Mrs. Twombley. I thought that if I let my defenses down she might do something, but I guess that I was wrong.

The last big event during my week in Washington was the Annual Meeting of the President's Committee on the Employment of the Handicapped, where President Johnson was to address the crowd. It was just before the start of this event that I was introduced to some very interesting people. Somehow, I had endeared myself to General Erskine and he took every opportunity to present me to the high and the mighty, including John W. Macy, the chairman of the Civil Service Commission, John S. Gleason, administrator of Veterans Affairs, Howard K. Smith, the NBC News commentator and journalist, and Harold Russell.

Mr. Russell was a former U.S. Army paratrooper who had just been appointed as chairman of the President's Committee on Employment of the Handicapped. Both of his hands had been vaporized when an explosive charge that he was carrying detonated prematurely. His personal experiences during World War II and his rehabilitation as a double amputee were one of the subjects of the hit 1946 movie *The Best Years of Our Lives* that won him an Academy Award for best supporting actor.

While I was standing with General Erskine I was introduced to the thirty-sixth President of the United States, Lyndon B. Johnson. The President shook my hand and, smiling the broadest of smiles, said, "Well, young man, it's so nice to see you here. Ya' know the U.S. Marines are always welcome in this town and I hope that you're enjoying yourself."

I assured the President that I was fine and in good hands with General Erskine. We then took our seats on the marble stage and listened as President Johnson addressed a gathering of nearly a thousand people. After the President's speech we attended the last of the formal banquets.

I said my good-byes to General Erskine, thanking him for his kindness and hospitality during my visit, and then returned to the Marine Barracks to pack my bags and catch some sleep before the return trip to Camp Pendleton. My flight heading west did not seem as long as the one that had taken me to Washington, and the memories I carried back certainly gave me a lot to think about. But from time to time I still sit and wonder what it might have been like to have taken that short walk with President Harry Truman.

SOG Duty in Vietnam

One morning in April 1965, I was walking through our new company headquarters building, when the shortcut I had taken brought me down a narrow hallway toward our work area. As I got closer to the S-3 office I could hear my name being used in the conversation that was taking place between the company's operations chief, a gunnery sergeant named John Freitas, and the company supply officer, Captain Gerry W. Turley. At the time, I was working for Gunnery Sergeant Freitas as the assistant operations chief, and until that morning I had thought of Freitas as a supportive friend. After all, we had served in this same company with one another for several years, and we had worked together every day. Hearing what Gunny Freitas was now saying to Captain Turley, however, my opinion about the depth of our friendship was suddenly altered.

"Captain Turley, I don't care what other people are saying about him. I don't think that Don Hamblen should be allowed to stay on active duty in the Marine Corps, let alone be allowed to remain in this reconnaissance company. I'll be the first person to admit that Hamblen has worked hard to stay in the Corps, but he can't do everything that the rest of us are expected to do."

At that point I had heard enough from Freitas's big mouth and I walked into the office and stopped directly in front of his desk. The conversation was immediately broken

231

off and the embarrassment on Freitas's face, like that of a little boy caught with his hand inside a cookie jar, made him look even more ridiculous than he sounded. He looked up at me and waited for my response, but before I could speak, Captain Turley stood up.

"Well, gentlemen, it looks to me as though the two of you probably have something to discuss. I was just leaving."

I waited until the sound of the good captain's footsteps faded down the hallway and then turned my attention to my pal, Gunnery Sergeant John Freitas. "Just what the hell were you talking about, John? Where the hell do you get off, offering your opinion of my worthiness to Captain Turley?"

"Well, Ham, I'll tell you exactly how I feel. Anyone can jump out of an airplane or learn to scuba-dive, but it takes more than that to be able to fight, and I don't think that you can do too much good in the field with just one good leg."

"Okay, Freitas, you've had your say, now let me tell you what I can do. I agree that it doesn't take too much in the way of brains to jump out the door of an airplane, but what good would *you* be if you jumped, and the first step that you took after landing was right on top of a land mine? *You* wouldn't be too much good either, would you? I don't have to be reminded by you that I might not be able to run twenty-five miles with a heavy pack on my back, like many Marines, but I can keep up with most of them. I do know that once I get on the ground I can do a lot of good. I can set up a radio, I can set up a terminal guidance system, I can adjust artillery fire, and I can still shoot a rifle. As long as I *think* that I can still contribute something to this glorious Corps of ours, then I intend to stay with it. Now, is that perfectly clear to you, Gunny?"

Gunnery Sergeant Freitas was the only Marine who ever told me to my face that he thought I shouldn't have been allowed to stay in the Marine Corps. However, I was not to learn the reason why Freitas had his knickers in a twist until several months later. Still, I began to question myself: If this one Marine thought that I wasn't qualified to remain in the Corps, were there others?

When the people from *Look* magazine had heard the story about what had happened to me they sent journalist Christopher S. Wren and a photographer named James Hansen to Camp Pendleton to do a feature story for their publication. They photographed many of the training events that I participated in, including scuba dives, a rappelling demonstration, and a static-line parachute jump. After the folks from *Look* had completed their assignment they decided to throw a party to thank the staff noncommissioned officers in the company for their help, and it was none other than John Freitas who offered the use of his home for the event. Several months later, when the story finally appeared in the pages of *Look*, there was not one single picture of Gunnery Sergeant Freitas—nor any of the party—appearing with the article. Freitas brought this news to my attention the day he stormed into the operations office and announced, "Your goddamned stupid magazine article finally showed up, over at the PX."

Oblivious to his anger and disappointment, I asked, "So why are you so pissed off about it, Gunny?"

"Because I offered the use of my house to a bunch of staff NCOs and to those people from *Look* magazine, hoping that they would take my picture, too, but they didn't. They didn't take one single picture of me. What a rotten deal."

So that was it. The gunny had decided to vent his frustration upon not finding his photograph inside of *Look* and over the inconvenience of that party, and had gambled it on our longtime friendship. And that is exactly what it cost him. I was mildly relieved in finally learning why Gunnery Sergeant Freitas had resented my presence, but until that time I had given very little thought to how my presence as an amputee might affect other Marines. I felt confident in myself, but I wondered about those Marines who might not share my optimism.

Little did I know that my abilities as a noncommissioned

officer were about to be put to the one test that every Marine must be ready to face—combat.

In late April, the current commanding officer of 1st Force Reconnaissance Company, Major H. A. MacDonald, directed me to drive over to the 1st Marine Division's G-2 (Intelligence) section to study a series of top-secret reports that had come into the division's message center. (As one of the company's operations chiefs I had the proper security clearances to read classified documents.) These intelligence reports detailed the Marine Corps' advisory role in operations that were conducted by an organization known as the Military Assistance Command Vietnam/Studies and Observation Group (MACV/SOG), which was requesting replacement volunteers from the Marine Corps for a six-month "joint tour" with the CIA's Naval Advisory Detachment (NAD) in South Vietnam. I was to study all of the MACV/SOG reports and, based upon what I learned, decide if I felt qualified to accept an assignment in South Vietnam—keeping in mind the restrictions that independent duty in such a remote area would place on a one-legged Marine staff sergeant.

Marines from 1st Force Reconnaissance Company had been used as military advisers in Vietnam since early 1964. Though previous volunteers had been sworn not to discuss the nature of these missions, the classified reports that came into the 1st Marine Division message center painted a very clear picture of the hazardous duty performed by our Force Recon advisers.

First Lieutenant L. V. "Reb" Bearce, Sergeant Jessie Giles, Corporal Dennis Blankenship, and Lance Corporal James Ranga had served as military advisers in Vietnam, and it was no secret that Lieutenant Bearce had been involved in one particular mission that helped to intensify the United States' involvement in the war. In July 1964, Lieutenant Bearce had been responsible for planning a crossborder, nighttime raid against the North Vietnamese villages of Han Mien and Han Met, with the raid scheduled for early August. As part of that mission, two South Vietnamese Navy PT boats armed with 57-millimeter recoilless rifles had begun to fire on the two villages when they were spotted by North Vietnamese patrol boats, which immediately gave chase. In the confusion caused by darkness and speed, the North Vietnamese patrol boats fired on the U.S.S. *Maddox*, a destroyer that was patrolling in the same area. The resulting firefight later became known as the Tonkin Gulf Incident, and was one of the most significant mileposts in United States military history.

When I finished studying those top-secret reports, I returned to Major MacDonald's office and told him that I didn't think that duty in South Vietnam could be any more demanding than the training was at Camp Pendleton. Fortunately, he agreed.

"Okay, Staff Sergeant Hamblen, if you think that you can hack it, I've got a set of orders for you and I'm going to quietly sneak you out the back door and over to Vietnam. Of course, I wouldn't think of sending you over there alone; you'll be in the good company of First Lieutenant Jerome Paull, and with your running mates—Sergeant Johann Haferkamp and Corporal Gene "Trigger" Graffenstein. The four of you have all the technical qualifications that're required, and I can only send volunteers who can act independently. If the Marine Corps says you're fit for full duty, Woody, then I'm certainly not going to treat you any differently from the next Marine. You'll report to First Lieutenant Paull and tell him that you've been given the green light to go. Good luck."

Following three weeks of Vietnamese language school at Camp Pendleton, our group assembled at San Diego's Naval Air Station, North Island, where, along with a dozen members of one of the Navy's UDT/SEAL teams, we loaded our gear onto a Navy Lockheed 10-49 four-engine R7V and flew first to Hawaii, then on to Guam, finally arriving several days later in Saigon, the capital city of what was then the Republic of Vietnam.

The headquarters for MACV/SOG was located on Pasteur Street, in downtown Saigon. It was the center for all planning and administration with an authorized strength of 275 men, broken down as follows: 108 officers, 3 warrant officers, 149 enlisted men, and 15 civilians. The actual SOG missions were launched from forward sites known as forward operating bases (FOBs), later known as command and control (C&C) sites.

After our group had been formally introduced to the leadership of MACV/SOG, code-named "The Plumbers," we attended a week-long series of daily briefings on our mission, use of supporting arms, and the specific areas of responsibility and interest to MACV. We were instructed to turn in all of our Marine Corps clothing and equipment, and we were sent to a tailor and fitted with new uniforms— three sets of khaki-colored trousers and short-sleeved shirts that would identify us internally as advisory members of a SOG team. All of our new individual combat equipment had been sanitized—the manufacturer's markings and country-of-origin stamps had been removed to prevent easy identification by the enemy.

I was assigned as the military adviser to a SOG team code-named Romulus. It was my responsibility to train with and accompany various members of this thirty-seven-man South Vietnamese Marine unit on its missions.

Now, twenty-five years later, the Top Secret classification that had been assigned to these covert missions has finally been removed. Accordingly, I can describe the history of these maritime operations and detail some of the more interesting events that occurred during the thirty consecutive months that I served as a SOG Marine adviser to Team Romulus.

Continuing small-scale covert maritime operations were conducted against North Vietnam with the primary objective being the collection of intelligence and the reconnaissance of the North Vietnamese coastal area. Harassment and short-term sabotage raids had been introduced as early as 1962 as a limited response to the escalation of North-South hostilities and as preparation for the future establishment of resistance activity within North Vietnam. Known as

OPLAN-34A, the Maritime Operational Concept evolved from these small-scale operations and commando-type raids.

Commencing in early 1963, a U.S. Navy SEAL team detachment consisting of two officers and ten Navy enlisted men, undercover as civilian technician advisers, assisted the South Vietnamese Navy and the South Vietnamese Marine Corps in recruiting and training a ready force of forty-five Vietnamese personnel and third-country crewmen (Chinese, Norwegian, and German) for their agent teams. Assets included a headquarters with modern communications facilities to monitor and control operations, separate messing and berthing areas for all personnel, motor pool and maintenance facilities, limited pier space, target ranges, a swimming tank, ammunition-storage bunkers, and an armory that was adequately stocked with a variety of sanitized weapons, demolitions, and special-purpose equipment. A value of $5.5 million was estimated as the start-up cost for the developed real estate, matériel, and associated industry.

MACV/SOG was activated on January 24, 1964, as a joint services unit that included U.S. Navy SEALS, U.S. Air Force special operations assets of the 19th Special Operations Wing, U.S. Army Special Forces, and U.S. Marine Corps Force Reconnaissance Marines. Working closely with the CIA, the SOG teams were assigned specific tasks that included small-scale demolition operations, intelligence-collection actions, ambushes, wiretaps, the temporary interdiction of lines of communications, and the taking of prisoners. Though supervised by MACV, SOG came directly under the control of the Joint Chiefs of Staff through the special assistant for Counterinsurgency and Special Activities (SACSA). These clandestine operations were directed for the President by Robert McNamara, who was kept regularly informed of the planned and conducted raids by memoranda from Major General Victor Krulak, who first held the position of special assistant, and then from Air Force Major General Rollan H. Anthis, who succeeded General Krulak in February 1964.

MACV/SOG missions ranged over all of Southeast Asia. Operations were carried out in Cambodia (originally code-named Daniel Boone and later changed to Salem House), Laos (originally code-named Shining Brass and later changed to Prairie Fire), along the Demilitarized Zone (code-named Nickel Steel), in North Vietnam (code-named Plowman), and within China. MACV/SOG also gathered intelligence about POWs and, whenever possible, carried out rescue missions of downed air crews and pilots (code-named Blue Light) in enemy territory. In addition to the in-sertion of agents into North Vietnam, MACV/SOG carried out a variety of covert psychological operations that in-cluded operating fake broadcasting stations inside of North Vietnam (known as Project Jenny), the kidnapping and as-sassination of key enemy military and political personnel, and inserting rigged ordnance into enemy arms caches (code-named Pole Bean).

Between 1965 and 1972, MACV/SOG conducted a total of 2,675 cross-border operations, during which time 103 U.S. Special Forces personnel lost their lives. Although the number of deaths may be considered by some to be rela-tively low considering the dangerous nature of the missions, after insertions some reconnaissance teams actually seemed to have disappeared from the face of the earth. Their fates remain unknown.

After the week of briefings at MACV headquarters in Saigon, 1st Lieutenant Paull and sergeants Haferkamp, Graffenstein, and I loaded our newly acquired uniforms and equipment into an unmarked airplane that was owned and piloted by the now-infamous CIA-run Air America and flew north to the coastal city of Danang. There, we were taken from the military airfield by jeep and driven to an old French-colonial compound located east of the city on a sandy peninsula that jutted out into the South China Sea.

The Vietnamese called the area My Khe (Me-Kay), but American servicemen assigned to the compound referred to it as Camp Black Rock, with the most dominant piece of terrain on the peninsula known as Monkey Mountain. This compound, surrounded by a twelve-foot-high wall, served as the training base for the cross-beach (CADO) mission teams and was home to the fifteen Americans and the fifty Vietnamese civilians who operated our supply and transportation section. An additional seventy-five-man special police force provided the necessary security to keep the compound protected from the eyes of the curious. The compound area was approximately ten acres in size and included eleven buildings that housed our communications bunker, armory, mess hall, and barracks. With 1st Lieutenant Paull assigned as the SOG officer-in-charge, Sergeant Haferkamp was assigned as the Marine adviser to SOG Team Remus and Sergeant Graffenstein was assigned to SOG Team Nimbus. Each of us was ordered not to discuss our individual team's missions, even with one another. This was to prevent any one of us from knowing the full scope of SOG operations if we were captured and interrogated by the Vietcong or the North Vietnamese army (NVA). As it turned out, this was a wise precaution.

After I had been shown to my quarters and given time to unpack, I asked my Vietnamese interpreter, a civilian nicknamed Twit, to gather the members of Team Romulus for our first meeting. I was sure that these men were just as curious to meet me as I was to meet them. The looks of surprise on their faces when they saw that I was missing the lower half of my left leg made me laugh. That helped to break the ice and I think that they accepted me as much out of curiosity to see how I'd do as they did because I was trained as a Force Recon Marine.

Team Romulus was made up of thirty-seven young men—One South Vietnamese Army 1st lieutenant was assigned to the team as the officer in charge of the thirty-six highly trained, well-disciplined, and extremely dedicated South Vietnamese Marine enlisted men, all of whom were jump-qualified. Several were scuba-qualified, as well.

The team's primary mission was to conduct nighttime prisoner snatches of North Vietnamese army officers, village or hamlet chiefs, and key political figures known to be living in the villages that dotted the North Vietnamese coastline. The methods for conducting these cross-border, over-the-beach raids were unique. With the assistance of the South Vietnamese Navy, the team was taken north in a Nasty-class PTF (patrol, torpedo, fast) boat or by swift PCF (patrol craft, fast) boat to a predetermined target area. Then, using Marine reconnaissance-type rubber boats (IBS, for inflatable boat, small) powered by silent-running Johnson outboard motors to take us ashore, we would execute our planned attack, return to the hidden IBSs and rendezvous with the Nasty boat for a fast trip back to Danang.

The Nasty-class PTF boats were constructed in Norway and propelled by British-made Napier Deltic engines. They had proven themselves to be operationally capable in service to several European countries before their procurement by the U.S. Navy. The boat was an 80-foot, 80-ton, diesel-powered, mahogany-hulled craft capable of speeds up to 40 knots, with a cruising range of 860 nautical miles at a speed of 38 knots, or 1,050 miles at 20 knots, which greatly improved the capability of SOG teams to conduct covert operations.

When I asked Twit why no South Vietnamese Marine Corps officers had been assigned to lead the South Vietnamese Marines on these missions his answer was short and to the point. "No South Vietnamese Marine officer will volunteer. They know that if they get caught up North, they will die up North."

Six of the thirty-seven men who made up Team Romulus were born and raised in the Danang area and visited regularly with their families. One of the team members was a native of Cambodia but, surprisingly, the remaining thirty team members had all come to South Vietnam from hamlets and villages along the North Vietnamese coast. Discouraged by the steadily more oppressive Communist rule in the North, they had fled south to join the South Vietnamese military, hoping someday to return to their homes and ultimately to live in a unified democratic country. That was one of their primary reasons for volunteering for this type of duty. Many of them had families still living north of the Demilitarized Zone. Their backgrounds were what made Team Romulus so valuable—as an intelligence-gathering force, these men knew the land, the people, the intricate coastal waterways, and the sea better than anyone else. Until recently our area of operation had been their home. Their determination to fight Communism was underscored by the fact that many of the team members of SOG Team Romulus who had come from North Vietnam, wore a dark-blue tattoo, the Vietnamese phrase SAT CONG ("Kill Communists"), inscribed above the heart.

As the new military adviser to Team Romulus, it was my job to watch, listen, and learn all that I could from this unique group of men. None of them spoke English very well, but every one of them tried to master key words and phrases that helped bridge the wide communications gap that existed between us. I did the same; my three-week crash course in the Vietnamese language had hardly prepared me to understand any of the at least dozen different dialects spoken by my fellow team members. But, with the constant help of Twit, I quickly began to learn about those things that we had in common and to understand the differences between us, the differences becoming apparent the first time I observed the team rehearse an upcoming mission.

Equipped with two IBSs, the team rehearsed their boat-handling abilities in the ocean's surf zone as part of the landing and withdrawal portion of the mission. The prearranged signal for the team's withdrawal was the firing of a yellow flare, but during the final rehearsal we discovered that we'd run out of yellow flares. Rather than assemble the team and simply explain that the new signal for withdrawal would be a green flare, the entire rehearsal had to be run through using the actual green flare, so that everyone in the team could *see* and *understand* the change in the plan.

I could see that some interesting communication problems would have to be overcome.

The standing operational procedures (SOP) for SOG

Team Romulus missions were well defined. Usually twice each month the SOG team advisers went to the Naval Advisory Detachment (NAD) command post, known as "The Tank," where we were briefed on a number of possible missions. From these we would make our selection based upon the weather, the traveling distance, the enemy's known security in the target area, the availability of continuous communications, and the extent of our internal knowledge of the targeted area. Once a mission was selected we would begin rehearsing at sites that matched the physical layout of the target area.

The NAD compound housed the administrative offices and our medical dispensary. Four permanent piers served the assigned afloat assets, including 14 Nasty PTF boats, three Swift boats, two LCM (landing craft, medium) pusher craft, one floating drydock, and one floating crane. A fuel farm was located at the southern end of the compound close to the support buildings where boat parts and our communications equipment were repaired.

My primary responsibility was to accompany the team on most of its missions and, as the observer and military adviser, be responsible for maintaining constant radio communications with all of our supporting activities and with SOG headquarters from the time the team departed Danang until we returned to friendly waters. After returning to the NAD, I would be debriefed by 1st Lieutenant Paull, who would then submit a written patrol report to the MACV headquarters in Saigon.

Since the capture of any knowledgeable American military officer by the North Vietnamese would have a disastrous effect on the security of future missions, all officers, including 1st Lieutenant Paull, were prohibited from accompanying any of the SOG teams north of the Demilitarized Zone. (This message was reemphasized in 1965, when the Joint Chiefs of Staff authorized the utilization of PTF boats in the interdiction of small-tonnage North Vietnamese shipping and stated, "U.S. personnel will NOT, repeat, NOT be aboard PTFs.")

My first mission with Team Romulus was not into North Vietnamese waters, but south of the city of Danang. We had learned from one of the local intelligence networks, often called the "bamboo telegraph," that a small group of Vietcong guerrillas had set up an outpost on one of the smaller islands located near the confluence of the Cau Dai and Hoi rivers. This outpost was thought to be commanded by two North Vietnamese army officers, and SOG wanted to talk to at least one of them. Our mission was to make this possible. By accompanying those men chosen to execute the plan, I could make my own determination of how well my team members had been trained by my predecessor in the planning, rehearsing, and conduct of such missions, and judge how well they were aided by the different outside agencies that helped support SOG operations. Since nighttime operations such as over-the-beach prisoner snatches were considered to be the most difficult to perform because they required the greatest amount of preparation, coordination, and rehearsal time to insure success, I was pleased to see how well Team Romulus did in demonstrating their capabilities.

Immediately after my return to My Khe from the briefing session at The Tank, the members of Team Romulus began to build a to-scale copy of the Vietcong island outpost based on received intelligence. Using bamboo, palm leaves, cardboard, communication wire, and scraps of plywood, the team members constructed a good likeness of the target area—all within several hours—while the details of the operational plan were being written. The complex plan called for a South Vietnamese Navy Swift boat to take us to a drop-off point approximately 2,500 yards offshore, where twelve designated team members and I would take two rubber inflatable boats to a point just outside the island's surf zone. We would then paddle our way to the beach. On signal, two scout swimmers would quietly slip over the side of their rubber boat and swim ashore. Once they had made a security check of the beach, an infrared signaling device known as a metascope would be used to flash an "all clear" signal to several of the team members whose special goggles allowed them to pick up the infrared signal. While the two scout swimmers remained with the rubber boats and provided our rear security, six team members, including myself, would move inland to secure the camp, while the four remaining team members would approach the suspected hooch of the two North Vietnamese officers. Then, depending upon how things went inside, the snatch team would return to the beach with one or two trophies bound and gagged for the trip back to Danang.

Dressed in the traditional black pajamas that were the standard uniform of the Vietcong, and armed with an assortment of silenced weapons, we left Danang the following afternoon and headed south toward the mouth of the Cau Dai River. Very close to midnight our Swift boat positioned itself far enough away from shore so as not to arouse suspicion, and under a quarter-moon sky, we paddled past the sleeping village of Thanh Tam, finally coming to shore on the western side of the tiny island. As had been rehearsed at least half a dozen times before, the team members moved quickly past our security guards. Aided by two Starlight scopes, we made our way to a vantage point that enabled us to see that the small outpost looked very much like our mock-up.

Barely audible spitting sounds of several silenced weapons could be heard near the camp's perimeter. Within seconds the four-man snatch team came into view as they made their way past us and headed back to the beach, dragging with them one very scared but well-trussed-up North Vietnamese captain.

As soon as those of us in the security force had assembled by the rubber boats, the green flare signaled the Swift boat of our immediate departure. We paddled through the surf zone and met the patrol craft for our return trip to Danang, where we handed over our "guest" to waiting interrogators from The Tank, who were most anxious to talk to him.

After the North Vietnamese captain was ushered away,

those members of Team Romulus who had participated in the prisoner snatch returned to My Khe to enjoy a well-deserved breakfast. We had suffered no casualties and had left the Vietcong stunned, wondering not only where we had come from but when we might return.

The two other groups of Vietnamese fighting men who lived and operated from our compound at My Khe also deserve to be mentioned for the contributions that they made in their participation in SOG operations.

The Civilian Irregular Defense Group (CIDG) were South Vietnamese men who were organized, trained, and equipped by U.S. Army Special Forces teams to defend rural hamlets and villages from the Vietcong. One detachment of CIDGs helped to provide security for our compound. Even more important, much of our information was obtained from these local citizen soldiers, who were to play a much larger role in the months to come, working with teams from 1st Force Reconnaissance Company.

The Nungs on the other hand were ethnic Chinese, residents of Kwangsi Province, but an appreciable number of them, approximately 2,500, inhabited the highlands of northern Vietnam. Long noted for their exceptional martial-arts skills and displeased with the prospects of Communism, many had served willingly with the French, and for this reason had emigrated to South Vietnam in late 1954 after the French defeat. In time, many of them converted from Buddhism to Catholicism. At one time, after the formation of the republic, the South Vietnamese army included a division of Nungs, but the unit was broken up because of its potential threat to the incumbent government composed mainly of South Vietnamese Catholics. The displaced Nungs then hired on as mercenaries, eventually came under the domain of the U.S. Special Forces and the MACV/SOG teams involved in unconventional and covert warfare.

An offshoot of Nungs were SOG's Chinese underwater swimmers. Trained by Navy SEALS, this particularly tough group of Chinese served as scout swimmers in the South Vietnamese Navy and South Vietnamese Special Forces units. These men were highly skilled at infiltration and in the use of underwater demolitions. Using the ocean and the many coastal riverways as their entrance and egress routes, they caused absolute havoc among the Vietcong, sinking countless supply-laden VC junks and destroying enemy supply and ammunition caches located along the shoreline and estuaries of South Vietnam. They prided themselves on a "take-no-prisoners" philosophy and were swift, silent, and deadly. The swimmers were greatly feared by citizens of North and South Vietnam alike.

When I went to Vietnam, the normal tour of duty for a SOG team adviser had been six months, but the short tour had caused problems; the Vietnamese had little regard for American military advisers who were not as committed as they were to the war against the Vietcong and the NVA. It was not uncommon to hear stories told of previous Navy advisers who had "inadvertently" been left behind on some unnamed island or isolated shoreline by the unhappy members of a SOG team eager to get out of harm's way. But, on March 8, 1965, when Marines from Battalion Landing Team 3/9 splashed ashore near Danang to provide security for I Corps Headquarters and the Danang air base, the mission of SOG was expanded, and with it the likelihood of my request for a six-month extension being granted was greatly improved. I was enjoying the type of duty assignment that dreams were made of—independent, hazardous duty that allowed me not only to teach, but to advise and to learn. All of this while receiving hazardous-duty pay, jump pay, overseas pay, temporary additional duty (TAD) pay, health and comfort pay, as well as my base pay as a staff sergeant, nearly all of which was deposited in a savings account back in the States.

Three of the enlisted Marines who had first been selected for duty with MACV/SOG in Vietnam had rejoined 1st Force Reconnaissance Company. When I learned that several platoons from the company were headed for Vietnam I was anxious to meet the advance party when they arrived. That group, consisting of the new company commander, Major Malcolm C. Gaffen, and most of the company's staff sections, had departed Camp Pendleton in such a hurry that all they had when they arrived were their M-3A1 submachine guns and their individual equipment. They had left Camp Pendleton for Port Hueneme, California, and stayed on Okinawa for several days before arriving in Vietnam. The two advance platoons of 1st Force Recon Company were billeted at the Danang air base for several days before they moved to the northern side of the foot of Marble Mountain to set up housekeeping in a camp made up of hardback canvas tents. This camp was later named Camp Merrell in honor of the first Marine from 1st Force Reconnaissance Company to be killed in Vietnam, Corporal Lowell Merrell.

I found some of the more select team members of 1st Force Recon Company gathered at Mrs. Long's bar, a local watering hole located alongside the shore of the South China Sea. Mrs. Long, a lifelong resident of Danang, served ice-cold beer and soda in her thatch-roofed establishment. Because her little bar happened to be located along our running route, the members of Team Romulus had adopted it as the most logical place to rest and recover after exercise runs along the beach.

Staff Sergeant "Val" Vialpondo, sergeants Jessie Giles and Clarence L. Johnson, and corporals Les "Bone" Herring, Mike Paget, and J. J. Brown had kept in touch with me. Because Giles had only recently returned to the States from his SOG tour a few months earlier, he knew where Team Romulus was likely to be found on a hot afternoon.

My tour in Vietnam would prove to be much different from that of these Marines. However, during the many months ahead I was able—with the help of Vietnamese friends—to supply the Marines of 1st Force Reconnaissance Company with extra equipment, ammunition, weapons, and with the most valuable gift that could be given to a reconnaissance Marine—timely intelligence information.

People and Politics

By early 1966, I had participated in at least sixteen SOG missions that had taken me from the southern boundaries of I Corps to the coastal villages of North Vietnam. During this time I was able to read the radio-message traffic and the classified patrol reports of the Marine Force Recon teams. They told of the recon Marines' many successes—and of some failures—as they learned to change and adapt their tactics after initially patrolling against the Vietcong, then later against the more formidable and better-equipped soldiers of the North Vietnamese army.

I often thought that my life as a SOG team adviser, although often hazardous, was a much more enjoyable experience than that of any Force Reconnaissance Marine team leader, who had the weight of responsibility for his recon team added to the seventy-pound pack he carried up and down the hills of northern I Corps. However, I do not want to give the impression that my tour of duty with Team Romulus was without its moments of difficulty and danger. There was plenty of that.

In the spring of 1966, I accompanied members of Team Romulus on a prisoner-snatch mission that we thought was well planned and thoroughly rehearsed, but as we began our withdrawal toward the beach, we were caught in a brief firefight with a heavily armed Vietcong reactionary force. We had done our homework and had planned for every contingency, but it is a well-known fact that things do not always go according to plan, even Marine plans. Although I was wearing a flak jacket, I still managed to get hit by a hot piece of shrapnel that entered my chest below my left armpit. Fortunately, the wound was not too serious, and upon returning to Danang I was taken to the Naval Support Activity near Marble Mountain to have the shrapnel removed. After that I returned to duty.

It was often the unknown dangers, the ones that could not be planned for, that proved to be the most perilous of all. The most memorable of these incidents, the one that angers me to this day, was the result of a Marine Corps officer who misused his authority and willfully disobeyed orders that endangered the members of SOG Team Nimbus. While his arrogance and ego nearly cost him his life, his stupidity cost him the respect of every member of MACV/SOG.

Major Smothers (not his real name), an enlisted combat veteran of World War II and the Korean War, fancied himself an authority on parachute operations. He had been commissioned after his service in the Korean War, and as he rose in rank he became a "prover"—a man determined to prove that he had a better way to do things. His reputation was well known in the Marine Corps and it preceded him to Vietnam. In 1966, after attending the Command and Staff College at Quantico, Virginia, he was assigned to MACV as one of the operations chiefs at The Tank. I can only imagine that he must have found his desk-bound administrative duties in The Tank too boring to suit the needs of his ego. That was precisely what made him dangerous.

Deciding to create some excitement, and ignoring the standing orders that strictly forbade anyone who did not have proper approval from accompanying a SOG Team north of the seventeenth parallel into North Vietnamese waters without authorization, Major Smothers donned a South Vietnamese naval officer's uniform and climbed aboard one of the Nasty boats that was headed north to locate Sergeant Gene Graffenstein's SOG Team Nimbus, which was wait-

ing to be extracted from the beach after making a successful prisoner snatch near the town of Vinh, approximately
twenty-five miles north of the Demilitarized Zone.

Only one Marine Corps officer, 1st Lieutenant Dick
Barba, had been given the authorization to accompany Sergeant Graffenstein to and from this dangerous recovery
mission. He, too, was very much surprised at the sudden
and unscheduled appearance of Major Smothers dressed up
as a South Vietnamese naval officer. The major assured
1st Lieutenant Barba that he had been given permission to
"go along for the ride" and, unchallenged by the South
Vietnamese Navy crew, he boarded the Nasty boat armed
with a Swedish M45 K 9-millimeter submachine gun.

When the SOG team made its offshore rendezvous with
the Nasty boat, Major Smothers decided to help in bringing
the hogtied prisoner aboard the stern of the boat from the
pitching bow of the team's rubber boat. In his haste to grab
the prisoner, Major Smothers placed himself between the
two craft, running afoul of the lines that connected them.
Waving off any help from the Vietnamese crewmen, the
major reached for a line that ran behind 1st Lieutenant
Barba. When the major yanked on it, it snagged on the bolt
of Barba's weapon—also a Swedish K submachine gun.
The bolt on Barba's weapon was pulled clear from the
locked position by the major's efforts. The submachine gun
went off, sending one 9-millimeter bullet straight into the
meaty portion of the major's left leg.

Fortunately, the major only suffered what is commonly
referred to as a "through and through" gunshot wound,
which did not result in his leg being fractured or in the sev-
ering of his femoral artery. But, nonetheless, the accidental
shooting had to be reported. The major required some immediate medical attention when the Nasty boat had returned
to the safety of Danang.

Less than a week after the accidental shooting of Major
Smothers I happened to ask Sergeant Graffenstein if he had
seen the major, and his response caught me by surprise.

"The major went over to the division command post,

Woody. He said that he was going there to attend an awards ceremony."

"Who's getting an award?" I asked.

Trigger lowered his head. When he finally spoke he sounded as though he was just too embarrassed to talk about it. "The major is being awarded the Purple Heart, Woody."

"What did you say, Trigger? Did you just say that Major Smothers is getting a Purple Heart?"

"There's more to it than that, Woody. The major already picked up one Purple Heart when he was being treated for his gunshot wound at the Naval Hospital. Today he'll pick up a second Purple Heart for the very same thing. It gets worse. The major also handed me this paperwork before he left, and asked me to sign it."

"What kind of paperwork are you talkin' about?"

"I was sort of hoping that you wouldn't ask, Woody, or at least that I wouldn't be around here when you read it, but Major Smothers has put himself in for the Silver Star, too. He wants me to sign off on his award recommendation as a witness to what, he said, happened aboard the Nasty boat. What am I supposed to do?"

I read the major's recommendation for an award of the Silver Star for heroism and my thoughts went back to the memory of those Marines I had served with on the lines in Korea, those who had been killed or wounded and those who had made so many personal sacrifices on a daily basis yet had received no recognition for their actions. In disgust, I threw the papers back at Sergeant Graffenstein.

"Trigger, not only *no*, but *hell no*! You will *not* sign that bastard's award recommendation. That shit-head should have been court-martialed for his stupid stunt last week. He's lucky that your prisoner wasn't killed, or even worse—that bullet could have killed one of your team members."

Later that day, Major Smothers limped into the SOG compound to see Sergeant Graffenstein, hoping to collect his award recommendation before heading back to The

Tank. Much to his credit, Trigger had taken my advice and had refused to sign the document, telling the major exactly what I had said. The major knew that his plan had been met head-on by one thick-headed Yankee and I thought that the issue would quickly die. I later learned that when the major returned to The Tank he took his award recommendation to several of his counterparts and tried to get them to approve it.

Much to the surprise of Major Smothers, Colonel A. L. Butler, USMC, who was assigned to MACV headquarters in Saigon, got wind of the incident and paid Major Smothers a personal visit. The major was told that not only would he not be recommended for the Silver Star, but that he would never set foot near another SOG Team for as long as he remained in Danang.

Vietnam's monsoon season began in late September and would last well into January, curtailing many of the SOG operations into North Vietnam. While SOG Team Romulus remained close to Danang, waiting for a decent break in the weather pattern, I used this valuable down time to help cross-train the team members by improving basic field skills, boat-handling abilities, individual and team tactics, and by constantly rehearsing our nighttime kidnapping techniques.

We started, as always, with the basics: As part of our jungle training we emphasized learning how to live off the land. We studied the various types of jungle and coastal vegetation and learned which plants were poisonous and which ones contained fresh water. Team members became familiar with the sonar and radar systems that were used aboard the Nasty boats and as part of those classes we practiced quick assembly and disassembly of the metal poles for the portable radar reflectors that were used to signal our presence to Nasty boats waiting offshore. Classes on map reading, the use of the lensatic compass, and interpretation of aerial photography were mandatory for all hands.

Between missions, much of our time was spent cleaning and preparing equipment for immediate use. Our salt-water environment required that all communications equipment and weapons be well protected from corrosion, making these cleaning details a daily ritual, but adding to each team member's ability to disassemble and assemble a variety of weapons and acquire knowledge through constant familiarity. As new weapons and ammunition became available, we incorporated their use into our team. Standard weapons at our disposal were: the Colt AR-15 rifle; the silenced Swedish K submachine gun; the U.S.-made M-1 Garand rifle; the M-2 carbine; and the Soviet-made SKS (semiautomatic) and AK-47 rifles. We also had several types of crew-served weapons in our armory—the 60-millimeter and the 81-millimeter mortar, the 3.5-inch rocket launcher, and the 75-millimeter recoilless rifle. Each team member knew how to use every one of these weapons, as well as being more than capable with a pistol and fighting knife.

SOG Team Romulus also participated in parachute training as often as we could. Using South Vietnamese CH-34 helicopters, U.S. Army Otters, and Caribous flown by Australian pilots to keep up proficiency, we tried to schedule at least four to six jumps per month. However, our best efforts were always subject to aircraft availability and the weather. If these factors were in our favor, we made as many water jumps and equipment jumps as we could get in in one day.

In 1966, the tempo of the war began to increase. When I had first accompanied the team into North Vietnam, the small villages along the coast were guarded by only a few members of the local militia, but our cross-border missions into North Vietnam had motivated the NVA to protect their villages by posting regular soldiers along the coast. To MACV's way of seeing things, the more NVA soldiers used as coastal security, the less would be available for infiltration south of the Demilitarized Zone.

As a part of a new MACV operation, we began a program that was designed to bribe the enemy. Working closely with the South Vietnamese Navy, our SOG Teams were tasked with commandeering the Vietnamese junks that sailed the waters between the coastal villages of North and

South Vietnam. We had, from time to time, boarded these types of junks, and after taking the crew members prisoner, we would leave them on one of the many remote off-shore islands and then use their vessels to carry our teams north disguised as crewmen. At the conclusion of those missions we would send the commandeered junks to the bottom of the South China Sea by placing one or two satchel charges of C-4 plastic explosives below the junk's waterline. The resulting explosion left little evidence of our activities.

The new plan that was introduced in early 1966 by those in charge of MACV incorporated the use of SOG teams to board the junks that randomly sailed along the coast. This time, though, rather than sink the junks we gave their crews blankets, fishing equipment, canned food, rice, and most important, radios. The Sony model 911 radio was to become the one most preferred by the Vietnamese fishermen because it had AM/FM capabilities. Though these men were extremely wary of their own South Vietnamese military, they accepted these "gifts" and agreed to pass along any and all information they thought might be of use to us. This gift-giving plan had only moderate success, but even some good intelligence was better than none at all.

To further enhance Team Romulus's capabilities a list of "nice-to-have" types of unusual equipment and ordnance was submitted to the MACV headquarters in Saigon. To our surprise many of the items began to arrive at the Black Rock compound. Claymore mines with variable-time fuses were a favorite toy that would give a hastily departing SOG team several minutes of valuable getaway time. Satchel charges, whose devastating explosion could be delayed for up to several hours with new-style timing devices, became another favorite item that we began to employ on a regular basis. While the standard (T/O) weapon for Marine reconnaissance team members in 1965 was the lowly M-3A1 grease gun—an overweight, inaccurate .45-caliber survivor of World War II—our SOG armory was considered a treasure house of exotic weaponry—Stoner 63A automatic rifles, silenced .22-caliber rifles and semiautomatic pistols, and various pistols of European manufacture were available to all SOG team members. The contents of our armory made Camp Black Rock a very popular place with a number of the Marines from 1st Force Recon Company who knew I was assigned to the SOG Group.

A close friend of mine, Gunnery Sergeant Maurice J. Jacques, came to Vietnam with his platoon in early 1966. He too was armed only with an M-3A1 submachine gun, which he and his fellow Marines had found to be unsuitable in the punishing jungles of South Vietnam because it lacked the range and accuracy to cope with snipers and failed to provide accurate covering fire out to any great distance. The additional weight of the ammunition and the length of the M-3A1's magazine also proved to be a problem in the dense jungle environment. I was able to help Sergeant Jacques and several of his Marines obtain those weapons that they felt would give them the firepower they required in the field. As grease guns were traded in for the heavier but more accurate M-1 Garands, and Colt AR-15s, a close relationship with the Marines from 1st Force Recon Company began to take shape.

My involvement with those Marines was, of course, limited, but on several occasions I tried to make their lives a little bit easier. Having a fairly open budget that was also augmented by large amounts of money from the government of South Vietnam, I was able to openly procure various items that the Force Recon Marines could not obtain "through channels." After visiting their camp one day and listening to some of their complaints about the "haves" and "have-nots," I returned the following day in SOG's only dump truck. As I approached the recon company's mess hall, I shifted a lever that slowly raised the bed and dumped three pallets of Hamm's beer at the feet of several dozen astonished but thirsty recon Marines. I had not forgotten my ties to the Marines of this special unit, and I let them know it.

When I had first arrived in Danang in 1965, I found it to be a beautiful, open, and friendly city. There were few if any restrictions on travel, and I was allowed to come and go at any time within the limits of the city. As I moved around Danang and became more familiar with my surroundings, I found the people to be happy, honest, and pleased at the presence of American servicemen. But by 1966, as more and more of us came to their country, the Vietnamese people began to be corrupted by material goods and began to resent our presence. The Vietnamese worked hard and were paid little for their efforts. We helped corrupt them with our seductive excesses and our money and made thieves out of their children.

When I was able to walk down the beach, away from our compound, I could encounter several different dialects within two or three miles. When I tried to speak to the people on the beach, in what I thought was their own language, my attempts were met with kind smiles from the adults and laughter from the children. They were amazed at a "round eye" trying to speak Vietnamese, but they were quick to learn our slang phrases and swear words. They also knew when they were being conned. One little Vietnamese girl who lived near the compound and who spoke English expressed her impressions of most U.S. servicemen when she said, "Americans eat too much, talk too much, and are too fat."

The possibility of a Marine SOG team adviser being taken prisoner by the Vietcong or the NVA if one of the cross-border missions was compromised was quite real, considering how obviously our physical appearance differed from that of the Vietnamese. Despite those differences, it was the quick thinking of my friend Sergeant Johann Haferkamp and the use of the language skills he had acquired as a boy that prevented him from being taken to Hanoi as a POW in the fall of 1965.

Again, some background information is necessary.

Sergeant Johann Haferkamp was born in Oberhausen, Germany, in 1938. The son of a German fighter pilot who was later killed during the war, Johann left his homeland in 1957 and sailed to Montreal, Canada, where he got his first

job as an iron-mine laborer in northern Ontario. Johann was
not a stranger to very difficult times. His family was forced
to evacuate its home and relocate in Jena, in the eastern
section of Germany, during the early years of World War II.
In 1942 they returned to their original home only to suffer
from the effects of allied bombings of Essen and the famous Krupp iron works. During the terrible years of
1943–44, his family was forced to move again, this time
into the depths of the Black Forest of southwest Germany.
As Germany began to recover from the devastation of the
war, Johann worked to support his family while attending
school, but he saw his future not in Germany but in North
America.

After working for a year in the iron mines, Johann had
saved more than $3,000 and began a working odyssey that
took him first to Buffalo, New York, then westward toward
British Columbia, through Banff National Park in Canada,
south through the states of Washington and Oregon, and
into California. Together with three German friends, Johann
continued his North American tour, descending south
through Las Vegas and into Mexico where he worked as a
deckhand on a shrimp boat for nearly nine months. He and
his friends made their way to Mexico City and then traveled on to Vera Cruz before reaching their southernmost
point, Guatemala.

The return trip finally brought the group back to San
Francisco, and it was there that Johann learned that he was
about to be drafted. The immigration laws of the United
States in 1961 stated that all immigrant aliens under the age
of twenty-six were subject to the draft within six months of
their arrival in the United States. Johann's number had just
come up.

In German, the word "Marine" means Navy, and thinking that he was enlisting in the United States Navy, Johann
signed a four-year enlistment contract believing that he was
going to wear bell-bottom trousers and see the world. He
said that it wasn't until the third week of getting the crap

beat out of him by a Marine sergeant in San Diego that he realized he'd joined the wrong organization.

Now, as the adviser to SOG Team Nimbus, Johann consistently demonstrated that he was an exceptionally well-qualified Marine. If anyone knew the problems associated with language difficulties, it was Johann Haferkamp.

Johann was responsible for his team's communications with supporting arms—helicopter gunships and long-range artillery—and he had to be most proficient in land-navigation and communications, too. Team Nimbus was, in fact, given missions that differed greatly from mine, and it is important to note that while Sergeant Haferkamp, Sergeant Graffenstein, 1st Lieutenant Paull, and I did not sit around and discuss our individual missions with one another, we *did* know the respective end results.

Specifically tasked with going after what is today called infrastructure, Sergeant Haferkamp's team was used as a deep-reconnaissance unit trained to seek out and destroy enemy roads, bridges, storage areas, and communications sites located along the western border of South Vietnam and Laos. Team Nimbus consisted of thirty South Vietnamese Army Special Forces soldiers and differed from Team Romulus in that the majority of its members came from the northwestern area of South Vietnam.

On one mission in October 1965, Team Nimbus was inserted into their area of operation along the Laotian border near a rubber plantation owned by the Standard Oil Corporation. Dressed in the traditional black pajama uniform of the Vietcong, Team Nimbus was in the process of moving through a grove of rubber trees when they saw a larger force of Vietcong soldiers heading straight for them. Johann's only chance for survival was to confront the men of the approaching unit and convince them that he was an East German adviser moving through the area with his own group of Vietcong. Highly suspicious of the blond-haired, blue-eyed adviser who spoke only German, the Vietcong interrogated Johann and his team members for two days before allowing them to leave the area. I believe that this is the only case on record of a United States Marine talking his way out of being captured by the Vietcong. Johann did not consider the SOG team's mission compromised and they were able to return to the safety of Danang several days later.

By the spring of 1966, the Vietcong had moved closer to the city of Danang, and had made their presence felt, beginning with a series of attacks on the outlying villages and within the city's limits. One particular instance comes to mind when, in the name of trying to help a fellow Marine, my efforts nearly cost him his life.

Many of my team members had brought their extended families with them to Danang and because they lived and worked with the local people they, too, knew when the bamboo telegraph had announced the likelihood of a surprise attack by the Vietcong or elements of the NVA. We knew that the Vietcong wanted desperately to win the hearts and minds of the South Vietnamese, and if they could actually *prevent* innocent people from being killed or injured it would only serve to further their efforts. When word came that both the Danang airfield and the combined U.S. Air Force/Navy Post Exchange had become the next predicted target, defensive precautions were taken.

Air Force Chief Master Sergeant Getchel and Marine Staff Sergeant Gonsowski were assigned as managers of the Danang PX, and over the course of the preceding several months they had become dependable friends, helping us to procure hard-to-find items through the exchange.

On a scheduled visit to the PX, I explained to Sergeant Getchel that according to our best intelligence network, his PX was high on the VC target list. However, he tried to reassure me that he was in no immediate danger and was confident that a group of Chinese Nungs that had been hired to protect the facility could handle any terrorist threat. Staff Sergeant Gonsowski, on the other hand, knew that there was no love lost between the Nungs and the Vietnamese and thought that it would not be a bad idea to send a fast message to Saigon requesting additional security.

What he received from Saigon the next day was a brown paper bag containing one .45 Colt automatic pistol and five rounds of ammunition!

When I learned what had happened I put together a "care package" consisting of four selective-fire M-2 carbines, three grease guns, several hundred rounds of ammunition, and two cases of hand grenades, and personally delivered it to the two SNCO's running the PX.

When I returned to My Khe later that afternoon, I learned that the probability of a surprise night attack had increased and went to our own ammunition bunker with two of my SOG team members to double-check our own security. Much to my surprise, I discovered that in my haste to get the ordnance over to the PX, I had provided Getchel and Gonsowski with a case of booby-trap hand grenades, the kind used on enemy trails and the streambeds they used as trails. These grenades would detonate as soon as the pin was pulled.

My attempts to send a warning to the PX using a hand-cranked field telephone proved useless. To complicate things, the one bridge that connected our peninsula to the mainland was guarded by South Vietnamese forces and was off-limits after darkness. My only hope was to go to the PX and hope that Getchel and Gonsowski would not become bored and start to monkey around with those deadly hand grenades.

Taking a case of standard hand grenades along, two SOG team members and I made our way to the river bank that separated us from the mainland. We hired a fisherman to take us across in his boat, and then commandeered three bicycles to carry us the remaining distance to the PX. And as the three of us pedaled madly down the dirt road leading to the PX, I expected at any moment to hear that familiar, muffled-crunch sound of an exploding hand grenade, telling me our race with time had been for nothing.

The dumbfounded expressions on the faces of Getchel and Gonsowski seemed comical to me after I had explained to them what had happened, but I was so pleased to find both of them alive that I didn't waste time hanging around apologizing for my mistake and making matters worse. I left them with the second case and told them that I would try to return the following day and retrieve the booby-trap grenades. I guess the road to hell really is paved with good intentions.

At the beginning of 1966, there were 180,000 U.S. troops in Vietnam, including more than 39,000 United States Marines. As the war began to escalate and our troop strengths climbed, the role of our SOG teams was expanded beyond that of covert military operations, and we acquired new missions to aid the government of South Vietnam. Some historical background information will help to explain how this happened.

With Vietnam's French-sponsored emperor, Bao Dai, living in France, leadership in South Vietnam had fallen into the hands of one man, Bao Dai's pro-West premier, Ngo Dinh Diem. Diem was the product of a prosperous and well-educated Catholic family from Hue, the former Imperial capital of Vietnam. He had served the French as a province chief prior to World War II, becoming a strong nationalist and anti-Communist politician. But because Diem had been unable to reconcile his anti-French attitudes with the Vietminh movement during the Indochina War he had left his homeland in the early 1950s to live at a Catholic seminary in the United States. There he had stayed until his appointment as premier in June of 1954.

During early 1955 the entire South Vietnamese government became engulfed in a crisis that threatened to disrupt the plans of the United States government to help build up this vital anti-Communist country. This crisis occurred as a result of the South's political instability when the leaders of the opposition, dissatisfied with Diem's refusal to accede to their various demands, formed the United Front of National Forces. By mid-March the disaffected leaders felt strong enough to test Diem's strength. Fighting between the government forces and UFN forces lasted through the summer.

Although Emperor Bao Dai had repeatedly ordered Diem to join him in France, the premier refused, opting instead to remain in Saigon and direct his forces against the rebellion.

On October 23, 1955, a nationwide referendum was held in South Vietnam to settle the issue of national leadership. The election, often criticized as being rigged, resulted in Premier Diem's receiving 98.2 percent of the total vote. Three days later South Vietnam's new president proclaimed the Republic of Vietnam (RVN).

President Diem's regime experienced a three-year period of relative political tranquility, but in 1959 political dissent had begun to reemerge from several influential segments of South Vietnamese society. The results of the August 1959 national elections, in which pro-Diem candidates captured every seat in the National Assembly, served to stimulate political opposition that had lain dormant for four years. Opposition to Diem's corrupt government mounted steadily within the military as well as in political circles in the months following the election, as many South Vietnamese senior military officers expressed their disenchantment with Diem's management of the war with the Vietcong insurgents.

Another problem, religious unrest, was to play a key role in determining South Vietnam's political direction as the new decade unfolded. Buddhist leaders throughout South Vietnam began protesting against various policies enacted by the Catholic-controlled government. The tensions mounted, and by early 1963 these protests were highlighted by spectacular and highly publicized self-immolations of Buddhist monks. In May, the problem erupted into violence when the Vietnamese police and military forces killed twelve Buddhist demonstrators who were protesting at a religious demonstration in Hue. This event triggered a protracted crisis of public confidence in the Diem government.

On August 21, Ngo Dinh Nhu, the president's brother and closest political adviser, ordered the national police to raid key Buddhist pagodas throughout the nation. Following these raids, which uncovered a few weapons, Nhu attempted to blame the attacks on several key South Vietnamese generals. His effort to shift the responsibility for the police raids served only to alienate many of the nation's most powerful military leaders.

On November 1, a military coup led by Major General Duong Van Minh reacted to the deepening political and religious crisis by deposing President Diem and seizing control of the government of Vietnam. Both the president and his brother were executed by an ARVN officer the following day.

The government takeover by General Minh opened the door for the flamboyant Vice Air Marshal Nguyen Cao Ky, commanding general of the Vietnamese Air Force, and General Nguyen Van Thieu to become, respectively, the "Commissioner in Charge of the Executive Branch" of the government and the "Chairman of the Joint Directorate," until another junta headed by General Nguyen Khanh ended Minh's reign in January 1964. On November 1, following two more months of political turmoil, Tran Van Houng became South Viet nam's premier, only to be ousted in June 1965 by Nguyen Cao Ky.

At two high-level conferences early in 1966, U.S. policymakers stressed that pacification in Vietnam should receive a greater priority. In January, representatives from General Westmoreland's staff, the American embassy in Vietnam, Commander-in-Chief Pacific (CinCPac) Admiral Sharp's staff, and their Washington counterparts met secretly in Warrenton, Virginia, to review the course of the Vietnam war. The conferees examined the South Vietnamese Rural Reconstruction Program, the label for pacification at the time, as well as the structure of the American civil assistance organization in South Vietnam. The most important result of this conference was its general focus and direction. William J. Porter, the U.S. deputy ambassador to South Vietnam, commented that the watchword in Washington, D.C., would soon become "pacification."

The truth of this particular statement became evident the following month at the Honolulu meeting between President Johnson and the Vietnamese chief of state, Nguyen Van Thieu, and Premier Nguyen Cao Ky. On February 8, 1966, the U.S. and South Vietnamese governments issued the "Honolulu Declaration." President Johnson renewed the American pledge to support the South Vietnamese in their struggle against the Communists, while Ky and Thieu promised renewed dedication to the eradication of social injustices, the building of a viable economy, establishment of a true democracy, and the defeat of the Vietcong and their allies, the North Vietnamese.

The buildup of enemy forces in South Vietnam in 1966, thus did not happen by surprise. I was soon to learn not only how determined the Vietcong were in their plans to terrorize the countryside, but just how determined Premier Ky was in carrying out his own plans for "pacification" into North Vietnam. It was our SOG teams that were asked to carry that message to the enemy in the north.

In the fall of 1966, two airmen stationed at the busy Danang airfield decided to leave the safety of the base and rented moped motorcycles to take them around the city. Their trip took them south, along Route 1 and to the outskirts of town near the entrance to our peninsula. There, a large wooden sign had been erected near the road junction to warn passersby not to proceed down the road toward Marble Mountain without the assistance of an armed military convoy. It also prohibited travel on the road at night. For whatever reason, the two young airmen chose to disregard the stern warning and continued down the road, unprotected. Several days later, after we'd been alerted to their disappearance, a half dozen of my team members who had been practicing patrolling techniques outside the compound, ran back into the camp to find me. They had found the airmen.

Well-armed and anticipating an ambush, we returned to the scene of my teammates' discovery. The two men had been brutally murdered by the Vietcong. The severed head of one had been impaled on a bamboo stake; the second airman had been emasculated, penis and testicles placed inside his mouth.

The bodies had lain there for only two days, but heat, blowflies, and maggots had already made them unrecognizable. The grisly sight and the stench made even the most seasoned team members sick to their stomachs. The message of the Vietcong was very clear—at night the area belonged to them.

We radioed back a report of our discovery and waited for the Air Force authorities to arrive at the scene. After we had given all of our information to the Air Force security officials we returned to our compound.

As the Vietcong became bolder, it was obvious to us that they were not as dependent as we were on the use of a multi-channel radio to help coordinate their nighttime attacks on the outlying areas. Still, their ability to communicate with one another appeared extraordinarily good. We finally discovered the reason for their communications success during the interrogation of a Vietcong who was taken prisoner, but his explanation proved to be quite a surprise. Their ability to coordinate silently was based on the placement of a pair of boots in a shoe-repair shop located on a side street in Danang.

The owner of the cobbler shop, who also happened to be a Vietcong officer, had devised a silent code that told his fellow guerrillas at a glance the date, time, and place of their next meeting. A particular pair of men's workboots would be strategically placed in his store window. If the boot laces were tied up to the third eyelet their next meeting was scheduled for the third day of the month. The number of knots in the laces indicated the hour of the meeting: For example, three knots meant 0300. The direction the boots pointed gave the location of their meeting, and if the boots were placed down on their side then the meeting had been called off.

Less than a month after the Vietcong had murdered the two young airmen, our compound at My Khe became the target for one of their nighttime sapper attacks.

I was awakened that night by the muffled sounds of several hand grenades exploding inside of some nearby buildings and I wasted no time in getting myself "assembled" before heading for the door to risk taking a quick look outside. There was no sound of rifle fire coming from within the compound, which was reassuring since we also used AK-47s. As I crouched in the doorway and listened for the sound of anyone approaching, the night sky was suddenly illuminated by a tremendous explosion that lit up the entire compound. The shock waves blew the glass out of the windows and the walls of several buildings collapsed. Then, only silence.

With the first light of morning came the realization that the target of the attack had been the demolitions bunker, the partially buried Connex box that housed most of our explosives. The hand grenades had been a diversion to draw the attention of the compound's interior guard force away from the area of the bunker while satchel charges were placed against the steel door of the box.

Fortunately, two of our SOG teams, Remus and Nimbus, were not in the compound at the time of the attack, and no one was wounded or killed. But the explosion had destroyed much of the compound and our only dump truck, which had been parked beside the bunker.

We reasoned that the attack could well have been an inside job. Four armed guards were always posted atop the walls of the compound and two armed guards were posted to protect the only entrance into the compound. How could VC sappers have gotten past them and then escaped from within a walled compound? Evidence of demolition materials that only our SOG Teams had access to—timing devices that depended upon dripping acid to release a coiled-spring firing mechanism—were found near the entrance to the flattened bunker. Now, even more attention to the security of our mission planning was required, for if just one SOG team member had gone over to the enemy side, we would never be sure who would be waiting for us the next time we crossed over a beach in North Vietnam.

* * *

In the spring of 1966, a series of public demonstrations by Buddhists, students, farmers, and workers occurred throughout the cities of South Vietnam. The catalyst for these events was Premier Ky's firing of General Nguyen Chanh Thi, the I Corps commander of South Vietnamese forces. The demonstrators demanded a national election and an end to the war, but Ky met this opposition with his loyal military forces. Riots broke out in Saigon, Quang Ngai, and Hue. The port of Danang was closed down when a general strike was staged against the government by the dock workers and, to make matters worse, the mayor of Danang joined the opposition against the Saigon government.

Premier Ky declared Danang an enemy-held city and arrived in the city with 1,700 Vietnamese Marines and his national police in an attempt to end the strike. When the American commander of the Danang airfield sealed his gates, Ky was forced to return to Saigon, having "lost face" across the country.

Ky retaliated on May 15, when he airlifted more than a thousand Vietnamese Marines into Danang and seized the city's key installations. After a week's worth of fighting, in which there were hundreds of casualties, Ky's forces invaded the city's Buddhist temples and then headed north, where they sacked and burned the United States consulate at Hue. By mid-June, the opposition forces there surrendered to Ky's army. He then declared that the "Buddhist struggle movement" was over, and that he remained in power.

It was just after Premier Ky's victory that we received notice he was coming up from Saigon to our My Khe compound to inspect his Vietnamese SOG Marines. The truth is that Prime Minister Ky had more on his mind than a simple review of his troops. When he arrived at the My Khe compound he did, in fact, inspect the SOG team members. Then he gathered them together and told them that there were certain individuals remaining in North Vietnam who he considered traitors to the cause of democracy. He supplied the team members with a list of their names, their photographs, and the last-known village in which each had lived. He offered a bounty of $500 in cash for the death of each of the men on his hit list.

Each Vietnamese SOG team member was paid a guaranteed salary and a stipend of rice as well as an additional $30 for his participation in each cross-border mission. Considering that the average South Vietnamese soldier received less than $25 pay each month, that was a significant sum. The added incentive of $500 for each successful assassination was, in Ky's mind, all the motivation the men would require to insure their loyalty, which Ky did not seem to realize that he already had. Actually, it was team members' weekly stipends of rice that caused the only problem I had during the thirty months I spent as a SOG Team adviser.

One day I happened to walk into the beach encampment several hundred yards south of our compound and found that the attitude of my team members was at an all-time low. When I asked my interpreter, Twit, to find out exactly what was wrong, he replied that the men had not received their rice and could not feed their families or supply the camp cook with any rice for their own meals. Since Captain Tony, a Vietnamese officer assigned as a senior adviser to SOG, was the individual who received the weekly rice shipment, I paid him a visit and asked him to explain why the men hadn't been given their rice.

"This is of no concern to you. I am sure that they will receive their rice when it arrives and that the problem will be resolved."

But we knew Captain Tony had already signed a receipt for the men's rice ration. Within several hours the rice magically appeared and harmony was restored within the encampment. But because of Captain Tony's loss of face, a line had been drawn between us and he would not be satisfied until he could make me suffer equal or greater personal indignity.

He didn't have to wait very long.

The next day, while I was napping in my quarters, several Romulus Team members crept into my room, stole the artificial leg that I used for "land navigation," and—boot still attached to the foot—hoisted it to the top of the flagpole located in the center of the compound. Upon waking and finding my leg had walked off by itself, I put on my swim leg and began to limp around the camp, searching for my "good" leg. Of course my team members had positioned themselves around the camp to watch my frustrated efforts. Just as I spotted my leg dangling from the flagpole, Captain Tony drove his jeep into the compound.

As I lowered my leg to the ground, much to the laughter of my fellow team members. Captain Tony looked on. "It seems as though the men are laughing at you."

"Yes, Captain. They're laughing at me, but I think that I still have their respect."

He walked away, unimpressed.

On the first day of October 1966, Major General Herman Nickerson, Jr., assumed command of the 1st Marine Division from Major General Lewis J. Fields, and moved the division's headquarters from Chu Lai north to Danang. His arrival in Vietnam and his plans for the tactical area of responsibility (TAOR) that he now commanded would, again, have a great impact on my life.

24

General Nickerson Calls

By the end of 1966, President Johnson and Secretary of Defense Robert McNamara had projected the strength of American Forces in Vietnam at 390,000 men. According to these projections, by December of that year General Westmoreland would have a grand total of seventy-nine maneuver battalions and supporting air and ground units under his command. The United States Marine Corps was committed to a 70,000-man force in Vietnam, which meant that by the end of the year, the entire 1st and 3rd Marine Divisions and most of the 1st Marine Aircraft Wing would also be in Vietnam. Compounding the difficulty for the Marine Corps was the fact that the tour of duty for the individual Marine was thirteen months. Not only were new units being deployed to Vietnam, but replacements for the Marines whose overseas tours were almost over had to be sent to Vietnam.

In July 1966, I was promoted to gunnery sergeant and in November I received orders directing me to leave Vietnam and proceed to the Marine Corps Air Station, El Toro, California, for further assignment. Having twice been able to extend my tour of duty with SOG Team Romulus for a total of seventeen months and not having a family to worry about, there was no place that I would rather have been than exactly where I was. In order to continue as an independent SOG team adviser I needed to get those Stateside orders canceled, and to do that required some outside help.

As an adviser sent to Danang from MACV headquarters in Saigon, I did not come under the administrative or the operational control of any Marine Corps command in I Corps, but I thought that if I could use the Marine Corps chain of command to let my desire to extend be known, I might stand a fair chance of getting my orders canceled. I had learned early on that when you go to a gunfight, you take along a big gun. Major General Herman Nickerson— who had personally helped me to remain on active duty five years earlier—was the man that I needed to see. After placing several radio calls to the office of the division's sergeant major, a meeting time was arranged for me to speak to the commanding general.

The jeep ride from the SOG compound at My Khe to the division's newly constructed headquarters took less than half an hour. After a brief meeting to personally thank the division sergeant major for his help, I was led into Major General Nickerson's office. The general was pleased to see me again, and after offering me a cup of coffee, he asked me to sit down and tell him about the type of work that I was involved in as a SOG team adviser. The General actually already knew a great deal about what I was doing. His familiarity with our missions, our area of operations, and with our successes in obtaining intelligence information from the prisoners we had snatched from North Vietnam surprised me. He was very interested in my team so I told him about the South Vietnamese Marines with whom I was working, absolutely fearless men who were totally loyal to me and to our mission. I explained to the general that although my SOG team members were well trained and highly disciplined, they still remained very superstitious: They had even painted eyes on the bows of each of our inflatable rubber boats so that the "spirit of the boat" would always be able to "see the way" into our beach objectives.

The general then commented that although our weapons and equipment had changed a great deal since his last days of combat in Korea commanding the 7th Marine Regiment, the one thing that had remained the same was the degree of suffering and pain that Marines endured in combat. While talking about this, the General never lost his sense of bearing, but his mood changed and his manner became almost paternal. The Marines who were being injured were *his* Marines, he said, with the compassion of a father describing his own children.

"General, I asked the sergeant major if I could speak to you personally, and that is to ask for your help, sir. I've been in Vietnam for seventeen months, sir, and I don't want to go back to Stateside duty. With the first and third Marine Divisions both in-country, there aren't any infantry or reconnaissance units back in the States that need me. I'm getting along fine—no problems with my leg—and I feel like I'm making a contribution to what's going on here. All that I'm asking is to be allowed to remain here and continue doing what I'm doing. The people at MACV headquarters don't know me from Adam, sir, so they can't go to bat for me with this request, but you do know me, sir, and that's why I've come to see you."

Major General Nickerson gave several moments thought to my request, before he spoke.

"Gunny Hamblen, it seems to me that every time you and I get together, I learn something new and you get what you come for. The last time we had a talk like this, all you wanted from me was permission to stay in the Corps. Now you want permission to stay in a combat zone with an SOG team. Well, I understand your request and agree with you. As long as I'm here in Vietnam, you'll be here too. The intelligence information that teams like yours are able to provide is invaluable. I'm pleased that you came to see me and explained this situation, but now I want to ask a favor of you.

"With the marked increase in the number of Marines fighting in Vietnam, there's also been an increase in the number of casualties. When I go to our field hospitals or to the Navy's hospital ship to visit our wounded men, I sometimes find myself at a loss for words. I don't think that I will ever get accustomed to seeing wounded Marines.

Gunny, I will need your help from time to time, and ask that you come with me when I make these hospital visits. Your presence and your example of having overcome injuries would be powerful medicine for these men. It would mean a great deal to me and to those Marines. I'll get word to you the next time that I go over to the hospital."

I thanked Major General Nickerson for his help and I assured him that he could depend on me to assist him. I did not realize how soon it would be before the General would call in his marker, nor that I had just accepted the most difficult assignment I've ever had.

The United States Navy was responsible for all medical assistance given to Marines in I Corps, and Navy personnel managed all of the Marine Amphibious Force medical facilities all the way down to the individual battalion and squadron aid stations. At the lowest level of medical responsibility was the Navy corpsman who accompanied each Marine rifle platoon into combat. As part of the division's organization, two medical battalions, the 1st and the 3rd, along with the 1st Hospital Company, were responsible for all of the Marines' intermediate medical facilities located at Chu Lai, Dong Ha, Phu Bai, and Danang. Commanded by a Navy doctor, each of these medical battalions consisted largely of Navy personnel who were reinforced by Marines for administrative and security purposes.

For the most serious and more complex cases, the Naval Support Activity at Danang ran its own hospital. NSA Danang, as it was called, opened its doors in January 1966 with only fifty beds, but by the end of that year the hospital had expanded to over 450 beds. With X-ray and modern laboratory facilities, the hospital had departments and clinics in neurosurgery; urology; eye, ear, nose, and throat ailments; dental; and preventive medicine. NSA Danang had a large helicopter landing pad located within several hundred feet of the triage and emergency operating rooms. After the introduction of the medevac helicopter, on average, a wounded Marine could expect to be at one of the emergency medical facilities within half an hour after the emergency evacuation request had been made. Of the 6,400 Marines and sailors of the III Marine Amphibious Force (MAF) who were wounded during 1966, only 214 died of their wounds, a mortality rate of less than 4 percent. To assist in the treatment of Marine wounded, the Navy's newly refitted hospital ship, the U.S.S. *Repose* (AH 16) arrived off the shores of I Corps in March 1966. With 560 beds, the *Repose* had medical facilities that could rival any modern hospital or trauma center in the States. Marine helicopters routinely evacuated casualties directly from the battlefield to the deck of the *Repose*, as many as 98 casualties a day.

I was at the SOG compound at Black Rock the first time that Major General Nickerson's office called and left instructions for me to meet him at the entrance of the Naval Support Activity in Danang. The general had scheduled a visit to the hospital after learning that several Marines involved in a company-size operation against the NVA had lost hands and feet due to traumatic amputation from mortar shrapnel or from hidden booby traps. After being briefed by the hospital's chief surgeon on each Marine's name, age, injury, and prognosis, the general, a colonel from his staff, and I were escorted into the intensive-care ward to talk with the men.

The first Marine the general spoke to was a young private first class, from the 2nd Battalion, 4th Marine Regiment, who had been in Vietnam less than two months. His right arm had been severed by a piece of shrapnel, and as he lay in his bed with the stump of his right arm elevated by a cotton sling attached to his stainless-steel IV stand, General Nickerson moved in close to him and held the private's left hand, assuring the boy that he was on his way home and that he would get the best medical care humanly possible. He told the private the date he was scheduled to leave Vietnam, and then told him that he was terribly sorry about his injury, but that he was very proud of him because it was Marines like him who would help to end this war.

The next Marine the General spoke to was a black staff sergeant who had lost his right leg when a booby trap exploded behind him. Married and the father of two children, the staff sergeant was on his second tour in Vietnam and had less than three months time remaining in-country when the patrol that he had been leading was ambushed, causing him and his Marines to take cover in an area that was rigged with booby traps. After talking with the staff sergeant the general introduced me to him, so that I could offer my own words of encouragement.

"Will I be able to walk as good as you, Gunny? I used to play a lot of football with my two boys, and now I don't know what they'll think. The general told me that you can still scuba-dive and jump out of airplanes. Is that true?"

"The general's telling you the truth. I was walking in less than a month after I lost my leg. If you want, I'll show you what you'll look like pretty soon."

I sat down next to the staff sergeant and rolled up my trouser leg, exposing my flesh-colored fiberglass prosthesis. His curiosity aroused, I tried to add some humor to our discussion. "If you like, they can make your leg the same color as mine, but that might confuse your family for a little while."

The wounded staff sergeant's laughter suddenly filled the ward and I could tell by the way it sounded that it was his first since being wounded.

Major General Nickerson's visit lasted no more than an hour, but he spoke quietly to every patient whose bed he passed. I know that it was as difficult for him to express his sympathy to each of those Marines as it was for them to express their thanks to him. After we had left the intensive-care ward and walked over to the general's jeep, he said, "Gunny, I will never get used to doing this, but I know that it goes with the territory. I hate this damned war and to see the suffering it has caused my Marines. I'm glad that you came over here today, as it made my job a damned sight easier. At least these men can see first hand that there's hope after losing a leg or an arm. You've helped them—and me—more than you might imagine. I don't look forward to the next time that we'll have to do this, Gunny, but I'll be counting on your help."

During the next few months, I accompanied Major General Nickerson to the hospital at Danang on one other occasion. As the General had predicted, the bedside visits did not get any easier. However, our second visit to the U.S.S. *Repose* was the most difficult trip of all.

The pilot of the Marine Huey helicopter that had brought us out to the *Repose* had been instructed to return for the general in one hour. As soon as the helicopter had cleared the landing pad, General Nickerson, his aide, and I were taken below decks so that the General could pay his respects to the ship's captain and crew, and to visit with those Marines most seriously wounded. As in the past, I spoke with several Marines who were waiting to be transported to Danang or to the naval hospitals located in Yokosuka, Japan, on Guam, or to the Stateside facility nearest their homes.

I was talking to several wounded Marines when I was informed by one of the ship's crewmen that General Nickerson had had to depart the ship unexpectedly. Transportation to my compound at My Khe was being arranged by the ship's air officer. While I waited for the arrival of the next inbound helicopter, I was approached by one of the ship's surgeons.

"Gunnery Sergeant Hamblen, my name's Dr. Jaslovac. I was introduced to you during your last visit to the ship with General Nickerson. I have a patient, a Marine sergeant, who has just been brought to the intensive-care compartment from surgery, and I was hoping that you would speak to him. Before you do, I should tell you that he has lost both of his legs, his right arm, and that he has also lost both of his eyes. He was caught up in a Claymore mine ambush, and when it exploded at waist-high level, it ripped him to pieces."

The M18A1 antipersonnel (Claymore) mine was one of the most lethal pieces of military hardware used during the Vietnam war. It was particularly effective in executing ambushes along jungle trails. The Claymore was a rectangular fiberglass box with spikes fitted to the base so that it could be anchored to the ground. An ominous instruction—FRONT TOWARD ENEMY—was embossed on the convex exterior. It contained seven hundred steel balls set in an explosive bed and was detonated by remote control. Hidden in the undergrowth, some distance away from the lethal zone, a soldier would complete a simple electrical circuit to set off the mine. Alternatively, the Claymore could also be set off by a tripwire hidden along a track. Once detonated, the Claymore sprayed its contents in a sixty-degree fan-shaped pattern that was deadly to a range of fifty yards.

Believing that I would go with the doctor to visit his patient, I entered the small darkened compartment only to discover that I was very much alone with a man who would probably have been better off dead than alive. Two intravenous bottles dripped blood and antibiotics into what remained of his body and a respirator pumped oxygen down his throat. And as I stood there next to him, I suddenly felt completely useless knowing that I was now supposed to say something to this Marine that would cheer him up a little.

I had been told during my own time in the hospital that the very last of a person's senses to go was hearing. Fearing that this poor bastard would hear me cursing my own stupidity in having promised that I would come and visit with the seriously wounded, I kept my mouth shut and thought about what I could say to him.

He must have felt my presence in the room, because when I moved, he turned his bandaged head in my direction. When he did that I spoke to him. I told him who I was and that I had come to let him know that he would be okay. My words came quickly and I realized they were meaningless. He and I both knew that he was in very bad shape, and I decided at that moment not to continue to insult his intelligence by telling him that he would improve. He wouldn't be okay, and I think that if he had been able to ask me to kill him, I would have done it. I would not have wished this Marine's misery on another living person.

The sense of pain and frustration at my inability to help this man turned into a seething anger when I thought about the recent newspaper and magazine articles I had read that applauded the efforts of American men who had opted to desert their country and hide across the border in Canada to avoid the draft. I wondered what the difference was between this Marine and those men who had run away, knowing that the chances of their being selected for the infantry and actually going into combat were less than one out of ten. I was sure that the young sergeant's mother must certainly love her son as much as those mothers who had excused their sons' acts of cowardice; that made me sad.

While I stayed in the compartment with that sergeant I simply held his hand in mine. It was all that I could do, but I hoped that in his drug-induced state of comfort he would still understand that someone was with him who cared. When a Navy nurse finally came into the compartment to check on the sergeant's vital signs, I wiped the tears from my face and went out onto the flight deck of the U.S.S. *Repose* to await my flight back to Danang.

Wounded Again

After we had loaded our equipment on board the deck of the dark green PT boat, we rested for a while and watched as the crew cast off our lines, allowing us to slip quietly away from Danang and head north to our rallying point off of the North Vietnamese coast. Eleven members of SOG Team Romulus—selected because they had lived in the targeted area—and I were to go ashore near a coastal village seventy miles north of the DMZ on a CADO-type mission in August 1967 and kidnap a North Vietnamese officer reported to be living in the village. If our information about this officer's whereabouts proved correct, we would return to Danang with our prize within twenty-four hours; if not, there was the possibility that we might not return at all.

Our plan was not too complex: Once we arrived on station, we would lower our two inflatable rubber boats over the side of the PT boat and then be vectored toward shore, guided by radioed instructions from the PT boat, where they monitored our progress on the radar system, to the exact point we had selected as our best possible landing site. The distance to shore was twelve miles, and aided by our silent-running, fifty-horsepower Johnson outboard engines, we would cover that distance in a very short period.

At 2300 hours we were in position to begin our trip to shore. Dressed in tiger-striped uniforms, faces camouflaged, we were armed with sanitized silenced weapons and explosive ordnance. We moved away from our PT boat to establish radio communications before starting our run. When we were less than a thousand yards from land, two of our scout swimmers lowered themselves into the warm waters of the Gulf of Tonkin and swam effortlessly toward the surf zone to get a better look at the beach. Diving underneath the breaking waves in the surf zone they made their way to shore and radioed back a warning that the beach was covered with hundreds of sharpened punji sticks that channeled our approach toward the village. As I studied the beach through my infrared goggles, I pinpointed the scouts' signal from their metascope, and motioned to our second rubber boat to follow us in through the surf to where our two scouts lay waiting.

As soon as we got to shore, we jumped out of the boats and carried them inland, over the sand, to prevent leaving any visible signs of our arrival. We withdrew our weapons and packs and then covered the boats with camouflage netting, leaving them under the protection of four of our team members.

This particular night had been chosen well—there was no moon and by taking advantage of a combination of reduced light and a high tide, we improved our chances of success. With the main portion of our group protected by the security team, we followed in trace as our two scouts moved through a break in the punji stakes and headed to the southern side of the little village.

One of my SOG team members, a corporal nicknamed Frenchy because of his gold-toothed smile, had spent several of his teenage years in the village, living and working with his grandparents. His memory of the few dirt trails and the exact location of its scattered bamboo hooches provided us with additional information that, combined with aerial photographs, had helped us to construct a mock-up of the village. Frenchy had told us that the villagers owned numerous dogs and to prevent these animals from alerting the residents to our presence, our two scout swimmers had armed themselves with silenced pistols, known for their intended use as "Hush Puppies."

The Hush Puppy (Mark 22, Model 0), developed by Smith & Wesson specifically for SOG Teams, was based on the Model 39 automatic pistol. It was equipped with a five-inch threaded barrel on which a noise suppressor developed by the Naval Ordnance Laboratory in Washington, D.C., could be screwed. To make the weapon even more quiet, the slide could be locked to keep the mechanism closed and silent while firing.

Since the 9-millimeter round was normally supersonic, and therefore would generate an audible crack—a sonic "boom"—in flight, a subsonic round was developed for the Mark 22, and the Super Val Cartridge Corporation, a leading developer of extralethal loads for pistols, was given a contract by the U.S. Navy to develop the special ammunition. The result was a green-tipped Parabellum-type projectile that, at 150 grains, was substantially heavier than the standard 9-millimeter bullet. It also had a reduced muzzle velocity of 274 meters per second. The pistol was equipped with special caps and plugs and could be carried underwater. The ammunition was packed in boxes holding twenty-two rounds and a spare baffle insert for the silencer. Each insert lasted for about thirty rounds before it had to be replaced. When used with supersonic rounds, the silencer had to be replaced after every five or six rounds.

Our scouts led us to a small grass-covered rise that provided a good view of the sleeping village, which had no more than a dozen huts making up its core. We studied the area and noticed that the one hooch of particular interest to us sat less than two hundred yards from where we had come to rest. As we waited, watched, and listened to the night sounds, we noted that a small amount of light was coming from within the target hut. We hoped to see the faint light broken from within the hooch—a sign of movement and hence occupation—but after several minutes of watching patiently and not seeing any signs of movement,

Frenchy signaled the four-man snatch team to move in closer for a better look.

Armed with silenced Swedish K submachine guns and carrying rucksacks of explosives, the four team members slipped away from the rise and began to low crawl toward the distant hooch. They hadn't been gone but a few minutes when the sound of machine-gun fire, coming from down on the beach, served notice that we were in very big trouble.

The snatch team covered the remaining distance to the hooch within a few seconds and finding an empty hut lit by a small oil lamp, they tossed two satchel charges inside and then raced down the dirt trail toward the center of the village and planted two Claymore mines along the trail that led to the beach. The satchel charges and the Claymore mines had been prepared with acid fuses, and by the time the snatch team returned to where we lay hiding, the first of our explosive charges detonated. The sound of machine-gun fire coming from behind us had stopped and, not knowing whether our security team had survived the brief firefight, we started back toward the beach just as the two Claymore mines exploded near the village.

Our scouts led us back toward the beach, angling off to the south to prevent us from stumbling into an ambush, but at a distance of less than a hundred yards from the crest of the beach three hand grenades exploded to our left. We answered the attack, several Swedish Ks spraying the brush that paralleled the trail. The sound of AK-47s firing on full automatic stopped our scouts from moving forward and, as we listened to hear the direction in which our unseen enemies were moving, another enemy grenade volley exploded nearby, wounding three men at the rear of our column.

I motioned to our two scouts to move toward the beach and started to help carry one of my wounded men when a bullet struck me in my left arm. As I struggled to regain my balance I was joined by Frenchy, who helped me, leading us back down to the boats. As we ran across the sand toward the water, I saw that both of our rubber boats were still there, held in waist-deep water by the security team. As we reached the water's edge we passed the bodies of three North Vietnamese soldiers.

The wade out to the waiting boats seemed to take forever, but as soon as we got alongside the inflatables, strong hands pulled us over the sides. Only our two scouts remained on shore, covering the withdrawal. We waved to them to make their way out toward us, and then swung our boats back toward shore to pick them up in shallow water. As we headed toward the surf zone and put some distance between ourselves and the white flashes of enemy rifle fire, the increasingly far-off plumes of water their bullets made told us that we were safely out of range.

Our outboard engines, though built to run quietly, still made enough surface noise to give away our positions as we headed out to sea. Fearful that the NVA might have motorized boats of their own, we put up our portable radar antenna and signaled the South Vietnamese PT boat that we had aborted our mission and were headed due east for a pickup.

Of the twelve members of Team Romulus who went on this particular mission, three were wounded seriously enough to require hospitalization and two of us were seen initially by our corpsman, "Doc" Robbie Robinson, before going over to the hospital. My X ray revealed what looked like a .32-caliber bullet lodged against the radial bone of my left arm. Because it did not warrant surgery to extract it, the little bullet still remains there.

Not long after the swelling in my arm had gone down, I received a radio message requesting that I pay a personal visit to the 1st Marine Division command post and meet with Major General Nickerson again. I knew that in Vietnam bad news traveled much faster than good news, and I was in no hurry to see the man who had earned the nickname "Herman the German." Nevertheless I found myself in the presence of the division commanding general the day after I had received his message.

"Gunny Hamblen, I read about your being wounded again, and I'm afraid that you're not going to like what I have to tell you: Your days in Vietnam are over. There's much more to this than my personal concern for your safety and I want you to listen to what I have to say before you give me a half dozen reasons why I'm wrong.

"This war has begun to sour the mood of the country. People don't like to see their favorite sons getting killed on the six o'clock news while they're eating supper. The media has made a three-ring circus out of Vietnam and they'll report on anything and everything. That has now become a problem for you and for me.

"Even though you are assigned to MACV/SOG, I'm still the I Corps commander and you operate in my tactical area of operation. Yesterday, we had two reporters in here, one from UPI and the other one from the Associated Press, who wanted to do a follow-up story on you. How they got wind of your being here, I can only guess, but you and your men do not need any more exposure than you already have.

"To make matters worse, if you should get killed on a mission north of the DMZ, there'll be hell to pay. The American public'll think that the Marine Corps has been forced to scrape the bottom of the barrel and has allowed amputees to do its fighting; that would not look very good for our Corps. I know that you want to stay here, Gunny Hamblen, and I admire your courage, but if even one person in your family should protest the fact that you are here, it could only lead to more trouble.

"Gunny, you and I go back a long way, but I have to think about what's good for the Marine Corps as well as what's good for you. If it were up to me alone, I would want a hundred more Marines like you, but I've been told to get you out of Vietnam as soon as possible. You've done thirty consecutive months over here, which is probably more than any other Marine in all of I Corps, but enough is enough."

Major General Nickerson's explanation did not give me much room to maneuver, and I understood his position. Before I left his office he told me that as his way of thanking me for my service in helping him visit with the wounded

Marines, I could choose any Marine Corps post or station in the States as my next duty station.

Before I departed Danang in November 1967, SOG Team Romulus was given one more mission that I was allowed to train, but not to participate in—a raid on Tiger Island (Hon Gio). Tiger Island was a piece of North Vietnamese property located forty miles north of the DMZ and thirty miles off the coast. Intelligence reports indicated that the North Vietnamese were possibly using the island as a POW camp. SOG teams Romulus and Nimbus were to slip ashore on Tiger Island and then determine if our most recent intelligence was good or not. After the teams left Danang, they commandeered a South Vietnamese junk that took them to an anchoring point several miles off the island. Using inflatable rubber boats, the teams made it to shore, but were detected by the island's security forces before they could move very far inland. During the firefight to cover their hasty withdrawal, six members of Team Romulus were killed and five were seriously wounded. With no South Vietnamese Marine replacements volunteering to take the place of the casualties, Team Romulus was reduced to only eleven men. However, I will be the first one to say that I have never served with a better group of professional fighting men than the thirty-seven South Vietnamese Marines who had volunteered to make up SOG Team Romulus when I first arrived.

I departed Danang on November 15, and returned to the United States after participating in more than sixty SOG missions—of which forty took me into North Vietnam—during the thirty consecutive months that I served in what was then the Republic of South Vietnam.

26

Final Stateside Duty

My orders to the duty station of my choice brought me back to Camp Pendleton, where I was assigned as the company operations and training chief in the newly formed 5th Force Reconnaissance Company, located by the ocean at Camp Del Mar. The company's staff comprised primarily dual-qualified (jump- and scuba-trained) officers and staff noncommissioned officers, all veterans of the Vietnam war. Although the personnel strength of the company varied from week to week, we were organized the same way as 1st and 3rd Force Reconnaissance companies, which were then still operating in South Vietnam. But, even with a very capable staff of combat veterans and a well-designed training schedule, we were not without our problems, the greatest single one being that once trained, the majority of our Marines were shipped to South Vietnam hoping to join the ranks of either 1st or 3rd Force Reconnaissance companies. Instead they were absorbed by Marine infantry units for their thirteen-month tours of duty. When word of this situation began to filter back to Camp Del Mar, the morale of our high-spirited Marine volunteers took a downward plunge.

In April 1968, I took one week's worth of annual leave and hopped aboard a military flight taking me from the Marine Air Station El Toro to Washington, D.C., to meet with the one Marine who had some degree of control over my future—my career monitor.

I had not been in Washington since 1964, and thought that it might be wise if I spoke directly to those Marines who actually helped plan my future and to learn from them what I could expect in the way of duty assignments in the months ahead. The office for the assignment of all enlisted Marines with infantry MOSs was where I was directed, to meet with a Major Duffy, the gentleman who would explain the "needs" of the Marine Corps and how those needs would impact on my future duty assignments. I was told that before I could speak with Major Duffy, I would have to pass through some of the bureaucratic "wickets" that are famous at Headquarters Marine Corps.

An old master sergeant, who sat behind a small oak desk that was hidden underneath the stairway leading to the monitor's office, was the first such obstacle. He informed me that the Sergeant Major of the Marine Corps, Sergeant Major Herbert J. Sweet, wanted to speak to me personally before I met with Major Duffy. The old Marine asked me to wait while he sent a private first class to get my official record book. When the PFC returned, I was escorted to the office of one of the true legends of the Marine Corps.

Born on October 8, 1919, in Hartford, Connecticut, Sergeant Major "Shifty" Sweet enlisted in the Marines on February 26, 1937. Following recruit training at Parris Island, his duty assignments took him to Quantico, Virginia, and then to Trinidad, British West Indies, before he saw combat in World War II. Sergeant Major Sweet was a company gunnery sergeant the first time he was wounded in combat with the 3rd Marine Division, on Bougainville in December 1943. In July 1944, during the initial landing to recapture the island of Guam, he was again wounded when an enemy artillery shell exploded next to him. When he came to, a Japanese soldier shot him in the arm. Evacuated to a Navy hospital in the New Hebrides Islands, he was awarded his second Purple Heart. In February 1945, then–First Sergeant Sweet went ashore on Iwo Jima and was awarded the

Bronze Star Medal for bravery, along with his third Purple Heart. In 1951, when he was assigned as a company 1st sergeant in the 5th Marines, Sweet was wounded for the fourth time.

Now, as the senior enlisted adviser to the Commandant of the Marine Corps, General Greene, Sergeant Major Sweet was interested in my future. He welcomed me into his office and as we sat and began to talk, he read my service record book. He asked me how I was enjoying duty with 5th Force Reconnaissance Company and as I began to explain the problems inherent with a new training company, he suddenly cut me off.

"What's this I see about you having new orders, Gunny?"

"I don't know what you're talking about, Sergeant Major. I don't know anything about having any new orders."

There, on the first page of my service record book, was a yellow piece of onionskin paper, the word "classified" stamped in bold letters at the top and bottom, that directed me to further assignment with the U.S. Army's Strike Command.

"What the hell is the Strike Command, Sergeant Major?"

"I guess you really don't know anything about these orders, do you, Gunny? Well, why don't you and I go down and see your monitor together. Maybe he can shed some light on these."

Major Duffy was the officer in charge of the enlisted assignment branch and was responsible for insuring that the Marine Corps infantrymen were actually placed in the hundreds of duty assignments that were required to meet the many needs of the Marine Corps. Some of those assignments included tours of duty with other branches of the service. Major Duffy was pleased to see that the Sergeant Major of the Marine Corps had accompanied me to his office and commented that he also was surprised to see that I was interested enough in my future to have come from California to Washington just to talk about it. He, too, read over my service record book before speaking.

"Gunny Hamblen, before you say anything, I just want you to know that you are never getting outside of CONUS [Continental United States] on us again. We were scared stiff that while you were in Vietnam you'd get yourself killed. That would have left us with a hell of a lot of explaining to do. It took a lot of arguing with Major General Nickerson's staff before he would agree to send you back here to the States, but your last wound was the straw that broke the camel's back. You now have these orders to Strike Command, at McDill Air Force Base in Florida, and you should consider this assignment as a real feather in your cap. They asked for you by name, Gunny, and since you have the required technical qualifications as a jumpmaster and scuba diver and are still single, you fit the bill. This tour of duty is a new requirement and will last for at least two years, so why don't you go down to Florida and see if you like it for at least one year. Then, if it's not your cup of tea, we can always move you to another command."

In May 1968, I left 5th Force Reconnaissance Company and reported to McDill Air Force Base, located outside of St. Petersburg, Florida, for what proved to be an interesting, if not unusual, tour of duty. I was assigned to the operations (J-3) division, as one of the Marine Corps' enlisted representatives to the chief of operations, and was responsible for assisting in the planning, training, and execution of those joint military operations that relied heavily upon parachute operations as the primary means of delivering men and equipment into areas of Strike Command operations.

The United States Strike Command was commanded by an Army four-star general named Q. J. Conway, whose love for parachuting made him a favorite of those of us who were jump-qualified. Fortunately for me, the time previously spent as an operations chief with a Marine reconnaissance company had prepared me for this assignment. General Conway welcomed me aboard and said that he would look forward to the two of us getting to make a few jumps in the days ahead. He wasn't kidding.

Colonel George Dwyre, U.S. Air Force, Lieutenant Col-

onel James Henslick, U.S. Army, Lieutenant Colonel
Marvin Hewlett, United States Marine Corps, Air Force
Staff Sergeant Stanley Bicksler, Army Specialist 4th Class
Russell Burnette, and I made up the nucleus of the Joint
Operations Center, and with so many different fingers in
the pie, our planning efforts were not always an easy evolution. Each of the services wanted to take credit for every
job well done, but few would accept the responsibility for
solving the complex problems associated with the coordination required of joint military parachute operations.

It was General Conway's desire that every member of his
Strike Command staff be qualified as an advanced parachutist. To insure this, the general designated every Monday
and Thursday morning for parachute training. Our operations section was responsible for preparing the command's
jump manifest, and we did this twice a week. But, one day,
less than one third of those men who were required to jump
turned out, and it became quite obvious to General Conway
that not all of the staff shared his enthusiasm for jumping
out of perfectly good aircraft.

General Conway scheduled a formation the following
day and with every jump-qualified member of the command present, he asked me to step forward and used me as
an example.

"I won't keep you gentlemen very long, but I do want
you to pay attention to what I have to say. Our job here at
Strike Command is to plan and conduct joint operations
anywhere in the world. To do that we rely on parachuting
to get us into the area. Yesterday, we had a scheduled jump
planned, but I saw less than twenty men on the runway
when we suited up. We have a one-legged Marine gunnery
sergeant on this staff and if he can find the time to suit up
and be prepared to jump, then so can the rest of you! From
this day on, if any of you fails to make a minimum of three
training jumps per month, you'll be out of a job and out of
a career. That's all."

General Conway wanted to be sure that he and his staff
were accustomed to jumping from as many different types

of aircraft as possible. Thus, it was not unusual for us to utilize Army Huey helicopters and Air Force C-130s and C-141s that flew in from Fort Bragg, North Carolina, loaded with parachutes that we used to prepare ourselves for operations within the United States, the Caribbean, Africa, the Middle East, and Korea. On several occasions we made as many as nine parachute jumps in one morning, using Army Hueys to take us to jump altitude.

It was during an operation code-named Bold Shot that I realized the seriousness of the U.S. Army's commitment in their planning for joint parachute operations. This operation called for a mass exit jump at dawn onto the Caribbean island of Vieques. Since the Army had overall responsibility for the operation, they supplied the jumpmasters, drawing them from various Army commands. Specialist 4th Class Russell Burnette, who was assigned to the operations section as a typist and messenger, sat next to me as we flew from Fort Bragg to Vieques in an Air Force C-141 Starlifter cargo jet. As we waited for the four-hour flight to pass, I removed my artificial leg so that I could rub out a cramp that was beginning to bother me. Not thinking that my movements had disturbed anyone, I was working on my leg cramp when I looked into the horrified face of an Army chaplain, who had been designated as our jumpmaster. He was, no doubt, as surprised to see me as I was to see him wearing a cross on each lapel and a jumpmaster's helmet.

"My God, who the hell has authorized you to make this jump? I'm not sure that I can send you out of this aircraft with only one leg, Marine. Are you sure that this has been approved?"

I persuaded the shaken chaplain that if in doubt to ask our pilot to contact the folks back at McDill, who would verify my ability to jump, but the word of the one-legged jumper on board had now been passed up and down the rows of the dozens of jumpers seated in our C-141. Their looks of personal discomfort only added to the excitement of the jump.

The Army's Strike Command prided itself on its ability

to keep our operations secret, but even their best efforts to maintain security sometimes fell short of the mark. Operation Sugar Bowl, one of the last operations I was involved in, was such an event. This joint operation required us to fly from McDill Air Force Base to Alaska, and then rendezvous with operating forces over Japan before we jumped into South Korea. With all of the planning for this operation having been accomplished in the "Green Room," our windowless building, we thought that we had done our very best to insure operational security. That thought went out the window when I received a clipping from a Japanese newspaper, sent to me by a friend, which gave the exact time we would depart from McDill Air Force Base, the exact time we would arrive in Alaska, the number of men involved in the operation, the exact location of our drop zone in South Korea, and the total cost of fuel for the aircraft involved in the operation. So much for top-secret security at the joint level.

In the spring of 1969, I was promoted to the rank of 1st sergeant of Marines. This event precipitated a congratulatory telephone call from my monitor at Headquarters Marine Corps. It was during this conversation, when asked how I was enjoying my assignment at Strike Force, that I again let the monitor know that if there was ever the chance of leaving McDill and returning to duty in Vietnam, I would do so in the blink of an eye. Much to my surprise, I was told that while duty in Vietnam was out, if I wanted orders to Camp Pendleton to be the 1st sergeant of 5th Force Reconnaissance Company, it would be possible.

I accepted on the spot.

After I had said my final good-byes to the soldiers, airmen, and Marines at Strike Command, I returned to Camp Pendleton once again, for what was to be my last assignment in the ranks of the United States Marine Corps.

In 1969, 5th Force Reconnaissance Company was tasked with training the replacements for the two Force Reconnaissance companies operating in Vietnam. As 1st Sergeant I worked to insure that the Marines who came to 5th Force

received the best training possible before they began their
tours in Vietnam.

The commanding officer of 5th Force Recon Company
was Major W. C. Shaver. His philosophy of training was
that recon Marines must be able to shoot, move, and communicate, and our training schedule was designed to support those principles. The exotic methods of entry and
extraction, parachuting, scuba-diving, and the use of the
SPIE (Special Purpose Insertion and Extraction) rigs synon-
ymous with Force Reconnaissance Marines were very much
a part of our training. But it was always the teaching of the
basics that we knew would insure the survivability of a recon team. By using the after-action reports from teams operating in Vietnam we constantly improved the quality of
our training. We knew from the after-action reports that any
recon team that stayed in one place for more than twelve
hours, no matter how good they believed their position to
be, stood an excellent chance of being attacked. This enabled us to teach the importance of map and compass work.
The use of supporting arms—long-range artillery, attack
helicopters, and fixed-wing aircraft—was routinely taught,
so that targets of opportunity could be engaged without en-
dangering the teams. The ability to communicate clearly
over long distances meant that every Marine had to become
familiar with the various types of radios found within the
reconnaissance companies, and those three elements—
shoot, move, and communicate—became the cornerstones
to our training.

In the summer of 1969, after returning from several
weeks of mountaineering training at Bridgeport, I was
joined by my old friend, 1st Sergeant Maurice Jacques, and
while we divided the duties of company 1st sergeant, we
also shared our experiences in combat with the junior Marines in the company. First Sergeant Jacques was a unique
individual, a veteran of the Korean War and a former combat engineer and demolitions expert. Maurice Jacques had
also made Marine Corps history by participating in the
Marine Corps' first combat parachute jump in Vietnam on

June 14, 1966. No combat parachute jumps had been conducted by the Marine Corps' parachute battalions during
World War II, and there were no combat jumps made during the Korean War. This first one ever, led by my former SOG team officer-in-charge, 1st Lieutenant Jerome T.
Paull, was conducted near the intersection of the borders of
Laos, Cambodia, and South Vietnam. First Sergeant "Boom
Boom" Jacques brought a wealth of personal knowledge to
5th Force and was always eager to share it.

In the fall of 1969, we received word that 5th Force Reconnaissance Company was to be disbanded because the
number of Marines being sent to Vietnam was to be greatly
reduced. First Sergeant Jacques received orders directing
him to Vietnam, and I remained at Camp Pendleton to help
case the colors of 5th Force Reconnaissance Company.

I retired from the ranks of the United States Marine
Corps on March 1, 1970, and felt honored in having been
allowed to wear the Greens for twenty years.

Epilogue

The idea for writing Don Hamblen's biography had its beginnings one summer Sunday morning in 1991 at Camp Pendleton's trap and skeet range. It was here that Don and I had met a number of years before, and in sharing similar backgrounds as New Englanders and Marines, and with a mutual interest in shooting, we soon became good friends.

After shooting several rounds of trap with Don and his wife, Reiko, we were joined by retired Sergeant Major Maurice Jacques, and Master Sergeant Dick Dossche, along with other former 1st Force Recon Marines, Bud Fowler and J. J. Brown. We began to discuss the quality of the books that had been published about Vietnam when Don commented that although he had started to read several books about the Vietnam War, he had quickly lost interest because he found them to be either greatly exaggerated, full of needless profanity, or both. His comments were met with nods of agreement from Bud Fowler and J. J. Brown, but my personal feelings and reputation as a writer were spared when Don said, "But, Doc, I must say that even though I didn't want to read any more books about Vietnam, I really did like what you wrote. I enjoyed the way you told your story about being in Vietnam with Force Recon because it was an accurate account of what happened there. And you didn't use the word 'motherfucker' in every other sentence."

Coming from Don Hamblen, that was high praise, so I asked him if he would allow me to write his biography. I knew from past conversations that Don was not very interested in having his life story told because of the many inaccuracies that had been printed in the past, but I assured him that I would write the story as accurately as he told it to me and my research would allow, and that he would be able to approve the contents before I sent my draft to Random House. With some added words of encouragement from Reiko, Don agreed, and we went to work.

I had always enjoyed listening to Don talk about his experiences in the Marine Corps and about his post-Marine years as a professional hunting guide, but it was not until I had finished recording and writing his story—a fourteen-month process that required the two of us to meet for three days each week—that I felt there were specific unanswered questions that needed to be asked of him, questions about his views on leadership, courage, and hope. His answers to these questions are exactly as he stated them.

QUESTION: How were your leaders selected when you first went into the Marine Corps?

ANSWER: When I joined the Marine Corps, back in 1950, I was told that there were two things that would help to get you promoted: either be a good shooter or a good boxer. I had used a rifle since I was very young and I felt confident that I could always hit what I was aiming at. I felt that if I were a good shot, I wouldn't have to be a good boxer. Our squad leaders were tough men because they were the ones who had to enforce the rules within the squad bay. If someone didn't move fast enough, or was lazy, or didn't do what was expected, he was called outside of the barracks by his squad leader and his attitude was adjusted very quickly. Sure, it was corporal punishment, but the thinking then was that it was better to get a black eye than get a black mark in your record book. That's how our enlisted leaders were chosen.

Q: What was your best day in the Marine Corps?

A: Just about every day was a good day, and I'll tell you why—I was spoiled, or maybe I should say I was blessed in that I always served with good Marines. The enlisted Marines and the officers alike were just good people. During my last eleven years in the Marine Corps, I was either in Force Recon or I was in units like Force Recon—all-volunteer organizations. The men in the company wanted to be there. If we were told to do something, we did it, and we did it to the best of our ability. That made the life of the staff noncommissioned officer much easier.

Q: Why was that?

A: It was a matter of respect and pride. We didn't have any trouble like we read about today. Because there were no long-haired, pony-tailed, earring-wearing, I'm okay–you're okay, have a nice day–, I did it yesterday–type of people tolerated in our outfits. There was always respect and a sense of self-discipline that did not allow for those who performed poorly to stay in the Marine Corps.

Q: You don't believe that it is the same, today?

A: Unfortunately, what I see when I'm at the Camp Pendleton PX, or even when I'm out in town, leaves a lot to be desired, because I don't see the respect that Marines used to have for one another. In fact, I think that some of them don't even have respect for their own mothers, let alone for themselves.

Q: Can you give any examples of what you're talking about?

A: Sure I can. In a recent column of the Camp Pendleton newspaper, *The Scout*, a question was asked of several Marines, "Do you think that the Marines who go out on liberty are holding up a good image of the Marine Corps?" One buck sergeant said that what really burned his ass was seeing Marines out in town wearing blue jeans with rips in both knees and looking like hell, but no one was doing anything about it.

In the same article, some gunny said that for him, growing up in the Marine Corps meant, "work hard and then play hard," but it seemed to him that now too much playing is getting done, and not enough work.

The last Marine interviewed, a young warrant officer, said he thought that Marines performed well in Desert Shield and Desert Storm, and that today's Marines presented a good image while they were out on liberty. There is no common answer and in my opinion there should be.

Q: Was life easier for you as a noncommissioned officer in a reconnaissance company or in a rifle company?

A: It was always more difficult for NCOs in a rifle company than in a reconnaissance company. In a recon company you have hand-picked volunteers, men who are in top physical condition and who have extremely high GCT scores. These are motivated young men who want to be there and will do their best to stay competitive. They think they are the cream of the crop.

In a Marine rifle company, you have young men who are from the mainstream of society, but they are not always in the best of physical shape, they are not always the brightest, they may not even want to be there, and they may not be competitive. However, despite all of these things they are the ones who will do the real fighting. That is where the real challenge is—to get these Marines to follow you into combat, and that takes more guts than being able to jump out of an airplane, or dive a hundred feet below the surface of the water.

Q: What advice would you give to Marines who wanted to become reconnaissance Marines?

A: I would tell any Marine who wanted to go to a reconnaissance company that he should learn his skills in the infantry first. That's where the rubber meets the road.

The obvious difference between infantry and reconnaissance units is the exotic methods of insertion and extraction that are used to get recon Marines in and out of their areas. Once they get on the ground, though, their mission is still the same—patrolling.

Q: In your opinion, what is good leadership?

A: Good leadership is having the knowledge to design plans that will succeed, and having the ability to persuade others to carry them out in the face of death. Leadership is also the art of dealing fairly with men. It is a real privilege and an honor to lead Marines, and they must be led by knowledgeable men who care for their fellow Marines.

Q: In your opinion, what is courage?

A: The way that I see it, courage is nothing more than will power. When a man loses courage it is because he has allowed his fear to become larger than his ability to overcome it.

Q: During your twenty years in the Marine Corps, there have been Marines who have stood out as good examples to you. Who were they, and what was the common thread that joined them into your group of good leaders?

A: Lieutenant General Lewis B. Puller and Lieutenant General Herman Nickerson immediately come to mind as two of the finest examples of Marine Corps officer leadership that I know. As a young man I read about the leadership abilities of General George S. Patton and General Erwin Rommel, but I learned about real leadership from enlisted Marines, too.

The Marines who I knew personally, men like Julian W. "Spider" Parrish, who rose from the rank of private to colonel, and John Massaro, who became the eighth Sergeant Major of the Marine Corps, are examples of two such leaders. Johann Haferkamp, who went from the rank of private to lieutenant colonel, and Danny Cook, who at one time was a parachute rigger in 1st Force Recon Company and later became its commanding officer, are two others. And not to leave out anyone when I think of professional Marines, Staff Sergeant J. Lundermo and Staff Sergeant S. L. Eakin, who was killed in Vietnam as a lieutenant, both hold high places on my list of real leaders.

Why were they leaders? To me the answer is simple. These Marines led by example. They shared their experiences with every Marine in the company. They answered questions truthfully, and if they didn't know the answer to a question, they'd find out and get right back to the Marine who asked it. Today, that just doesn't happen. Young Marines ask a question of a senior and they expect an answer, but what they usually get is, "I'll get back to ya later." But, later doesn't come. At that point they've just lost the respect of their Marines.

Q: Was there ever a time when you gave up hope?
A: No, I never did. I always thought that if things got too tough someone would come and lend a hand. And that's what happened.

Q: If you could have just one wish, what would it be?
A: I'd like to have all of my left leg back for just two months out of the year. You know that we go each fall to fish and hunt, and I sure would like it if I could have my leg back for just those two months.

Q: Are we going to see any elk this year?
A: If you stop asking these questions, Doc, we might just see some.

Index